T0272572

TEAM

OTHER GTD BOOKS

Getting Things Done

Ready for Anything

Making It All Work

Getting Things Done:
64 Productivity Cards

Getting Things Done for Teens

Getting Things Done Workbook

TEAM

Getting Things Done with Others

David Allen AND Edward Lamont

VIKING

VIKING
An imprint of Penguin Random House LLC
penguinrandomhouse.com

Graphics by the authors.

LIBRARY OF CONGRESS CONTROL NUMBER:
2024000351
ISBN 9780593652909 (hardcover)
ISBN 9780593652916 (ebook)
ISBN 9780593832257 (international edition)

Printed in the United States of America
1st Printing

Book design by Daniel Lagin

*To all of you who are working
with others to get good things done*

Contents

TEAM

Introduction

hen *Getting Things Done* was first published in 2001, it was a game changer. By uncovering the principles of healthy high performance at an individual level, it offered a reliable road map out of overwhelm and transformed the experience of work and leisure for millions.* The book continues to transform lives around the world and has spawned a global network of professionals who bring to life its principles for thousands of learners each month in coaching and seminars. Decades later, we know that GTD® works for individuals, but it has also become clear that the best way to build on that individual success is at the team level.

THE TEAM GAME

This book is about teams, what can go wrong with them, and our perspectives on what to do to restore effective teaming. In this book we want to do for teams what David originally did for individuals: clarify the principles of healthy high performance, then offer a road

---

* For a concise overview of the GTD methodology, see appendix 1.

map for leveraging them in organizations seeking productive collaboration and effective leadership. We'll share our experience of ways to enhance your awareness of the "field of play" and offer tools and interventions that will bring a new level of flow to how work gets done on teams. The goal? To free up good people to do great things with their lives (or nothing at all, if that is what feels right once they are no longer underwater in a sea of overwhelm).

Most of what we do that is productive, creative, inventive, interesting, and even fun involves some level of coordination and ideally cooperation with others. That could be as big as landing on the moon or as ordinary as a family picnic. What is ironic is that despite the organizational or personal importance we place on these projects, most of the ways we manage them are suboptimal.

We wanted to write a book about teams but not ignore anything that might be relevant in understanding, improving, highlighting, or simply enhancing the experience of working with other people to get cool things done. After our collective sixty-plus years of working with individuals on teams, we were drawn to write this book because it became clear to us that teams are the future of how work will be done well in the twenty-first century. We believe that helping teams work more effectively is the biggest opportunity to positively impact individual performance, team outcomes, and the organizations in which both operate.

We have also seen how the terrain has shifted. For decades the emphasis on human development has been very much about individual change, but in the past few years the context or system in which the individual operates has begun to receive more attention. None of us works in isolation, so no matter how good our personal practices are, we all are affected by the environment in which we work and live. Even when individuals have their own stuff in order, it doesn't necessarily make collaboration among individuals as effective as it could be. When something has gone wrong with the system in which those individuals are operating, even offering a bulletproof solution at an individual level can only partially resolve the issue.

In our work teaching workflow management through the Getting Things Done® methods to individuals, we've seen the frustrations of trying to do great work inside of teams that don't work. We've seen all too many people make amazing changes to their own lives, but eventually leave their organizations for greener pastures because of the lack of structure and the inefficiency in the team around them.

THE HURT

This has consequences. When Gallup finds in its 2022 *State of the Global Workplace Report* that only 21 percent of employees are engaged with their work, it is unlikely that the other 79 percent are the source of the problem; the sheer numbers point to their team or organization as a more likely suspect for where the real problem lies. The global average includes significant variations, but even in North America only 33 percent of people report being engaged, while in Europe the figure is just 14 percent.

Numbers like that led us to some questions we just couldn't shake: Decades into the twenty-first century, why can't we figure out how to organize large numbers of people in the workplace? What prevents us from working smoothly with one another? Why can't we identify a way whereby a larger workforce equals an increased ability to fulfill organizational purpose? Adding more people doesn't always equal more output. On the contrary.

More than 130 years after the first "scientific management" initiatives by F. W. Taylor, it seems we still can't reliably coordinate human interactions in a way that doesn't strain the physical, mental, and emotional health of the people working within organizations.

Not all organizations, of course. There are outliers. But the rare successes serve only to highlight the random and ephemeral nature of their results. Surveys consistently show that most people are disengaged and demotivated by their work, even when it pays them extremely well. In the worst cases the experience of working in some organizations is so bad that it has earned its own descriptor: toxic.

THE FIX

We believe there is a better way. It's not complicated, but it isn't always obvious or necessarily easy, either.

We suggest getting back to first principles and steering away from complicated software-heavy solutions to what are mostly human challenges. We believe it is possible for teams to take simple steps that lead to a culture of work that supports both individual and team performance.

A culture of healthy high performance is rare, but that doesn't mean it's impossible. This book is an exploration of what it takes to build on the proven principles of GTD to create and nourish such a culture as a team. By respecting those principles, it is possible to develop and maintain the space and perspective to plan quickly based on new inputs, prioritize in a dynamic environment, and execute in a way that keeps you ahead of your competition and in control of your life and work. By identifying some simple standards, structures, and processes at a team level, the individuals on the team have less team noise to contend with, and can get on with doing the work of collaborating efficiently to achieve team aims.

In our now infamously volatile, uncertain, complex, and ambiguous (VUCA) world, organizational success comes down to the ability to plan quickly, prioritize on the fly, and then execute on those priorities. Without planning we are directionless. Without prioritization we are lost in a sea of possibilities. Without execution we can't move forward.

If you get planning, prioritization, and execution flowing, then your team can move up the food chain in terms of the quality of problems it can deal with—away from reactivity into consistently moving forward on things the team cares about. As recent events have repeatedly demonstrated, one of the critical survival skills for organizations is how quickly they respond in moments of radical change.

Those last sentences were written with a global pandemic and an unexpected war in Europe in mind, but the speed of change in our world means that by the time this book is in your hands, your mind may have gone on to focus on more recent crises—our world is not shy about offering us events that demand quick and creative responses to survive and thrive.

WHY THIS BOOK? WHY NOW?

The idea for this book first came about when we were working with a division of a national carrier in Europe. After a few years of our running Getting Things Done seminars in the organization, our client was interested in seeing whether their investment in training was having any impact. We were asked to survey the hundreds of participants we'd worked with up until that time, and to find out what they felt they'd gained from participating in the seminars. The results were impressive: productivity was up, stress levels down, and people felt they were getting more quality time with their families.

Those were impacts we expected at an individual level, but we were surprised to see positive systemic impacts we hadn't anticipated. For example, in our seminars we set aside several hours for the participants to work through their backlog of "stuff" and take their email inboxes to zero. When we started our work in the organization, most participants were turning up with thousands—sometimes tens of thousands—of unprocessed emails in their inboxes. They needed all the time we gave them to clear their backlog. After we had been working for a few years in the organization, many of the participants started turning up with only hundreds—and sometimes only dozens—of emails. That was a bit of a problem for us—we needed to find them something else to do during the time we'd allocated for clearing up thousands of mails—but it was a pleasant surprise in terms of what was happening in the organizational culture. The people who'd already been trained by us were "infecting" their colleagues—who hadn't yet been trained—with the benefits of remaining on top of their inboxes. The standard for what was "normal" for inbox management had shifted in the organization. That realization provoked a question: What if rather than have those impacts occur "accidentally," we could amplify them at the team level with slightly different interventions?

Another reason for this book is that, while sending smart, motivated people back into the trenches with better tools is rewarding, at a certain point we began to feel we were not speaking to a big part of the problem they faced. It became painful to watch them return to teams where the structures and processes were so poorly thought through that the individuals—even those who'd acquired world-class skills in what we teach—could only ever protect themselves against the encroaching chaos. It started to feel as if we were doling out bandages in a situation where a machine gun nest was causing all the carnage. Bandages can be welcome in such a situation, but they are nowhere near as helpful as preventing the carnage in the first place.

> There comes a point where we need to stop just pulling people out of the river. We need to go upstream and find out why they're falling in.
>
> —DESMOND TUTU

It's not that our work had no impact—our clients were grateful for any support we could offer—but we could see that to help them get the full benefits, we needed to address what was happening at the team level.

Too often, the structures and processes on a team can make it more difficult to work and collaborate, not easier. Once individual effectiveness has been addressed, the solution to what ails most teams is obvious if not easy: designing and maintaining a team environment that minimizes the noise and friction of collaboration. If we get both of those things right, the efforts of the whole can equal much more than the sum of the parts. In designing teams we need to remove the things that get in the way of their members doing their real work and to create environments that allow them to perform at their best. The genesis of this book was in the realization that there are simple—almost mechanical—steps that teams can take that will both ease collaboration and support individuals in doing their own work.

Finally, the market has repeatedly asked us for a book with this perspective. As soon as our clients have understood the power of GTD to help individuals to work more effectively, one of the most frequent questions we hear is, "How do I get the rest of my team to do this?"

That question points to a pressing need: to connect and align individual excellence and wider team performance. By building on what optimal productivity principles do for individuals, this book will offer a better way of working with others, while simultaneously nourishing an environment that fosters creativity and the flourishing of skills.

Many of the principles of team productivity are based on ideas explicit or implicit in the earlier GTD books, but others are entirely new. This book builds on those earlier ideas, or at least on some presumption of individual skill in handling the volume and complexity of modern work, but we don't think it's necessary that you be currently using GTD. We've tried to write this book so that anyone can pick it up and benefit from it without having read the other books and still be able to do useful things with their team.

We both have made a substantial investment of our life energies in GTD, of course: David as creator of the methodology and author of previous books, and Ed as the founder of two of the largest GTD franchises globally. We *do* care that members of your team have some systematic approach to handling their workflow, as we believe that the foundation of team productivity and coordination lies in individual prioritization and reliability. The effectiveness of the suggestions that we make in this book about teams will be completely undermined if you have individual team members who are unable to find their bottoms with both hands. But if you are aware of some other approach that enables people to make, track, and deliver on their commitments in a way that makes them dramatically more productive but significantly less stressed, then feel free to use that approach. Apart from a condensed refresher of the original material (see appendix 1), we won't go deeply into the specific principles and skills covered in *Getting Things Done, Ready for Anything*, and *Making It All Work*. If you are looking to improve your own game, or the game of a particular member of your team, then we strongly suggest having a look at those books as well.

LESSONS FROM FOOTBALL

To understand the focus of *Team*, it might be helpful to think of the different ways you could improve a sports team. Any team sport will do, but let's use football—or soccer—as our example. The football metaphor is apt: as we write, there is no sport played in more countries and cultures than football. Over the past thirty years the GTD model has proven its ability to impact effectiveness in any country or culture where it has been tried. Better still, on multicultural, geographically dispersed teams, it has provided a common understanding and a common language for getting things done together.

There are several levels at which you could start to improve a team: you could work on raising individual skills, training each individual to play better; or you could go to work on how those individuals play with one another as a team, on passing and trapping the ball and how individuals collaborate to score or defend; or you could focus on the identity, or culture, of the team.

Individual skills development is an obvious place to start, as it is relatively easy. Everyone wants better players, and time and consistent deliberate practice will enhance individual performance. No one can do the practicing for players; it is the responsibility of each individual to put in the time to raise his or her own game.

But a group of individuals—even technically excellent ones—with no training on how to play with one another will not perform to their potential as a team. Think here of a group of eight-year-olds, all chasing the ball in a clump, everyone wanting to do everything and mostly just getting in one another's way.

Give those same players some relatively simple guidance about how to play together, and team performance will improve. Self-created chaos is reduced, wires remain uncrossed, and the team has more space to expend its efforts strategically. Not only will each individual play better, but the team will move around the pitch more effectively as a group. The skilled individuals who can dribble, kick, and pass the ball masterfully are given specific roles on the team. Some are good at scoring and are developed as strikers. Others are better at undoing attacks and are trained as defenders. Strikers may defend, and defenders may score, but they know that is not their primary responsibility. By using players with different strengths and skills in different positions, the team becomes more efficient at undoing their opponents' defenses and shutting down their attacks. The players are not only given a team structure in which to direct their efforts but also the freedom to improvise within that structure, and within the framework of the team's playbook.

Well-deployed individual skills begin to enhance performance and reduce the effort necessary to play well as a team. For example, accurate passes mean less effort for the person receiving the pass. Passing precisely to where a teammate is sprinting means there is no need for them to break stride to pick up the ball, which enhances the likelihood of taking the opposition by surprise. Set pieces—corner kicks, free kicks, and goal kicks—are all designed and rehearsed so that the team doesn't have to invent them from scratch each time, with all the costs in creative energy and attendant errors that constant improvisation would bring.

These are advantages that will not be improved by simply increasing individual skills. They can only be achieved by coordinating individuals on the team level. Smart teams don't just play the same game harder. They are already playing as hard as they can. What they do, rather, is to step away for long enough to change the nature of their game. They don't just play the same game better; they play a better game.

This sort of work on the tactical organization of the team is clearly important to raising performance, but improvement at this level is more challenging than simply training individuals. Factors like ego needs, team mood, and personality conflicts make advancements much more difficult to control and direct than just attending to the skill development of an individual.

If you improve both individual skills and team tactics, you begin to change the team in another way, too: its identity and culture. This particular aspect is difficult to describe, but everyone knows when it is in place. It is present on all teams that put their stamp on their era:

the Montreal Canadiens ice hockey team of the late 1970s; the Chicago Bulls basketball team of the early 1990s; or, in football, the Manchester United team of the late 1990s. All these teams had great players. They also had impeccable teamwork. But beyond that they also had an identity that lifted performance well beyond what either of those elements would have predicted. A collective self-belief made them so unbeatable that as Ken Dryden, the Canadiens' goalie during their unparalleled winning streak, recalls in his book *The Game*, "Sometimes we'd lose just to remind ourselves how bad it felt."

A prime example of the impact of this aspect of a team was when Manchester United beat Bayern Munich in the Champions League in 1999, despite trailing 1–0 at the end of regular time. With only a few minutes of injury time left to play, many teams would have given up. The game was technically over. But that Man United team was used to winning. They *expected* to win. They'd already won the Premier League and the FA Cup in the UK that year, and they were not going to accept a loss in the European competition. In the three minutes of added time, they scored twice and took home European glory.

Was it their culture and identity that led them to triumph? Hundreds of other teams with a strong identity lose in similar circumstances. Maybe they just got lucky. Maybe. But it was certainly their identity as winners that had them persist, even when the cause seemed clearly to be a lost one. That was the lottery ticket that had them claim the jackpot.

You could think of it this way: each player gets better, then the team learns to play better together, and that starts to shape the culture and identity of the team. Then—once it is strong enough—the identity of the team begins to impact both individual and team performance. Any of those three interventions will lift performance on the team, but it will attain its best performance if it can find ways to hack them all. When it can put individual technical skill alongside collective strategic effort in a culture of high performance, incredible things can be unlocked. With clear goals and standards in place for how they play together, they will start to play to their real potential.

The original *Getting Things Done* book was primarily directed at the first of these three aspects—helping people to deal with the chaos around them and perform at a much higher level as individuals. It was a much-needed response to the astonishing increase in volume and complexity that individual knowledge workers faced in the early years of the twenty-first century. It was also, in organizational-change terms, the place with the most obviously low-hanging fruit. It was clear that while ambitious people were all working very hard, there were wide disparities in their productivity. As David did his research for that book, he came to recognize that a significant chunk of the gap between high and low productivity was traceable to the understanding—or ignorance—of a few fundamental principles. When *Getting Things Done* was first published, its ideas spread like wildfire via word of mouth. A whole generation of smart, hardworking people had finally been given the code on how to best position themselves in productivity terms. Like the individual players on a team, these people saw it as their responsibility to put in personal practice time, to improve their own personal systems and workflow.

In this book we are moving away from the individual level to cover ideas that will, in the end, benefit the individual as well as the team by helping teams do a better job of minimizing friction, enhancing collaboration, and reducing the organizational equivalent of bad passes: messages answered late, or not at all; delayed starts on meetings; undocumented processes; and inaccessible information.

A PERSON IS NOT A TEAM

Many books have been written on the individual aspect of workflow, and we won't seek to cover that ground again here.

Teams that have gotten things right have been doing elements of what we propose for years. When individual leaders have put two and two together for themselves and have seen the possibilities of a critical mass of their people improving together, pockets of team sanity have sprung up. But like high-performing individuals with no training, they usually stumble over some pieces of a larger system, without being aware of how that system fits together. We want to pull together all the elements of the model and clarify the best practices in each of them.

FROM "MIND LIKE WATER" TO "HEALTHY HIGH PERFORMANCE"

One of the concepts from the first *GTD* book that caught the attention of millions of readers was the idea of working and living with a "mind like water": that your mind—like a pond of water—can react appropriately to what is in front of it, then return to calm, rather than constantly rehashing what has been done or fretting about the future.

Enabling that way of working is still central to this book, but we are tackling it from a different perspective. At a team level, we see the equivalent of "mind like water" to be something we've come to describe as "healthy high performance." This is a way of working together that is not just able to keep pace with, or outrun, the competition, but to do it in a way that is sustainable—fun, even—over the longer term. Many think a "mind like water" is something you achieve accidentally, but the first GTD books showed that it is something you can create for yourself by doing some simple things consistently. Similarly, we believe that developing healthy high performance on a team is not a crapshoot. There are easy steps that can be taken to dramatically enhance the probability that the team will spend much more time working that way.

Some talk a good game on health, but when push comes to shove, health takes a back seat to hitting a team target. That's fine for the first effort, and maybe even for a few years after that, but eventually there are consequences for the team. The first case of burnout shows up. And then another. *Hmm, that's odd. But we can replace them.* Of course you can, but at what cost? A better question is, "How do we perform with excellence in a way that is more human than what we've been doing until now?"

Just as the original five steps of GTD produce both more productivity *and* less stress at an individual level using the same set of behaviors, there is no need for a team to do one set of things for health and a different set for performance. We believe that the practices, standards, and processes described in this book will produce health *and* high performance on a team.

In principle the concept is easy to understand. And there is nothing not to like about it—in principle. Everyone wants high performance, and everyone wants sustainable good health. The challenge comes from the tension that exists between the two. For many they are effectively opposite goals. *I can have high performance, or I can have health.* So pervasive is this belief that many exchange health for wealth by working in a way that gives them financial high performance in lives that are seriously out of balance. And when we speak of health we are not just speaking of physical health. There is a mental and emotional aspect to it, of course, but also the health of our primary work and personal relationships.

On the one hand, there is plenty of unhealthy high performance. People perform incredibly well but remain dimly aware that it is costing them more than they like: "I'd love to spend more time with my kids, but I'll get to that once I've hit this year's sales target." Much of our work has been done with teams that are already high performers. We often get a call when they have been performing at a high level for far too long, and the wheels are beginning to come off.

Some teams are just too busy to be truly successful. So much so that no matter what amount of success they have achieved, they are too busy to enjoy it. And they are so busy that they don't have the time to look up and scan the horizon for the next big thing in their industry.

We have worked with clients on Wall Street who expect their high performers to retire by their late forties, so they can finally "have a life." Often they get a lot right. Take, for example, a purpose-driven team, with a leader who has high expectations. They are successful, but success requires twelve-hour days. So be it. That's what it takes to hit challenging targets. Twelve-hour days become normal. The following year's targets are set even higher. To meet the increasing expectations created by their own overdelivery, it feels as if more time is required, so gradually people start putting in thirteen hours a day. Within months there is a new normal for the team. There are obvious limits to that model, and we get a call when someone clocks the unsustainable nature of it.

It's time to accept that we no longer live in a time when it is acceptable to make fast growth the be-all and end-all of our activities. As a look at any newspaper will show, even our planet is offering daily feedback that infinite growth exists nowhere in nature without cost. Why would that be any different for a team, a company, or an economy? We must adopt a more sane and human approach to how we work if we are to survive and thrive. The question we should be asking is this: What level of performance can we sustain over time without damaging the people on the team, their relationships, or the environment?

On the other hand, there are those who are using "self-care" as an excuse to not go after things they want for themselves, their families, and their communities. There are plenty of teams that are working sustainably from a health perspective but not performing anywhere near to their potential. A desire for harmony puts paid to performance, and they can work for years—decades—with an acceptable level of mediocrity that betrays both their potential and the impact they could be having for their clients.

Both of those outcomes are suboptimal and missing a trick. We believe it is possible to have both sustainable team culture that nourishes the health of its members and the kind of performance that most teams only dream of. Is that a high standard? Absolutely. But why would you want any other when the stakes are the health of the team members and the sustainability of our planet?

We acknowledge the tension between performance and sustainable good health but believe that the tension can be a creative one—a bit like the tension between being focused on appreciating the present moment, and still being willing to plan and create an attractive vision of the future. Accepting current reality as it is, and still choosing to work on improving it for tomorrow.

We see both health and high performance as partners. The trick is to notice when one or the other has come to dominate in unhealthy ways. It is not that we can achieve some balance that then remains unchanged. Everyone and everything gets knocked off balance at some point. The key is to notice the lack of balance more quickly, and to take steps to get back on.

We think the only sustainable way forward is to embrace the tension and to know that striving for both health and performance will produce better results over time. In any given team both goals will have their advocates. The conflict between them will be creative as long as it is understood and tolerated as the path of growth.

In this book we assume that the team wants both: high perfor-

---

Power is so characteristically calm, that calmness itself has the aspect of strength.

—EDWARD GEORGE BULWER-LYTTON

---

mance, because that is what it takes to be competitive in most industries these days; and health, because that is what it takes to stay that way over the long haul.

A note about the text from us as coauthors. There will be a few instances where the stories or examples we tell are unique to one of us. If so, we'll flag it using the [David] and [Ed] designations. For instance:

[DAVID] Most of the heavy lifting for the text within the book was done by my longtime friend, *Getting Things Done* colleague-in-arms, and coauthor, Ed Lamont. I had many years of experience with teams in my early years as consultant, coach, and trainer, but he's put more miles on his tires in the last two decades working in this arena than I have. He has an awareness, a style, and a demeanor that has made him a very trusted resource in global companies for some of the most senior and sophisticated teams around. Plus, he's a brilliant writer. And though he "hates thinking" because he thinks it's so hard, he has done it better than me in many respects on this topic. I can attest, however, that we are in total agreement and alignment with everything in this book.

[ED] Working with David to create this text has been a useful exploration of many of the ideas described here. As we mention further on in the text, the book has been written using the ideas contained in it, and it has been a pleasure to work with David on the evolution of his original thinking. Discussing, debating, and agreeing how principles that were life-changing for me as an individual expressed themselves in teams with a friend who originally pulled them together has been a worthy challenge. For those of you who've ever wondered if David eats his own dog food, I'm here to tell you that he's been a joy to collaborate with: quick with feedback, full of ideas and inspiration, and great fun over lunch as we discussed the ideas in the pages that follow.

Many of you reading this will already be familiar with David's story from his other books, interviews, and podcasts, but you may not have any idea who I am. For context, let me give you a bit of background on myself.

Growing up, I would never have been accused of being organized. When a classmate in junior high school described his process of laying out his books and clothes for the following day on the night before, I thought he was Einstein. Mostly, I just did things as they showed up on my radar. For much of my life, that was fine. School wasn't all that challenging, and I chose occupations that didn't require too much skill with organizing myself. I learned to juggle on a trip around Europe, discovered the art of street performing, and turned that into my first career. It's not one that is known for its rigorous scheduling. An injury led to working in commodities and eventually to working as a trainer and coach. It was only then, when my world encountered some of the world's largest and most successful organizations, that problems began to show up.

Viewed from the outside, I was a success, professionally speaking. The problem was that I couldn't feel the success I was having. I had great clients, was being asked to serve them in cool and exotic locations, and was earning good money . . . but the stress was killing me. A very short list of negative impacts would include the following:

- I was running on three to five hours of sleep per night during the week, and trying to convince myself that a solid meditation practice and extra shut-eye on the weekend was going to keep me healthy.

- Although I was a fit guy in my twenties, by my early forties I was weighing in at 249 pounds, or about 66 pounds heavier than my fighting weight.

- To manage my stress I was smoking five good-sized cigars a day, which is a serious commitment when also spending up to twelve hours a day in seminars and coaching sessions.

How did I end up there? There was no drama. I was simply a bright, committed guy who was out of his depth in the volume and complexity of twenty-first-century life. I had no system for dealing with what was coming at me. Well, that is not quite true. I did have a system; it just wasn't very good. It was mostly comprised of the organizational equivalent of string and binder twine, things I'd learned in the 1980s at university. It certainly wasn't *systematic*, so I was being sucked into the same whirlpool as many in my generation, and my only strategy for dealing with that was to try to work longer and harder to get on top of it all. It kept the show on the road, but the costs—in cigars, sleep, and energy—were way too high.

I'd already read Covey, bought the best Filofax going, and read every book I could find on time management. I bought a Psion, then a PalmPilot, then a Palm Treo, then a BlackBerry. They didn't help. In fact, the way I was using them seemed to make the problem worse, as did the Post-its I had sticking to any open space in my workspace. I was checking my device constantly and trying to cram "catching up" into any free space that turned up in my day. I tried multitasking to see if I could fit more things into the same period of time. I'd sit in meetings and try to do emails to "save time." I got an assistant, who did what she could, but because of my chaotic approach I couldn't really direct her to how she could help me. And I thought all of that was normal, just what it took to be "successful."

Then, somebody gave me a book called *Getting Things Done* and—after putting it off for several months—I skimmed it on a flight to New York. I didn't understand much of it on that first pass, but I did get this: there was a systematic approach that would enable me to get more done, with less stress. It sounded too good to be true, but I was desperate enough to double down on my investment. I read the book cover to cover, twice. Then a third time. I gave it to my assistant and blocked a couple of days to put it all in place. Within a week I was a convert. Not only was I getting way more done, but I felt better about my work than I had in years. In the way of new converts, I started handing out copies of the book to friends and family. Eventually, I got myself to a seminar with David. Twice. I got myself coached, then trained as a trainer.

In my existing practice of working with teams and individuals on purpose, vision, and strategy, it became clear that I'd found a missing link for my clients, too: GTD was what would put legs under vision and move things forward for them and their teams. In 2009, I got the license to distribute GTD in Europe, and over the subsequent years with my partners built teams in two companies that became the largest international distributors of David's work in five countries. This is the book I wish I'd had when working with teams at the beginning of my consulting career.

Any of the following chapters could hold its own as a standalone topic, if not even its own book. Many authors and consultants have articulated these topics in the thousands of business-oriented publications published in the last century. What we have attempted to do is to curate the best of the best practices and give a complete map of the topics and techniques that could be relevant in any situation— formal and informal, personal and professional—when coordination and cooperation with others is essential.

Not all of you are going to identify with all of this, but we've tried to cover the material in a way that includes all of you who might. We guarantee that situations will show up in which you'll find this a useful manual, but you don't need to use all of its practices with every team you're on, only the bits that feel useful to you in the moment with a particular team facing a particular challenge.

Most of our examples and suggestions in the book revolve around the most typical of "team" environments—the organizational world of corporations, not-for-profits, start-ups, etc. However, "team" can mean any context in which more than one person is involved in dealing with a situation or a project. This could include marriages, family situations, local committees, sports groups, etc. All the principles and best practices we elaborate apply equally to all of them.

It's fine for you to just "snack" on the book. From the index or a quick thumb-through you'll probably find something of interest from your past, current, or possible future experiences. Some of it will be immediately useful to you, and some of it might come in handy later. The more of it you use, the more it will help, but don't feel you have to do all of it at one time. Pick off the pieces that are most relevant for your team now, implement and integrate them and get the success from using them, then come back for more when your team has achieved bandwidth again.

Some topics may be tackled here more than once, but that will usually be through a different lens or viewpoint. There are many ways that any of these perspectives and suggestions can be understood and utilized.

We've done our best to make this an evergreen manual—something that will still resonate a hundred years from now. The nature of work, teams, and technology will undoubtedly be fluid and shifting, and with increasing speed. So we've done our best to be careful with buzzwords and technical detail that could get out of date with the changing times. We think what we describe here are universal and timeless principles and practices that will withstand that.

In *Team* we champion clear standards and processes that offer guidance on how we can work with one another in a way that minimizes organizational friction while maximizing the results of the collective efforts.

As with *Getting Things Done*, we are mostly steering clear of the personal and interpersonal. We know you need to have great relationships and navigate difficult conversations on a team. Those "soft skills," like being present and *really* listening to what your teammates are saying rather than just reloading your own opinions, are critical but are not the subject of this book. Given the scope of what we are trying to do—taking teams from chaos and despair to hope and clarity—there isn't space to deal with all of that here. There is enough to cover in the scope that we've set ourselves, and to cover all aspects of team success would make the book heavy enough to be a murder weapon. What we can do is attempt to reduce the frequency and gravity of those difficult conversations when they happen.

We are also not doing team building, conflict resolution, or any of that other extremely valuable stuff. We encourage you to find resources to do that elsewhere. We are doing team mechanics. We believe that we can make a significant contribution to how people work with one another in organizations. Our aim, finally, is to reduce burnout, to restore integrity, to decrease flare-ups caused by the stress of being overwhelmed, and to help leaders and teams to generate sustainable cultures of healthy high performance.

SECTION ONE

THE LANDSCAPE

Chapter 1

When "Teamwork" Doesn't Work for the Team

When one of our clients joined the leadership team of an international financial institution based in Germany, there was a standing item on the executive team's meeting agenda: burnout cases. That was costly from a time perspective, of course, but that they were spending time on it in each of their meetings was the least of the costs—human and financial—for the organization.

In Germany burnout isn't just a watercooler complaint. It is taken very seriously by the authorities and has real consequences for organizations where affected individuals work, and for the economy. Employees who are suffering from burnout are signed off as sick but continue to be paid by their employer or an insurer for up to a year and a half. Their jobs must be held for them if they return, and when they do there is a structured process for ramping up their workload; ten hours in week one, fifteen hours in week two, and so on. From a human standpoint it is a well-designed process for reintegrating burnout cases. Often it works. And still, long after they return, there remains uncertainty: Will they be able to take the pressure again? Someone who was once a stalwart resource has become a question mark on the team.

As far back as 2015, Gallup estimated that burnout was costing the German economy roughly €9 billion annually. It's not just affecting Germany. The same trends are being seen elsewhere, particularly as people came back to a new world of work after the COVID-19 pandemic.

And contrary to received wisdom, it isn't happening only to those at the bottom of the organizational pile. A recent survey by Deloitte showed that more than *two-thirds* of C-suite executives were thinking of quitting because of burnout.

Even prepandemic, the trend was clear. Our client in Germany described it this way: "I found myself in conversation after conversation in which people were telling me that they were overworked, this person was overwhelmed, and that one was off sick. The conversation was always negative. It was, 'We need this' or 'Why don't we have that?' rather than, 'Here is what we're going to do with the available resources.' People were falling over from overwhelm."

WHAT MAKES WORK UNHEALTHY?

We see numerous factors at play. One is volume. Research done by Martin Hilbert and Priscilla Lopez showed that in the mid-1980s, we were taking in about the equivalent of forty newspapers' worth of information per day. By 2007, that number had more than quadrupled. It won't have shrunk since. The time available to process all that additional information had, unfortunately, not kept pace.

Much of that increase is due to advertising, and some to viral cat videos, but it is no less exhausting for that. In our experience the obvious actionable inputs per se have not increased significantly. What has increased are the inputs on which we might decide we want to act—e.g., cc'd emails, group chats, FYIs, and social media rabbit holes.

Workwise, these days we are all trying to keep our feet under ourselves in the digital equivalent of a powerful current. Without a strategy for dealing with it, we get swept off our feet. No matter how smart you are, this current is—like an ocean current for a swimmer— much, much stronger than any one individual can withstand on their own. As in the ocean, without a plan you will be swept out to sea. What does "swept out to sea" in this digital riptide look like?

For individuals, it looks like checking your device first thing and last thing every day; being late and underprepared for meetings; scrolling up and down in your inbox flagging and re-flagging mails; prioritizing interactions with people who are not present over people who are; and searching terms in Google such as "anxiety," "depression," and—yes—"burnout."

People are switching primary inboxes as a solution to their overwhelm, but mostly they are just accumulating inboxes, which only contributes to it. They stagger from Zoom meeting to Teams meeting and back again with overfull bladders and often little idea of why they are in the meeting in the first place.

Individuals live consistently in overwork and overwhelm for so long that it feels "normal." Comfortable even. They go blind to what it means for their family that they are not home for significant occasions, or able to reach out to friends in need, or volunteer in their communities. With the amount of work they have on deck, how could they fit it all in?

With the increase in volume, our minds are so overwhelmed by incoming info that we can't cope. The constant demand for reactivity has reduced our ability to discern what is truly important and what is simply new and clamoring for a quick response, leaving many worrying about immediate responses to things that have little meaning. Immediate responses are often required because of someone else's inefficiency and lack of control. Interrupt-itis becomes the order of the day. It's as if we've lost the ability to make sense of a situation for long enough to get our bearings and navigate out of the problem. Instead we are stuck scrolling, swiping, and flicking to keep up. When we're

> Drive thy business,
> or it will drive thee.
>
> —BENJAMIN FRANKLIN

overwhelmed by the volume, scrolling offers what feels like a bit of peace. Unfortunately it's not peace; it's numbness. But when we've not felt genuine peace for a while, most of us will readily accept even a very poor simulacrum.

For teams, too, there are plenty of signs and symptoms of burnout.

THE CHANGING NATURE OF TEAMS

Subject to the same always-on, digital response time pressures as every other structure in society, teams and the very idea of teams are changing. They can be powerful engines of transformation or a sort of organizational purgatory. For example, as long as teams have existed, individuals have always come and gone from them. What has changed in our world is the speed at which people are moving in and out of them and how often the team needs to reevaluate what it should be doing. Personnel switches that were once an occasional inconvenience have now become a revolving door of personalities. Team boundaries are often so ill-defined that leaders struggle to be able to say how many are "in" or "on" their team. One of the trends we've observed recently is that people are coming and going in and out of teams so quickly that even people on the team struggle to be able to say who is going to be at the next team off-site.

We've also seen situations where leaders—in a desire to get everyone on board—name a leadership team of twenty, dooming themselves and the "team" to excruciatingly long meetings with endless repetition of points as everyone makes sure they are heard, which results in sticky, tricky decision-making processes. Not only that, but many of those twenty will be working on multiple other teams as well.

The speed of change and rapidly shifting cast of characters means that the old "-ming" model for team development—forming, storming, norming, performing—is being challenged like never before. That model implies that a team remains together long enough to move through all the stages, when now the team often won't have enough stability to move through the stages at all. In the current state of the world, teams need better guidance on how to move quickly to performing, before its members are reshuffled again or reallocated to a new business unit.

Another of the largest problems teams are facing is the amount of friction and noise in their communication and decision-making processes. Monitoring and responding in multiple channels have led many to simply throw up their hands and declare a kind of communications bankruptcy.

One of our coaching clients recently described her attempts to stay on top of her work with her team: upon arriving she consults a customer relationship management system (CRM) to look for updates on any of the shared projects she is collaborating on with others. She goes through them all, reviewing the actions others have taken and checking whether she is "it" and needs to do something in response. If so, she does it there and then, independent of its importance in her priorities. She then consults a separate series of shared spreadsheets to see what others have updated and what needs attention. That done, she goes to look at another digital collaboration tool used by teams she works with, where the title of the entries usually doesn't represent what is in the detail and it is often unclear what are simple next actions and what are larger outcomes. Finally, she consults team calendars that have deadlines listed for cyclical work that needs doing monthly. All this is in preparation for planning out what to do with the rest of her day. She is not alone. As we listen to our clients describe their team function, we can't help but cringe. As one of them told us, many teams are running around like headless chickens rather than holding strategic goals alongside the urgencies of each day.

Most teams remain caught in the busy trap, reacting to the world rather than acting on it. There isn't time to plan, prioritize, and execute systematically because they are constantly so far underwater with their commitments. The leader casts the longest shadow here. If the team leader is saying yes too often because she has at best a vague idea of what the team has already taken on, then the culture of the team will reflect that. Individuals on the team will say yes too often as well, and the resulting broken promises and incompletion leaves the team subtly demoralized about its efficacy, and its stakeholders seriously unsatisfied with its performance.

It is tempting to attribute an unhealthy work environment to some nefarious driving force—someone, or some group, usually at the top—actively planning a negative experience for employees. But in our experience, it is just what happens when not enough attention is paid to the structure and culture in which individuals come to work each day. It isn't that the people at the top are bad people, or have bad intentions. They are typically under more pressure than most, and their way of leading and managing is mostly a reaction to that pressure. So consumed are they by tactical and operational matters that they rarely find time to do the strategic work on structure and culture that would unleash the talent and motivation latent in their organization.

> **If you find yourself in a hole, the first thing to do is stop digging.**
>
> —WILL ROGERS

They'd do that work if they had time, but as tactical problems drift inexorably up the hierarchy of an organization, those at the top are consumed by firefighting. Despite others' perception of their power to make things happen, they often have little sense of control over what they are doing. While on the board of a major multinational, one of our clients once found himself in earnest conversation with his peers on how "someone should do something" about what was taking place in the organization. It was as if there were still some higher authority that prevented those around the table from doing what they already had the power to do.

It is not just the boardroom. We see the same sense of lack of control at all levels in organizations. From secretaries to CEOs, in organizations as diverse as listed companies and nonprofits, everyone complains about how little control they have.

How has this come about?

For one, we are offered next to no clear guidance on how to work effectively. In schools and universities, we teach math, science, and languages, but not how to handle the flow of information and assignments that come at us when we learn those subjects. At work we are sometimes given technical training on particular aspects of our jobs, but rarely given any support for how to manage the complexity of our work. Of course, highly motivated individuals have always cobbled together systems that support them in their desire to outperform, but it is rare that teams or organizations provide that training systematically. Since it was first published, GTD has been the go-to solution for helping individuals close that gap. The improvement at the individual level has highlighted the next challenge: finding a way to reduce friction and enhance productive collaboration among individuals on a team.

Because at a team level, there is even less instruction on how to work *together*. Two people can both be in control of their individual workflows and inventory of commitments. But when they want to achieve something together, the complexity of workflow management increases exponentially. They will now have agreements to manage (implicit as well as explicit) about who's doing what and by when. Any changes that affect one party will invariably influence the relationship. Given the speed of the workplace these days, this can easily become a swirling mass of unclear agreements, finger-pointing, or simple numbness to the reality that is present.

A FOOL WITH A TOOL IS STILL A FOOL

Another contributing factor is that the speed of technological development has long since outstripped our ability to think about and decide how we want to use that technology. Each year we have new tech, more tech, and then more newer tech. Everyone hopes that the next software purchase will sort things out. Each new development seeks to make life more convenient for us, but that convenience often ends up costing us our autonomy. Some people look forward to artificial intelligence (AI) easing the painful parts of work, without understanding that if AI actually starts doing those things, their current role may be redundant. It is because we haven't developed better ways of thinking and deciding—which would enable us to harness our technological advances in service of our humanity—that tech can't serve us. In many cases it seems we've ended up serving it.

> The goal of all inanimate objects is to resist man and ultimately defeat him.
>
> —RUSSELL BAKER

Because everyone is so overwhelmed and desperate for solutions, there is often little evaluation of the new tools and whether the solutions they offer will fix a problem or simply smear it around different parts of the company cloud. We need a more reflective, more strategic way of using the tech we have, and of integrating (or rejecting) developments to come.

WHEN AUTOMATION IS CONSTIPATION (OR DESPERATION)

Don't interpret that last section wrongly. We are fans of technology, and it's true that some of us are working faster and better with technological assistance. But if the model was really functioning as promised, we'd be working less, not more. That is clearly not happening for most of us. Tools are piled on tools to help resolve the problem, some offering helpful automations. But if you automate a mess, you only end up with an automated mess.

If we don't know this already, we should: tech is not the solution to the problems that we have as teams and organizations. If that were the case, each new piece of equipment and each software update would lead to an improvement. But they don't. They are put in place, and after they don't solve the problem they're supposed to, they end up on an ever-growing junk pile of erstwhile latest-and-greatest tech toys.

If tech really were the solution, we'd have all breathed much easier when messages were made small enough to fit on the leg of a well-trained pigeon. Or once the postal system was created. Or when the telegraph went up. You get the point. Our problems were not resolved with a new means of communication, because the medium is not the issue.

We have the most sophisticated technology in history at our fingertips, but people are still sending emails with five minutes' warning, saying, "Hey, would be good if you read this ahead of the meeting." It's the digital equivalent to serving up warm photocopies as handouts in the late 1980s. Going mobile was supposed to help, but most are beginning to have their doubts. Research shows that people are touching their phones hundreds of times per day, but we're not so concerned about them. It's the people who never let their phones leave their hands who concern us, the ones stumbling down the street trying to keep pace with messages and notifications coming at them from dozens of helpful apps.

Even when tech appears to be an unqualified boon—as with the relatively seamless move to online working in the early stages of this century's pandemic—it brings challenges. The ability to untether work from geography is a tectonic shift in how humans work with one another. Offices have their uses, but no one is going back to spending ten hours per week commuting, now that it is clear that most formerly office-based work can be done from pretty much anywhere. That seems like an unadulterated plus, but it has left many struggling to find a structure that both supports and contains their work in the way that office life once did.

INEFFECTIVENESS IS EXPENSIVE

Part of the problem is that no one—whether individuals, companies, or countries—is fully costing out the current way of working. If they did, we'd likely see much more energy invested in initiatives to reduce the amount of waste. As it stands there are no real objective reference points for good or bad, only a lot of human carnage and a vague sense that it really shouldn't work this badly.

Companies are missing golden opportunities that are available in their markets because no one feels they have time to think or act strategically. How could they, when they are stuck fighting daily fires? One of the biggest costs is in employee engagement. And the indirect costs of a lack of engagement are pretty much incalculable. Too often initiatives are launched with great fanfare and get money and attention thrown at them for a month or a year, but then they are buried by a new set of initiatives. As layer after layer of "initiative patina" is laid down in the organization, ultimately no one really knows what to focus on. When an organization has 118 "key initiatives," it effectively has no clear priorities. The consequences show up in a lack of alignment and—worse—priorities that conflict within the organization.

> Anyone can do any amount of work provided it isn't the work he is supposed to be doing at the moment.
>
> —ROBERT BENCHLEY

HERE, TAKE THESE,
AND CALL ME IN THE MORNING . . .

This has implications for the maintenance of the culture of the team, and points at some helpful fixes. A culture of healthy high performance will not simply manifest in a team out of nothing. Such a culture requires an investment of time to create, and then consistent time and attention to maintain. What is required is a way to facilitate team performance quickly, and a way to sustain key ways of working even when all the members of the original team have departed.

Our client from the beginning of the chapter found a way through. His personal experience of GTD helped him see that there was a possible solution to the problem. Over the course of several years, he drove an initiative to introduce GTD to a critical mass of employees. By the time he left the organization several years later, the burnout conversation was a rare phenomenon, and it had disappeared entirely as a standing agenda item for the management team meetings.

THE POSSIBILITY OF TEAMS

When clients have implemented the recommendations in this book, they describe feeling that they have more control over what's going on in their teams—that they're not being constantly overwhelmed by the amount of work in front of them, and they sleep better at night. They feel that they're having more meaningful relationships with their colleagues and family.

Imagine working on a team where you all clearly know why you're doing what you're doing, where the team is heading, what its key priorities are, and what your role is in making that happen. A team where you expect—and usually get—twenty-four-hour turnaround on requests you make. Where you are assessed on outcomes you produce, and not on how long you work. Where most work is done asynchronously so you have the control to flex your day to be able to prioritize both work and personal topics as necessary. Where your teammates sometimes say no to new requests, and it is seen as a positive sign of people choosing to stay focused on key priorities. A team on which your colleagues usually deliver what they say they will, and—because of a shared language and agreed-upon standards for teamwork—manage their promises in a timely manner when they see they won't be able to deliver as planned. Where meetings are few, and they far more effective than most you've ever attended. Meetings in which everyone in the room knows why they are there, and what they are trying to get done in the time allotted. Meetings that start— and end—on time, with clear action points about what happens next. Where everyone shows up with their issues ready to go, and all topics get handled clearly enough for the team to move forward on them after each meeting.

Sound utopian? It's not. It's how the two of us have worked on our respective teams for years, and it's what we'll show you how to do through the course of the rest of this book. We can't promise there will be *no* stress, but we can promise that the combined impact of what we propose will result in much less stress and much more productive use of effort in the pursuit of team goals.

It's not hard to switch from the experience most people are having on teams to the one we describe. The process is probably much easier than you think. You don't need to change the entire organizational culture to change the experience of working on your team. For many teams, agreement and adherence to some simple adjustments in working practices will be a huge step forward.

There are countless success stories from sports teams, the military, and charitable organizations that use these practices. Some of them appear in the pages that follow, and some are already familiar to you from your own experience. If we get this right, much of what you read in the following pages you'll recognize in some form from effective teams you've worked with in the past. These are not necessarily new concepts, but they have not been formulated as a repeatable model. Some people have had the ingredients, but not necessarily the recipe. The beauty of a recipe is that once you have it, you don't have to follow it slavishly. You can play with the ingredients in ways that suit your particular needs and still get great results—better results, even, because the fit is more suited to what you need. And you now have a formula that you can apply at any time in the future, in new team experiences.

> "Management" means, in the last analysis, the substitution of thought for brawn and muscle, of knowledge for folklore and superstition, and of cooperation for force.
>
> —PETER F. DRUCKER

Chapter 2

New World, New Work
WHAT'S HAPPENING?

I n a world that is changing as rapidly as the one we've just described, the world of work has had to change, too. As the nature of work itself is shifting, quickly and dramatically in some cases, it has major ramifications for teamwork.

Some historical context will be helpful here. Only relatively recently have people left home to "go to work." It was only an evolutionary heartbeat ago that the Industrial Revolution first required that people go elsewhere for work, because the tools and machinery necessary to do their jobs were in the factories. Before that, work was mostly done at home or on the farm.

The pandemic of 2020 to 2022, along with advances in technology, shifted our understanding of where work could be done. The shift was already happening in a small way—digital nomads and remote teams were already a thing—but it got a huge boost when repeated lockdowns meant that organizations could no longer have people come to offices as before. Those few prepandemic digital nomads simply represented the leading edge of the future of work. A future where it doesn't matter where you are in the physical world if you can get a decent connection to the digital one. As knowledge work became untethered from a physical location, in many cases it also began to be loosened from an organizational hierarchy.

The world of work was already moving away from "command and control" to a more open, flexible, and dynamic model. Experts have long predicted that independent contracting would become the norm, and that shift is already visible. In much of the developed world, many professions are staying nimble by hiring freelancers when they are needed. People are taken on for a project, not for a job. In the future more and more workers will be effectively self-employed and simply come together on specific projects, before going off again to work with a new team (and often for a different organization). With organizations becoming more widely distributed networks of free agents, the fundamental practice of collaboration—the ability to align upon and then deliver agreed outcomes together—will become even more critical for organizational success.

Parallel to this shift has been the rise of what has been termed "New Work," a variety of workflow methods that give much more agility and autonomy to a team and its members. Lean, Kanban, Six Sigma, Agile, and Scrum are the best known, but they are only a few of the approaches on offer. Wikipedia lists thirteen varieties of Lean alone.

> ## The only thing worse than a man you can't control is a man you can.
>
> —MARGO KAUFMAN

What follows is our assessment and comments about the more structured models of optimal teamwork that have emerged over the last few years—either for your information or for your recognition, if you have already been engaged with them. Even if these approaches are unfamiliar to you, you may find the perspectives here useful.

WHY NEW WORK?

All these approaches were a response to some of the classic dysfunc-
tions of the large organizations of the twentieth century: hierarchical
structures with multilayered decision-making processes; a silo men-
tality that fostered internal competition and misalignment; and rigid
planning cycles that were just one sign of an internal focus that led
to a lack of awareness of customers' needs and desires. These turned
once world-beating companies into Darwinian dinosaurs as their
markets and more nimble competition adapted and accelerated away
from them.

A striking example of the need for change came to us from one
of our clients. In his organization, the approval process for international sales had six levels:

1. The salesperson sent a form describing the deal to the sales
   manager.

2. If she was okay with it, she sent it to the finance department of
   the country where the deal was being done.

3. If finance approved it, they'd send it to the country head.

4. If the country head was a fan, they'd send it to the finance team
   of the sales department at the head office.

5. If they got on board, they'd forward it to the global head of sales.

6. The global head of sales would then take it up with the managing director of the global organization in their weekly meeting.

After those two had made calls on the dozens of such deals that
had drifted up out of the regions, the "gos" and "no-gos" would—like

aging salmon—begin their journey back to their source. In a world where same-day deliveries had become the norm, the process was a ponderous anachronism.

Apart from the deafening noise this approval process—with accompanying horse-trading at each level—generated in the organizational communications system, the main problem was that none of the salespeople felt accountable for the deals they were making. They were simply shoveling whatever agreement they could get done with the customer into the system and leaving the responsibility for deciding whether it was actually a good deal to someone higher up in the structure.

Why all the to-ing and fro-ing? Because inherent in a hierarchical pyramid like the one described is an underlying belief that effectively says, "Sure, you people doing the work know your customers and your market, but our folks at headquarters are smarter and have more experience in the ways of the world. Be sure to ask them before you do anything new, and they'll let you know what you should do. If they are busy, just hang about, wait for a decision, then get back to work." In the twenty-first century it seems crazy when you see it laid out like that, but that is how big things have gotten done for much of human history.

So much for hierarchical decision-making. That those decisions were happening in silos only made things worse. These silos—in sales, marketing, operations, or HR—were often working at cross-purposes with no knowledge of the efforts of the others, which made the situation worse still. But even that was not as bad as when silos knew of one another's work and were actively competing to win kudos for their part of the business at the cost of efficient collaboration and use of organizational resources. If one layers onto this a planning procedure engineered like a Soviet five-year planning process—with internal coherence but little accounting for market realities—it is a wonder that many organizations ever got anything done at all.

IS NEW WORK REALLY NEW?

Yes and no. Elements of it have been around forever. Whenever people have worked together, someone—often a work-shy bright spark irritated by clumsy processes—has gone looking for ways to make things easier, faster, and more efficient.

And when conditions made it possible, people always worked in this way. Take this book, for example. Without any conscious planning to do so, *Team* was written in an "agile" manner by sharing increasingly less-bad drafts between us authors. That back and forth continued until we were ready to show what would—in agile terminology—be called a "minimum viable product" to our customer, the publisher, to get a sense of whether we were on track with what they wanted for you, the readers. With that feedback, we went back to working on less-bad drafts, until they were decent drafts. We showed it to the publisher again. And so on. After a few rounds of feedback, we had what our customer wanted. That process is not rocket science. It doesn't need to be; it just needs to work. And if we stumbled upon it as a way of working, then many others will have, too.

Contrast this with what a tempting alternative might be: minimizing collaborative touchpoints by sharing only "good" drafts with each other and holding off until the manuscript deadline to find out whether the publisher liked our best thinking. We might have hit that nail on the head with our first swing, but the potential downside—having the manuscript refused or being sent off

> High courage and consideration are both essential to win-win. It is the balance that is the mark of real maturity. If I have it, I can listen, I can empathically understand, but I can also courageously confront.
>
> —STEPHEN R. COVEY

for epic rewrites with a very tight deadline—would have been extremely high.

What *is* new with New Work is its systematic approach, which makes more effective and efficient ways of working together easy to understand and implement, so that the benefits can be scaled and spread widely to appropriate teams and projects within an organization. Whether you like them or not, all of these approaches share a common desire to make teams and organizations easier to lead, and more rewarding to work in.

A BRIEF HISTORY OF ATTEMPTS AT SYSTEMATIC CHANGES TO THE WAY TEAMS WORK TOGETHER

Lean and its flavors

Lean production—or what is now known simply as "Lean"—might be called the grandfather of New Work. The basis of it was developed by W. Edwards Deming in partnership with Toyota in the post–World War II period, and the approach was eventually called the Toyota Production System (TPS). Toyota had become very focused on the removal of waste in its manufacturing processes. Fixing such problems was nothing new, but Toyota began to look for improvements in their manufacturing not as a finite project, but as an ongoing initiative, a constant search for what we might now call marginal (or incremental) gains. The goal was to identify what the customer values in what you are producing, maximize that, and concurrently reduce non-value-adding activities. At Toyota the customer in the equation might be a car buyer, but it also could be the person—or team—in the next phase of the manufacturing process on the way to a finished vehicle.

When James Womack and Daniel Jones were building on those

ideas to create something applicable outside of the Toyota organization, they called their adaptation of TPS principles "Lean," to distinguish it from the more ubiquitous "mass" production.

Lean approaches seek not only to reduce or remove wasteful activities but also to bring fresh—and critical—eyes to processes that seem to be working well. As with GTD's five steps for completing work, Lean is centered on the idea of "flow": that you move from stage A to stage B to stage C as smoothly and efficiently as possible with the least amount of wasteful effort. Improving flow involves a process of mapping the current steps in the flow, then challenging what is being done in each one of them to reduce friction at every step. At its core, removal of inefficiency, or non-value-added work is a key focus of Lean.

Not everything can add value, of course. Some things don't add value to the customer but are still necessary to be able to stay in business. In Lean there is a concept called "necessary non-value-adding work." Customers don't care about things like keeping company accounts and filing accurate tax returns, but they are nonnegotiable. This non-value-adding work is the most challenging form of waste to deal with, because everyone is convinced that their way of doing things is critical for the team's survival. Lean's approach is to challenge whether that is true by mapping processes in a way that allows for a fundamental review of why things are being done at all. Externalizing and reviewing each detail of the process is critical, because you can't challenge and interrogate what you can't see.

Once Lean was successfully launched, other variations came into being. Six Sigma emerged from a different strand of Deming's thinking and is pointed more at the idea of reducing variation in a process—and the quality of the resulting products—than on removing waste. "Lean Six Sigma" brought these two expressions of Deming's thinking back together again under one banner.

Unfortunately, Lean has come to have negative connotations in some quarters. The word itself suggests that its aim is cutting fat, and when combined with a restructuring of a business, many think its objective is simply to squeeze more work out of all the skinny folks left after cutting. That's a logical concern, perhaps, but not really aligned with Lean's philosophical fundamentals.

At its core Lean has a strong focus on respect for people and their well-being. Lean gives them the power to improve their work, which increases their autonomy and engagement, and gives them more time to then focus on other value-adding areas of their jobs. Enabling people to do their best work—and to be fully engaged in it—is a huge component of the Lean philosophy. From a Lean perspective, asking people to do wasteful tasks is disrespectful to them and their time. Similarly, not offering them the opportunity to use their skills to the best effect is not honoring their talents. As a simple example of how radical this empowerment can be, when line workers at Toyota see something wrong, they have the authority to halt the whole manufacturing process until the problem is dealt with.

Holacracy

As hierarchies were trimmed, and decision-making moved closer to where the work was actually being done, the concept of "self-organization" emerged. A leading light in this movement is Holacracy—a business practice developed by Brian Robertson and his partners. Brian came across GTD and loved the simple methods it described for handling individual workflow. The clarity he achieved through the implementation of GTD got him thinking: Could similar ideas be scaled to an organization? He wondered whether a group of people could organize themselves in such a way that the organization could achieve its aims without politics or overreliance on a strong personality to drive things forward. After several years of experimenting, he pulled together an organizational operating system with no job titles—only roles and accountabilities for those roles. That might seem a minor point, but it opened an interesting possibility: removing the responsibility for certain actions from a person and job title and allocating them to a role. The bad news about having a job title is that unless its specific accountabilities and decision-making authorities are extremely clear (which is seldom the case), all kinds of stuff roll upward from below to be dealt with by those at the top, given the amorphous hierarchy. When the role versus the title is rigorously clarified, it becomes much easier to move decisions and actions to the appropriate people.

Holacracy (and similar models that have shown up since) distributes authority. In Holacracy it is "circles" that have autonomy to define and fulfill their own purpose within the overall business purpose. Anyone in the organization can surface what are referred to as "tensions"—challenges or opportunities—they identify, and have them processed and resolved quickly, at as "low" a level as possible without everything needing to creep up—and clog up—some chain of command.

FROM TITLE-BASED TO ROLE-BASED

The big shift in a role-based organization is the focus on the desired result and specific accountabilities versus a generalized and too often vague sense of responsibility. What does "chief financial officer" really mean? They're considered to have done a good job when exactly *what* is true? What does "head of human resources" mean? They are accountable to ensure *what* happens? It's fine to keep a title, if that's needed for external relationships, but few of the owners of those kinds of titles can instantly tell you what specifically their jobs involve.

> **When it is not necessary to make a decision, it is necessary not to make a decision.**
>
> —LORD FALKLAND

[DAVID] When I heard Brian Robertson speak at a conference in 2010 about Holacracy, I had been searching for a way for our small company to "run itself" without me having to be the "boss." I knew I wasn't the best player for that role anyway, and the stress of decision-making that consistently escalated onto my desk was more than I could tolerate, given the book I was then writing and other big projects for which I held the reins. I considered closing the company but instead decided to implement Brian's model. Our group has maintained elements of that system ever since. Its flexibility, freedom from needing to do "predict and control" forecasting, and egalitarian way of working has served us extremely well as we've weathered the changes in the economic environment and our business model over the years.

Immediately after we implemented Holacracy in our company, I hired someone to take over the role I had been holding as CEO. However, there were some things I had been responsible for that I couldn't hand off yet to the new person. He got the CEO title (useful in our communications to others outside the organization), but I had to think about the specifics of what I had been handling in a more discrete way, and define the subroles and accountabilities for them. Once that was clarified we were able to move forward with little ambiguity about who would be dealing with what, steering the company forward.

Changing to this kind of organizational operating system is not for the faint of heart. The primary obstacle is usually the owners' willingness to trust the self-organizing process enough to hand off final decision-making to it. Owners can still maintain the authority to decide about things strategic and financial if that authority is acknowledged and vetted by the distributed power structure. But as soon as someone plays the "founder's card" to overrule a decision coming from the self-organized structure, the initiative loses credibility and likely collapses.

Conversely, while many find themselves more inspired by having more control over their areas of focus, some employees are put out of their comfort zone by the increased responsibilities they are accorded in this way of working. Some would rather show up from nine to five, be told what to do, and just get a paycheck.

A related issue is that as workers are being asked to be more outspoken with their concerns and ideas, more self-confidence is required. If they feel anxious about their own competence, or struggle to speak up when they see problems, it's difficult for them to play in this much more engaging way.

Though this kind of organization may be a radical shift for a typically hierarchical enterprise structure, it is a harbinger of things to come. Work is of necessity becoming more of a conscious event, for all players. The popular models of efficient workflow were designed to bring enhanced best practices into relatively stable organizational structures, which are now diminishing if not disappearing entirely.

Agile et al.

"Agile" is without a doubt one of the buzziest buzzwords of the past decades, but what it actually means can be a bit of a mystery for the uninitiated. As the term has come to be used—and abused—to describe initiatives with little relation to its original intent, some definition of terms will be useful.

ARE YOU AGILE, OR MERELY AGILE?

As we'll use the terms here, capital "A" Agile is a rigorously defined approach, whereas small "a" agile simply means working in a way that enables quick delivery of small iterative enhancements, each of which on their own deliver some value to the client. If that sounds familiar, it's probably because some form of agile approach is the dominant means of delivering pretty much all software production these days.

Capital "A" Agile—and Scrum, the best-known framework for implementing it—is, like Lean, based on ideas like "flow" and "pull" and focuses on things that are of value to the customer. It's a more prescriptive framework for delivering value through rapid iteration. Rather than spending a year planning and building a new product only to find the customer doesn't want it, or discovering that the whole market has moved on, the idea is to identify smaller chunks of what the customer wants, then deliver consistent increments of value frequently until the final product is ready. So far, so familiar.

But don't let the similarity between agile the adjective and Agile the framework deceive you. Going down a formal Agile route is quite rigorous and means substantial changes to how all or parts of an organization structure themselves.

What does rigorous look like? Agile teams are dedicated to "epics" or the big-picture overall mission. Epics are broken down into "stories," like "improve billing for retail customers." "Product owners" have authority around overall direction, and "Scrum masters" are responsible for the correct execution of Scrum "ceremonies." Teams meet after each "Sprint" of two to three weeks and do a retrospective: this is what we achieved in the last Sprint; this is what went well; that's what didn't go well. Then, looking forward, this is what we want to take out of our "backlog" and really focus on in the next Sprint. As is clear from the description, there is a use of language that is specific to capital "A" Agile that works for those in the know but can be slightly confusing for those on the outside.

Most organizations are simply trying to get people to be more small "a" agile by adopting some of the lessons and principles of Agile (Scrum), without going through all the rigor involved in that approach. As is often the case, they want the results, but not all the change and effort required to achieve them. And even with a less rigorous approach the results can be impressive. The word has become buzzy because it has produced meaningful results for those who take the approach seriously.

When our client from the beginning of the chapter moved to apply an agile approach to their sales process, the managing director of the global business simply made clear that he no longer wanted to be where the buck stopped on all nonstandard international deals. Henceforth, only in an extremely limited set of circumstances were sales deals to come back up to the highest level to them for approval.

Using the Agile (and Lean) idea of moving decision-making and accountability closer to where the work was getting done, the sales-force was given clear guidance on minimum profitability and em-powered to do whatever they felt was best to achieve that. Three times per year they had "wildcards" that allowed them to ask for ap-proval to go below that level of profitability, but everything else was decided by the salespeople themselves.

In theory this was a change that should have been welcomed by all along the chain, but pretty much everyone resisted it, from sales to finance. Why? Because everyone loved the protection inherent in the existing system: the assurance of knowing that someone else was going to be taking ultimate accountability for the decision on each of the deals. Of course, no one said so in as many words. Each person claimed to be personally in favor of the change; their only concern was that so-and-so further down the line just couldn't be trusted with the responsibility.

Still, the management team stuck to their guns, and the process change went ahead. In the end it wasn't just the sales approval process that changed. The organization was able to do away with several boards and committees that became redundant as a result of the change. The risk committee got the chop, along with the sales committee and a markets committee, all of which resulted in huge savings of time, attention, and energy.

When misunderstood, agile as dogma can bump up against reality in some very unhelpful ways. As part of a new strategic approach, one of our clients was told to stop booking seminar rooms for trainings a year in advance, because it was not "agile" to do so. Trying to book rooms closer to the training dates, however, meant that all the good and reasonably priced spaces in the area had been long since booked.

Because Agile/Scrum is quite a rigid framework, it works best for groups that are working on a limited number of large projects, and where the work done—and also left undone—can be easily identified. It's also particularly helpful for the people working on those projects who don't have great workflow practices themselves. For them the approach can seem revolutionary because it externalizes a workflow system. Where once they were lost in a swirling mess of commitments that were only logged between their ears, they can now suddenly see how to move forward methodically on their projects. The challenge comes from the default prioritization implicit in this approach. If they don't have a system for the rest of their work—or their lives—the projects being run according to Scrum get outsize attention; everything else is left in the swirl until a fire starts in some other part of their life to grab their attention.

Another aspect of Agile that generates resistance is its tendency to force simplicity into a complex environment. True Agile is an ideal world, which is perhaps why everyone who works on teams where true Agile is being practiced loves it. They love it because the organization has slimmed down the scope of their work to something very specific and taken away the aspects that everyone else must battle through before getting to their real work.

It's not for everyone. As with Holacracy, if people really do just want to come in and be told what to do or just want to move their widgets in peace, then this approach won't be right for them. You can cause big problems if you try and push staff who have no desire to be empowered into a fast-moving workplace with high accountability. But for those who want to be accountable, take risks, and create things, it is a great way to work. Fortunately the agile model is not necessary—or even appropriate—for all parts of an organization. It is fine to have a diversity of approaches, given the nature of the tasks at hand. Many organizations are now moving beyond mastering a particular agile methodology, and on to mastering a "vocabulary" of interventions from different agile approaches to solve different types of problems they encounter.

> A really contented man has his yesterdays all filed away, his present in order and his tomorrow subject to instant revision.
>
> —UNKNOWN

NEW WORK AND KNOWLEDGE WORK

One of the odd things about the shift to New Work is its uneven application in different industries, and even within a single organization. Agile working, Lean, and Six Sigma, for instance, have seen much greater adoption in manufacturing and software production (which might be thought of as a process of manufacturing code) than by those doing knowledge work.

Part of what we hope to do with this section is to show how the principles of GTD can bring some of the benefits of Lean and Agile approaches to the nonstandard issues that make knowledge work distinctive and extend the benefits that manufacturing and software development have gained to a much broader population.

Even within a manufacturing organization, adoption of New Work is uneven. The shop floor may have elaborate supports to facilitate Agile or Lean working, while in the same organization knowledge workers are abandoned to their fate. Likewise, process-heavy occupations like manufacturing will have documented procedures for capturing the benefits of all the improvements made by all those previously employed in that department, but knowledge workers doing nonroutine work are often expected to find their own way each time a new person steps into a role.

It is all the more striking that those same businesses that have been successful at adopting improved ways of working in routine, process-based activities have often ignored—or failed at—finding those benefits in their nonroutine activities. A company's knowledge workers are in its sales, management, market research, and product development departments. They are equally critical to the success of the business, but their work consists of unstructured, infinitely varied, rarely repeated tasks that arise in response to dynamic market forces. Often these tasks are unique to an organization, role, or even individual. They may occur only once, or infrequently, but are not small in terms of their impact.

On a high level, knowledge work requires teams to manage their attention and energy to be productive as individuals, teams, and organizations. It's about how we apportion time, handle commitments, answer emails, and complete meetings effectively and on time; how we go about defining goals and making plans to achieve them; how we handle interruptions to our plans; and when and how we choose to prioritize responding to those interruptions—or not—with reference to our existing commitments (assuming we have any idea what these are . . .).

In many ways this kind of work has become more critical to success in manufacturing companies than simply making process-based improvements. If all your competitors have adopted the same Lean and Agile approaches to process-based work, then it is in how non-standard work gets handled that an organization can really differentiate itself.

Because of the nonrepetitive nature of knowledge work, it is difficult to document and to measure and as such can seem impossible to manage or improve systematically. It is so challenging that some choose to ignore it as an area for systematic improvement entirely; if they hire smart people, they reason, it'll work out somehow. But it isn't about smarts, and it can't really be worked out without support.

The application of approaches from New Work are equally important to knowledge work, perhaps more so, as the problems are harder to see. As one of our colleagues says, "If you work in a tomato canning factory, you know that something's going wrong if you've either got a big pile of tomatoes, a big pile of cans, or something's on fire. But in an office, somebody having a good day sitting behind the computer looks very similar to someone on a bad day sitting at a computer. And if you don't have ways of making the work visible then no one knows how you are doing."

HOW GTD SUPPORTS AND COMPLEMENTS NEW WORK APPROACHES AND COMPENSATES FOR THEIR WEAKNESSES

In a world of de-layering and increased empowerment, the demands have increased for the participants in teams to manage themselves, without direct oversight. No one has the time or bandwidth to hold people's hands and find out how they're doing on project X. The assumption is that team members are managing their own accountabilities for their role(s) on the team—the outputs and actions they have taken on or been given.

This is where GTD can supercharge a team that has already adopted one of the new approaches to work. An alignment between New Work and GTD is in the "mapping" of all current work. In most new work approaches, the expectation is that the team has a total inventory of all its projects and can regularly determine what it has committed itself to. Without it, the team can't be confident that it is working on the right things. This visualization of all the systems and approaches we've described above addresses the flow of work through a team, and this can be extremely effective in streamlining those processes. They all depend, however, on the optimal practices of the individuals involved. It is the flip side to Deming's point about a good person always being beaten by a bad process. The corollary is that an amazingly optimized team process will be torpedoed by substandard work practices of individuals running the process. You need both: a great process, and individuals who have a grip on their own workflow. Lean, Agile, Holacracy—or any other of the approaches under the banner of New Work—may succeed without supporting knowledge workers to structure their nonstandard work, but they all function better if people have a personal system that helps them fulfill the commitments they make in the teams' meetings. All of these approaches rely on individuals consistently delivering their part of a larger whole. But without a way to manage their promises effectively, there will always be leaks in the system. In other words, if you want to be a self-organizing team, you need all the selves to be organized so the team can work optimally. Because of this, there is a huge complementarity between GTD and all of the approaches to New Work.

Defining work is, of course, already a vital part of GTD. Maintaining complete lists of all your commitments has been a key to the power of the system from day one. When you visualize your own work (in a list, a graphic, or some other form), you can organize it, speak about it more clearly, and structure it to become much more manageable. But in the same way that, if you don't look at your lists as an individual, even the best lists can't help you, so, too, a team with great individual lists stored only in individuals' systems will struggle to coordinate activities. In a team context, if you consolidate the team-relevant elements of individual lists and share them visually with everybody else, the team's sense of what it has on its plate is dramatically improved.

We're beginning to touch on some of the principles of what makes for healthy high performance on a team, and in the next chapter we'll expand and deepen that discussion.

Chapter 3

What Is a Team?
Why Are They Important?

t wasn't looking good. The clock was ticking down, and the exercise was not going well. A small team of senior managers in a global conglomerate was attempting to solve a simple problem together, ahead of making a presentation about their solution to a group of peers back in the main room.

As part of a management development course, we'd split the full group into teams, briefed them on the exercise, and put a camera in the room to record how things played out. We'd been explicit that their performance would not be part of their annual evaluation, but they seemed to forget that almost instantly, along with the camera. While it was true that they were not going to be evaluated on the quality of their presentation, the exercise was not without purpose. Analysis of their interactions and the process they used to arrive at a solution would be used to help them identify opportunities for developing their collaboration and team leadership skills.

The group started the exercise with enthusiasm but quickly ran into turbulence. It was the first exercise of a weeklong program, and all were keen to make their mark. At first everyone was friendly and played to their strengths. The more introverted types started out saying less, while those who thought by speaking took up more of the airtime. Suggestions were made and discussed, and everyone made an effort to listen to one another.

But as time went by in unstructured conversation, tempers frayed. Initially cordial relations were corroded by the lack of visible progress. Overusing their initial strategies became a liability: the introverts became quieter, the extroverts louder. Everyone began interrupting one another. People accustomed to making decisions rapidly made attempts to reach a conclusion, any conclusion. Others jumped up to start sketching out possible solutions on a flip chart before being shot down. When someone finally noticed the allotted time was nearly up, it was too late to prepare anything coherent for the presentation. So, the person most comfortable improvising with limited support material got the nod to present their last-minute solution back to the larger group.

That dynamic played out—sometimes worse, sometimes a touch better—in nearly all the other groups we've observed over the course of several years at such events. Some of the teams did a reasonable job with their presentation, but most drove it into the wall. Even the best of them were not much better than what would be expected at a school science fair. If you didn't know that all of them were running businesses with turnover in the hundreds of millions of dollars—and some of them were running businesses that did billions—you'd never have guessed it.

These were smart, motivated people, most of whom were running organizations with thousands of employees. But it wasn't smarts or motivation that was missing. It was structure.

Pretty much every time we ran the exercise, the groups plunged in too quickly, forgetting—or ignoring—the basics of collaborating on a team. The time limit on the exercise lent a whiff of urgency so that—

like in real life—fundamentals were skipped over, because it felt better to be in motion. Easy wins like filling simple service positions were overlooked: a timekeeper to limit discussion or highlight the approaching end of the exercise; a facilitator to keep the discussion going and make sure everyone was heard; a team leader empowered to make final calls when the group couldn't align; and a scribe to capture thoughts they could use for their presentation to the larger group. Having those roles in place didn't guarantee success, but they certainly enhanced the likelihood that a better result was produced.

> The more technique you have, the less you have to worry about it. The more technique there is, the less there is.
>
> —PABLO PICASSO

Over the ensuing week, subsequent team exercises became more effective and harmonious. Not because anyone got smarter, but because after debriefing their performance and getting feedback from their coach, each team adopted some very simple structures that supported their discussions, decision-making, and execution.

This exercise and others like it are part of a growing trend, both in organizations and in business schools, to equip leaders with better tools for leading their teams to more effective collaboration.

THE TREND IS TO MORE TEAM WORKING

In the world in which we now work, teams have become the fundamental unit of productive collaboration. Skilled individuals still have a huge role to play, but—apart from a few hermit geniuses—pretty much all significant achievement happens in teams. And even the hermit geniuses, if they are to have real impact with their ideas, will need a team to go to work on bringing those ideas to life. Teams are getting fresh focus, and teaming well is a key skill for those wanting to thrive in this new environment. Teaming—with others and with AI—is *the* skill that will keep us from becoming redundant in the near future.

Today the challenges that we face as a society and in our organizations require such a diverse mix of skills and personal qualities that teams are the most efficient and effective way to address them. Solving big problems together demands multiple skill sets and more effort than any lone human can deploy. And that is just to find a solution. Guiding that solution through the politics and interdependencies of a modern organization is often too much for any one person to navigate. People collaborating in teams produce the coolest stuff, and we have identified the principles that will make it easier for them to do so.

The team level is also a great leverage point at which to make changes. Many initiatives try to bring about change in large organizations by intervening at the organizational level, but getting traction there is unbelievably difficult. Those with experience know that genuine culture change in a large organization could take a decade. Not so for teams. Just as soldiers don't fight for their country but for their foxhole buddies, members of a team will make commitments and changes with and for one another at a speed that would be next to impossible in a larger system. We're hopeful that if many teams within an organization adopt the principles and practices in this book, it will have a positive impact on organizations, but we are not targeting the whole organization in this work. We believe the point of highest leverage is the team, and that is where we will direct our focus throughout this book.

WHAT IS A TEAM?

There are probably as many definitions of a team as there are consultants serving them. Some definitions (and consultants) are more useful than others. We choose to keep our definition simple. For us a team is any group that comes together regularly or ad hoc to achieve a common aim that is far more easily achieved together than anything the parts might achieve on their own.

The definition is broad, but using our definition, many groupings that don't immediately occur to people as constituting a team can be seen as one and, as such, profit from the simple structures and processes that more obvious teams enjoy.

> We must indeed all hang together, or most assuredly, we shall all hang separately.
>
> —BENJAMIN FRANKLIN

Some teams are easy to identify: sports teams, of course; military and corporate teams, for sure. But how about an executive and her personal assistant? They might not commonly be regarded as a team, but we believe that there is value in treating them as one. Any such executive has already been identified as someone capable of having an outsize impact on the results of the organization she works in. If she doesn't pay attention to how she coordinates her work with her PA in the way that great teams do, tremendous amounts of energy and inspiration can be lost in a farrago of misunderstandings, unspoken expectations, or missed communications. A working relationship that should be a means of expanding the impact of the executive's talents becomes an inefficient passive-aggressive mess instead. This isn't hypothetical. Both of us have been called in to sort out precisely such situations dozens of times. Most executives don't think of themselves as being on a team with their PA or executive assistant, but in our experience, this is one of the most important teams in which any executive is a member.

How about a couple with a baby on the way? What are they but a team dealing with a new entry to their marketplace? If they don't find a way to work together effectively, the infant might put them out of business, or at least out of their minds. It might not be the stuff of fairy tales, but small things like getting a joint projects list on the go and keeping it visible might just preserve their sanity.

Families are not often seen as teams, but we have years of positive feedback from parents who've profited at home from the same simple principles of the GTD workflow approach that they are using at work. In the same way we believe families will also profit from integrating best practices from the world of teams. To be clear, while families can benefit from some aspects of how teams work, we are not saying that teams are—or should be—families. (Even when relations are strained, it is difficult to get fired from your family.) By using the same team structures, principles, and processes as teams do, families can fulfill their purpose—offering safety, love, and belonging to their members—even more effectively.

Using our definition, even a pairing like you and your taxi driver might be called a team—one joined together to get you where you are going. That might seem a stretch, but the same principles apply. And as noted in chapter 1, many modern work teams aren't called into existence for much longer than a crosstown ride.

As the example of the executive and assistant shows, we don't set a lower limit on numbers. But from experience over many years, it seems that once a team gets too large, the practices we propose in this book become unwieldy. What is too large? There will always be exceptions, but six to ten members is probably optimal, and twenty is well on the way to becoming more of a herd than a real team.

We don't think a team even needs to be employed full-time for it to be effective. There are volunteer teams, of course, but even in the corporate world teams can function well with members who work only part-time for the team in question. We have run successful teams for over a decade with none of their members employed full-time, or at all. A loose group of associates, united by a common purpose and the principles and techniques we describe here, has spread GTD to individuals and organizations in seventy-five different countries over the course of a couple of decades.

Perhaps even more extreme, the executive learning event described at the beginning of this chapter was run by a "team" of professionals who had never actually worked with one another before. In just a few hours they came together, allocated responsibilities, and agreed to handoffs and how they wanted to work with one another during the event. With clear documentation about what needed to happen and clear agreements about roles and responsibilities in place, the participants were never aware that they were in the hands of a team that hadn't actually met until the day before the event started.

That example of team may sound extreme, but it has been the norm in many industries for years. What is a film set but a collection of experts, pulled together for a short period of time, focusing their talents on a given objective before moving on to work on other projects?

While teams can increasingly be fleeting, longer-life-cycle teams still do exist in many companies and industries. There is no one-size-fits-all way to run a team, though certain businesses require particular structures and approaches. What is important is having an appropriate team structure and agreements for the activity of the team. You'll want a different framework for a family picnic or church committee than for sending a rocket to Mars. The principles will remain the same, but the way they are expressed may be radically distinctive. But any and all of them, no matter how informal or short-lived, will profit from the simple approach we propose.

Our purpose here is not to describe *the* way to run any team, but to uncover the principles and practices of effective teamwork and offer them up in an easily understandable framework so you can design a solution that works for *your* team.

WHAT ARE PRINCIPLES, AND WHY?

We've referred to principles several times now, so we should define what we mean. A principle is often seen as a fundamental law—like the laws of physics—that determines outcomes independent of time or location. Gravity is an example of a principle. If you drop something anywhere on Earth, gravity works in exactly the same way. All objects—stones, apples, whatever—are going to drop to the ground. You can play with that principle, as trapeze artists do to thrill their audience, but if you ignore it entirely, there will be trouble.

In the original GTD books, David uncovered and explained the principles of personal workflow. For example, a key principle of "Capture" is that getting things out of your head that you want to do something about will lead to better outcomes. That is consistent for humans regardless of time or place. It would have worked as well in medieval France as it does in modern-day China, and as it will in an eventual colony on Mars.

The same is true for "Clarify." The principle here is that you'll get better results if you protect time—sooner rather than later—to think about what the things you've captured mean for you. Nothing *can* happen until you do the thinking to know what the next action is. The only question is what state you'll be in when you do the thinking: stressed, because it's become an emergency and you're having to consider it while a bunch of other topics are on your radar, too; or relaxed, because you've protected some time to think each day.

You can certainly be flexible with these principles. We don't particularly care *how* you capture—paper will do it as well as a digital device—or *when* you clarify, but if you ignore either of them entirely, a price will be paid in missed opportunities or unwanted stress.

In this book, we're using the idea and practice of "principles" in several sections, and although the word is used in different contexts, its meaning remains the same: the activities or behaviors that optimally support what we're doing as a team and how we are being, together. Just as understanding gravity allows trapeze artists to work their magic in the air, understanding the principles of personal workflow has enabled an entire generation of knowledge workers to get more done with less stress for years at a time. Similarly, understanding the principles of healthy high performance on a team will enable you and your team to find your own way of applying them to create similarly positive results—no nets required.

PRINCIPLES THAT MAKE TEAMS WORK

We've identified five principles that are critical for teams, and a longer list of factors that are desirable and helpful but not absolutely necessary for a team to perform sustainably at a high level. The core principles are as follows:

- Clarity

- Sufficient trust

- Open communication

- Learning

- Diversity

PRINCIPLE: CLARITY

Sometimes referred to by other names, such as "transparency" or "line-of-sight," this principle expresses itself in myriad ways on healthy and effective teams. On such teams there is a strong commitment to continuously clarify *what is so* on a variety of different levels and parameters.

Getting the appropriate data on the table is a critical starting point for any project or decision-making process. This all comes down to determining what, exactly, is the world the team must currently navigate.

To expand on our football analogy in the introduction, the most obvious thing that will immediately draw a player's attention is where they are on the field of play. That puts the goal and the next play in the optimal context. Even if you and I have total agreement on the goal, we could be at terrific odds if we don't have alignment on where we are with respect to it. From where I stand, we need to go left. From where you stand, we need to go right. Whoops. We think we're an aligned team, but we're not.

> A problem well stated is a problem half solved.
>
> —CHARLES KETTERING

To counter that, a team needs clarity on purpose and direction. A team is defined by its purpose and most effectively operates using well-defined standards and processes. Often those need to be revisited, because they may have changed, or (more likely) the team standards have slipped, and course correction is needed. The same is true of other directional guideposts, such as alignment on what "success" would really look like (vision) or what we need to make happen to achieve it (goals and objectives). These represent the top three Horizons of Focus that GTD identifies, enabling clearer priorities. We give each of these more attention in chapters 5 through 8.

Then there is role clarity—without it, there is confusion about who's responsible for what and who needs to be informed about it, as well as the risk of double work and eating up the attention of people who don't need to know. Implicit here is clarity of ownership. There always needs to be one person to go to, inside or outside the organization, when clarity is needed on a problem or situation which involves the team. More on this in chapter 9.

One of the big wins in terms of clarity is knowing—and accepting—how much the team is already trying to do, and having some view on whether it is humanly possible to achieve it. This is so critical that we've dedicated all of chapter 12 to it.

In our consulting roles there are times when progress seems "stuck" in the team conversation and focus. There is no better way to "un-stick" the process than having an honest discussion about current realities and getting everyone on the same page about them. Clarity can only be achieved if the team doesn't hide things from one another.

[DAVID] In my years of consulting, one of the prime exercises I've facilitated for a team is one that gets them on the same page in terms of the current realities of their situation.

A magical way to do that is to create a visual timeline of significant events leading up to the present. When did the enterprise start? By whom? What, then, happened that changed things? What challenges and opportunities appeared, and when? What was added, what was stopped, when? etc. I have always been fascinated by the clarity of focus and discussions that followed such an event.

People are often influenced by the stories they have heard and simply accepted. And many times, those are generalizations and exaggerations that need to be curated. "All the good people are leaving." Well, who, exactly, is leaving? "Well, Juanita said she was thinking of changing jobs."

"We're losing money in the company." How do you know? Based on what metric? How much money? "Well, they're cutting some budgets."

"Our competition is gaining on us." How do you know that? How much, how fast? "They've put big ads in the paper."

Ad infinitum.

PRINCIPLE: SUFFICIENT TRUST

In any team discussion about performance, this principle will be mentioned in some form. It is clearly important for humans working together, but as a word "trust" is a "big" concept and is understood in different ways by different people. Like the word "love," "trust" is so loaded with everyone's personal understanding and expectations that it is hard to know precisely what it means in the situation you are in. With respect to love, the ancient Greeks developed six separate words to represent the different kinds of love (passionate, friendship, for all mankind, etc.), which contemporary society parks under one banner. That lack of distinction can, of course, lead to misunderstandings. The same is true for trust. What many desire is the kind of total trust that a child has for a loving parent. Some get luckier than others in the parental sweepstakes, but however things played out in your family, we don't think it's helpful to be looking for that kind of all-encompassing trust in your team. When we speak about trust, what we mean is a willingness to commit to common goals, and to trust that there is enough mutual interest in achieving those goals that we can rely on one another to make best efforts to do what we have committed to doing to get there. Trust is built by making and keeping promises. Trust is both an input—you need to invest some to get a relationship going—and an output. It is as an output that most people refer to when they speak of being able to trust someone—the re-

> It is clear that if people anywhere are to willingly follow someone—whether it be into battle or into the boardroom, the front office or the front lines—they first want to assure themselves that the person is worthy of their trust.
>
> —JAMES KOUZES & BARRY POSNER

sult of certain commitments being met consistently. On an effective team you need at least that minimal degree of trust. Your agreements may be renegotiated (a simple example from your taxi driver team: "There's a roadblock ahead. It will cost more if I go this way, but will be faster"), but the intent to deliver remains constant.

PRINCIPLE: OPEN COMMUNICATION

This is the stablemate for what is now known as psychological safety— the ability to speak freely about things that impact the team without fear of punishment. We are not suggesting that the team must communicate openly about everything, but rather that there is clear support and positive feedback for disclosures of any sort, from any source, that might affect team performance. Without this, the likelihood of getting the consistent clarity defined by the first of these principles is dramatically decreased.

In Holacracy, for instance, it is crucial that anyone, at any level in the organization, feels free to surface any "tensions"—perceived problems or opportunities—as soon as they are noticed, so they can be appropriately evaluated and resolved in a timely manner. The system is set up to foster trust so that no negative judgment will be made about the person themselves for simply raising the point that there is something that deserves attention. Whether people trust one another as individuals is not at issue here, but whether they trust the process of getting things out in the open.

A friendly and conflict-averse team might feel nice, but withheld information can disrupt a team's coherence and morale as much as anything. And too often the information or feedback isn't actually withheld; it is simply misdirected into triangulations and gossip in forums that have no power to address the issue or opportunity.

Though it's great to like people you work with, you don't have to like them to work well together—you just need clear agreements. Without those, "liking" can turn uncomfortably bitter when the pressure is on.

PRINCIPLE: LEARNING

In the quote below, Hoffer makes his point succinctly, but the impacts on a team that doesn't make the effort to learn are worth elaborating. Teams that are unwilling or unable to take time to review, reflect, and learn from what they do are condemned to repeat their mistakes. If your team does not integrate this critical skill, then it won't be able to adapt in a dynamic, fast-changing environment. There will be no innovation, and no ability to respond to the evolving demands of the market and your stakeholders. It is only by continuously learning about their needs and desires that you can have any hope of partnering with them long-term. Without learning, groupthink and unconscious bias go unchallenged, and the team becomes stuck in reactivity, rather than creating strategies to deal with what they can see coming at them from the horizon. Trace any of the major industrial or corporate disasters back to the source, and usually you'll find a team that had stopped being open to the potential of learning.

> In a world of change, the learners shall inherit the earth, while the learned shall find themselves perfectly suited for a world that no longer exists.
>
> —ERIC HOFFER

The good news is that teams that have committed to the previous principles we've covered are a long way down the road to embracing this one, too. If there is a commitment to facing reality and sufficient trust to engage in open communication about it, then all that is necessary for learning is setting aside the time to discuss recent performance and a willingness to look for ways to improve it.

PRINCIPLE: DIVERSITY

This is perhaps the most controversial principle on our short list, in part because of how the word itself has become so tightly linked to debates on race and gender. Some say that diversity isn't really a principle, because there was a time not too long ago when many successful teams didn't appear to be diverse at all. But while there was less *visible* diversity because of the time and place in which those teams operated, we posit that there has always been plenty of diversity (of thought, approach, skills, etc.) on high-achieving teams. But too often everyone on a team went to the same schools and came from the same socioeconomic background. Including diversity of race and gender on any team represents a huge step forward, as ideally a team should include a rich mix of culture, experience, and viewpoint. Only then do you get the differing perspectives and feedback that lead to greater resiliency and more creative solutions.

The diversity of a team needs space to express its utility. As one of our clients noted, GTD creates space for diversity to flourish, because the potential of a diverse team can't be harnessed if everyone is so flat-out fighting fires that they can't raise their heads to get perspective on what is going on or make time for the conversations needed to hammer out robust solutions. Organizations actually need more "controlled explosions," more unusual people, more lack of symmetry in members and practices in order to deliberately challenge themselves before the market throws them a curveball.

NICE TO HAVES

What follows here are some "nice to haves" that we'd both love to have on any team we played on, but that are not principles per se, because we've seen so many teams work successfully without any or all of them in place. To be clear, all of them are desirable, so try to integrate as many as possible into your own teams.

Fluid leadership—In our experience, there always needs to be leadership, but it doesn't always have to come from the hierarchical head of the team. Effective teams pass the role to the "right player for the play," whoever has the best skills or experience to do the job in question.

Rigorous prioritization—While not a principle, this one is so important that we've dedicated an entire chapter to it. You can jump ahead to chapter 12 if you want to know more now.

Ownership culture—Team accountability for successful execution—where each member is responsible for the results of the team, and not just their own area—is the gold standard for team accountability. When everyone feels they are on the hook for the results of the team, they will all pitch in to help when things go wrong. We've seen teams function well without such a culture, but this is certainly a more fun and engaging way to work.

Fun—As the previous point illustrates, another desirable is having fun when performing together. This comes partly as a result of moving fast with trust to achieve team goals, and partly from a willingness to create time to

> Those who enjoy responsibility usually get it; those who merely like exercising authority usually lose it.
>
> —MALCOLM FORBES

> It's amazing how much people can get done if they don't care who gets the credit.
>
> —SANDRA SWINNEY

celebrate both effort and achievement. Even teams that thrive on conflict need occasional harmony, because otherwise the team can produce great results but in a dysfunctional, miserable work environment.

Proactivity—The willingness to quickly and consistently move toward both opportunities and problems is a hallmark of great teams.

Common language—One of the factors that reduces friction and noise on a team is having both a common understanding of the work to be done and how to do it, and a common language that permits clear and concise communication.

> The real challenge is to make good communication a handy and well-used tool. Then you are likely to pick it up and use it without thinking.
>
> —MAX DE PREE

TEAM VS. INDIVIDUAL (WHO'S BRINGING WHAT TO THE PARTY)

In our conversations about team performance, it became clear that a fundamental transaction needed clarification: namely, what the individual needs to bring to the team for the team to perform well, and what the team needs to provide to the individual to enable them to do their part. The first GTD books dealt mainly with the former—how individuals could improve their performance and maximize their contribution to the team. This book is aimed primarily at the latter—what the team should provide to the individuals.

WHAT SHOULD THE INDIVIDUAL BRING TO THE TEAM?

In this "contract" what should the individual provide? That is often unclear, because only a small proportion of this responsibility is captured in even what seems like a well-crafted job description. A job description—when it exists—usually details a short list of the requisite professional skills, along with the expressed desire that the candidate brings above-average competence and a wealth of real-world experience in the role for which they are being considered. Unfortunately, much of what a team needs from individuals never makes it into a job advertisement and is rarely brought up in an interview. These are the expectations that remain unspoken because of overoptimistic assumptions about what humans will consistently do while exercising their professional skills.

For example, teams need individuals to bring a degree of self-mastery and, at a minimum, an ability to make, track, and deliver on agreements they commit to. No one delivers everything on time, so when circumstances dictate that won't happen, they need the skills to renegotiate those agreements in a way that minimizes disruption on the team and in the organization. Beyond that they should show up when they agreed to, occasionally generate ideas about possibility, and have some minimal ability to add energy and motivate themselves through difficult patches. Ideally, they bring enough courage to be honest but civil in tough conversations, and a willingness to keep their ego in check in service of the team purpose.

Have you ever seen a job description that lists those as qualifications? Probably not. But all we've done in the preceding paragraph is clarify actual expectations. Any team interested in healthy high performance would welcome all of them in a heartbeat. These qualities are assumed, deemed too obvious for inclusion in a role description for skilled professionals, but the carnival of nonfulfillment on most teams demonstrates that it is an unwise assumption.

A longer list of desirable qualities would include the ability to be truly present in conversation, and to listen without interrupting the ideas of others. That means having understood what they are saying, then navigating the line between appreciation for what is useful in those ideas and giving constructive feedback, in order to build on them rather than simply criticize them. It means that through it all, being always willing to speak truth to power when the mission of the team is at risk.

Those last might seem like overkill, but they are in fact what many hope for when they bring new people onto their team. That the qualities seem idealistic when written out does not diminish their utility, and just because most have given up on getting what they want doesn't mean those qualities are undesirable. Whatever list you choose to articulate for your team, we guarantee you that doing so on the front end will save years of heartache and conflict. Having those abilities exist as unspoken, unclarified expectations can lead only to disappointment, resentment, and misunderstanding on the team.

> Courage is what it takes to stand up and speak; courage is also what it takes to sit down and listen.
>
> —WINSTON CHURCHILL

Even if it is typically as poorly articulated as we've described, the individual's contribution to the team gets most of the explicit focus in this contract between individual and team. But it is only half of the equation.

WHAT SHOULD THE TEAM OFFER TO THE INDIVIDUAL?

If you agree that the first part of the equation could do with some sharpening up, unfortunately the team's obligations to the individual are even less well defined. And unless the team gives some explicit thought to what individuals need from it to be able to do their work well, then the team itself can become a stressor. A structure that should foster collaboration, reduce friction, and decrease stress for its members can wind up doing just the opposite. The team needs to have developed clear guidance that helps individuals know what is expected from them, how they are doing in delivering their part of the team goals, and how to collaborate effectively with others on the team. Only then can they get more done, more quickly than they could as a group of individuals. What is wanted is consciously developed and clearly communicated standards, processes, and practices that make things easier for those on the team.

A simple example from the domain of GTD workflow: while it is for the individual to manage their own workflow, the team must decide how it will *collectively* handle its workflow so the individuals can work well together. For instance, how will the team systematically capture things that have its collective attention? What is the right forum in which to raise those topics? How will the team ensure those things are addressed in a timely manner? Where will the results of any team decisions be kept, so that everyone can find them? How often will the team review its work, and how will it prioritize that work in a way that helps protect its members from being overwhelmed?

> Most teams aren't teams at all but merely collections of individual relationships with the boss. Each individual vying with the others for power, prestige, and position.
>
> —DOUGLAS MURRAY MCGREGOR

Beyond that, the team should provide efficient structures, clear processes, defined roles, guidance on prioritization, a defense mechanism for handling stakeholders who ask for more than was originally agreed, and support to protect both time to think and time to get work done.

As in our football analogy, these go well beyond what increasing the individual skills of the team's players can resolve. Even if all the individuals have great skills with their own workflows, if the above questions aren't clarified at the team level, there will still be time and effort wasted attending to repeated misunderstandings. Clarifying how it wants individuals to work *together* is the responsibility of the team, and the subject of much of the rest of this book.

In the next section, we'll delve into how the existing GTD frameworks for individuals can be used to promote better collaboration on a team. We'll start by looking more deeply at how the five steps of GTD apply in a team environment.

KEY ELEMENTS OF PRODUCTIVE TEAMING

CONTROL	FOCUS	PLANNING
Capture	Horizon 5: Purpose and Principles	Purpose and Principles
Clarify		
Organize	Horizon 4: Vision	Vision
	Horizon 3: Goals	Brainstorm
Reflect		
Engage	Horizon 2: Areas of Focus	Organize
		Next Actions
	Horizon 1: Projects	
	Ground: Next Actions	

n this section of the book, we'll be focusing on the three original GTD models (listed vertically in the columns above) as they relate to working on teams. The five steps of GTD (Control), the Horizons of Focus (Focus), and the Natural Planning Model (Planning) are outlined in more detail in appendix 1, so if the above graphic currently registers for you only as a lightly structured word salad, you might want to read that now before going on. For those who are familiar with the models, the graphic is a guide to which element we are focusing on in this section. We'll repeat the map at the beginning of each element of a model and highlight the relevant part in **bold**.

Chapter 4

Maintaining Control and Focus
THE FIVE STEPS FOR A TEAM

The original GTD books offered guidance for resolving the issues of personal workflow at an individual level. Some possibilities for teams were implicit in the principles of those books, but we see there is value in making them explicit and offering a road map for implementing them on a team.

CONTROL	FOCUS	PLANNING
Capture	Horizon 5: Purpose and Principles	Purpose and Principles
Clarify	Horizon 4: Vision	Vision
Organize	Horizon 3: Goals	Brainstorm
Reflect	Horizon 2: Areas of Focus	Organize
Engage	Horizon 1: Projects	Next Actions
	Ground: Next Actions	

The five steps listed on the left in the table above are necessary to get any situation under control, and apply equally to teams and to individuals. For the most part what distracts people's attention represents something with which they are not yet appropriately engaged. So, whatever is not yet on cruise control for a team—or on track to getting done—will take up team energy. Such things need to be captured, clarified, and organized, with appropriate reviews in place, to ensure optimal team focus and engagement.

As with individuals', team workflow is only as good as the weakest link in the chain. If you personally are great at capture, but don't get around to clarifying your digital and physical piles of "stuff," it won't really matter how well organized you are, or how often you conduct a review, because you'll only be getting a fraction of the benefit. The same is true for teams, which is why we want to take some time to review the five steps as they apply to a team context. If you understand the best practices and minimum standards for each step,

STEP ONE: CAPTURE—IDENTIFYING WHAT HAS TEAM ATTENTION

CONTROL	FOCUS	PLANNING
Capture	Horizon 5: Purpose and Principles	Purpose and Principles
Clarify	Horizon 4: Vision	Vision
Organize	Horizon 3: Goals	Brainstorm
Reflect	Horizon 2: Areas of Focus	Organize
Engage	Horizon 1: Projects	Next Actions
	Ground: Next Actions	

and the relationships between them, you'll already be a long way down the road to better team functioning.

If you've ever sat in a meeting where actions are being decided upon, but no one is writing anything down, you'll already have some idea of why this step is critical to the functioning of a team. Because if you've then had the misfortune to attend the follow-up meeting, you'll have seen the results: inconsistent delivery of commitments made, and—as everyone has only a vague memory of what was agreed on—the near impossibility of holding anyone to account. If trust is one of the principles of healthy high performance on a team, then capturing is one of the main inputs to building that trust. Team commitments that are captured in the moment are dramatically more likely to be delivered in a timely manner.

A negative example is perhaps more easily illustrated: broken agreements corrode trust. If I tell you that I'll deliver X thing by Y time, but when Y rolls around you still don't have X, I will have undermined trust between us. If on-time deliveries are like deposits into a trust "account," then delivering late or not at all is a withdrawal from my trust account with you. If I do it often enough, you'll no longer be willing to trust me at all. You might love me to bits as a human being, but you'll go looking for someone else to get you your Xs. Conversely, preventing broken agreements builds trust. As outlined in *Getting Things Done*, it is relatively simple to prevent agreements from being broken in a damaging way. All you need to do is

1. not make the agreements;

2. complete what you agreed to; or

3. renegotiate agreements when you see they can't be delivered as promised.

Arrears of small things to be attended to, if allowed to accumulate, worry and depress like unpaid debts. The main work should always stand aside for these, not these for the main work, as large debts should stand aside for small ones, or truth for common charity and good feeling. If we attend continually and promptly to the little that we can do, we shall ere long be surprised to find how little remains that we cannot do.

—SAMUEL BUTLER

All of these options are significantly more difficult to act upon in a team that isn't capturing consistently. If you don't know how much you already have committed to, you'll say yes to things you can't accomplish. And if as a team you don't know *what* and *when* you agreed to deliver on a project, you'll struggle to complete it on time, or manage your promises in a timely manner.

Given all the difficult items that teams have on their plates, it would be a shame to fail at the simple stuff, like making a note in a meeting about what was agreed on, who is going to do it, and by when it is due. As a team you don't want to be futzing around with easily avoided misunderstandings when there is serious work to do.

CAPTURE AS TEAM—THE TEAM MIND SWEEP

Day-to-day team capturing won't look all that special. As individual team members notice there are things that need the team's attention, they'll capture them for themselves, then clarify them and put them either on their own agendas list for the upcoming team meeting or on a team agenda list that has been created on a shared drive for the purpose of capturing topics for the next team meeting.

The above process is probably already being used on any team where a majority of members are using GTD, but for those who don't have the system in place, any simple, easily accessible repository for ideas, inspiration, and concerns would do the trick for the normal daily capture of team topics. Members of the team just need to know where to place topics they want to get in front of the team, and the team just needs to go through those topics on a consistent basis so that everyone has confidence that they will be handled in a timely manner.

One manufacturing organization we worked with had implemented a new and exciting total quality management (TQM) process for their on-the-floor workers. The factory had two full shifts, with the changeover at midday. In a moment of inspiration they established a central inbox (literally a box) with pad and pen next to it. Anyone in one shift who noticed something the next shift ought to pay attention to would write a note and put it in the inbox. Unfortunately, no one was tasked with reading and doing anything about the notes on the next shift, so they just piled up. Oops.

A team mind sweep can be useful just to help get its members present and ready to think together. For those unfamiliar with GTD, the mind sweep is a way of emptying the brain of clutter and capturing topics that might require action. The exercise is as simple as asking the group, "What has our collective attention, right now?" If that doesn't provoke a rich stream of topics, issues, and pressure points, the questions can get more granular: What is it we're trying to do here? What are we worried about? What's going on that we should be aware of?

A team mind sweep would be useful at any point, of course, but we've seen them be especially valuable in relieving tremendous pressure and stress in critical situations. The cathartic nature of simply

> Out of intense complexities intense simplicities emerge.
>
> —WINSTON CHURCHILL

capturing everything that has the team's attention is a very useful prelude to being able to sort through that pile and make sense of it in a way that offers relief.

Capturing it all is only the first step, but simply getting it out of the collective team brain so everyone can see the scope of it is a massive advantage. Just as with an individual, a best practice is to simply capture things, without worrying—at this stage—what is going to happen with them. If the team moves too quickly to begin clarifying, organizing, or assigning accountabilities to the team's captured stuff, the process will begin to seem too long and drawn out, and the team will develop an unconscious resistance to capturing topics at all.

What currently adds more complexity to this relatively simple first step is when teams institute multiple channels of information and input that capture potentially meaningful stuff that needs to be

STEP TWO: CLARIFYING— DECIDING WHAT IT ALL MEANS

CONTROL	FOCUS	PLANNING
Capture	Horizon 5: Purpose and Principles	Purpose and Principles
Clarify	Horizon 4: Vision	Vision
Organize	Horizon 3: Goals	Brainstorm
Reflect	Horizon 2: Areas of Focus	Organize
Engage	Horizon 1: Projects	Next Actions
	Ground: Next Actions	

assessed. What do the team members need to see and react or respond to, relative to the purpose of the team? Just emails, or other channels like the various instant-messaging apps and team-related software? We suggest some solutions for reducing that complexity in chapter 6, on working standards.

The late, great Peter Drucker suggested that the biggest challenge for knowledge workers was in defining what their work *is*, specifically. Emails seldom appear telling you what they mean or what to do with them. Knowledge work is not immediately and obviously self-evident as the work of making or moving things was. The GTD methodology provides guidance on making work explicit—a senior consultant once labeled it "knowledge work athletics." At its core, "work" can be reduced to outcomes desired, and actions required to achieve them. What is the result that we're after, and how do we allocate physical resources to make it happen? But as natural and simple as this seems, outcome-and-action thinking is not something we automatically or naturally do in our relatively sophisticated world. It's a simple question, but by asking specifically, "What's the next action on this?" we've watched thousands of teams unblock projects that had become stuck. And if one action doesn't complete that project, "What's the desired outcome?" gives them a clear finish line. This thinking requires a cognitive muscle that most people avoid using until it is forced by urgent or pressing circumstances. When engaged proactively, however, it produces clarity and appropriate relationships with commitments, initiatives, and intentions of any sort.

We've seen whole teams and even organizational cultures move up to a new level of productivity by simply installing those two questions as standards for themselves and group thinking and decision-making.

The team will want to be able to clarify things as a team at regular intervals, but one of the biggest interventions it can make to its effectiveness and efficiency is to let all team members know that they not only have permission to protect time to clarify their own work, but that it is an expected part of their job. Ensuring that each team member is comfortable taking time each day to clarify their own incoming stuff will mean that all team interactions will have better preparation and be more complete than if the individuals are stuck firefighting.

Assuming that is in place, how will a team clarify topics brought to a team meeting to be thought through together? The same questions hold as for individuals:

- What is it? A new request? Does it relate to an existing team project? What—if any—team dependencies are in play with this item?

- Is it actionable? Is it aligned with our mission, vision, purpose?

- If it is actionable, what is the next action?

- Is there a clearly defined, desired outcome we want to track as a team?

- Who is doing that? By when?

For topics that make it to the agenda of a team meeting, the team is on the hook to clarify the expected desired outcome. Some teams choose to go further and clarify the next actions as well, while others leave that entirely up to the person they've made accountable for delivering the outcome.

You'll want to be ruthless with saying no at this stage. If you are reading this book, it's a fair guess that your team already has far more to do than it has capacity to deliver. So, you need to establish: What's really mission critical here? What's superfluous? The best teams we've seen are great at making those calls on the front end and protecting themselves from taking on too much. We've devoted the entirety of chapter 12 to how to do so effectively.

If the team is running a shared inbox, it will need clarifying, too. Our strong suggestion is to clear it out on some regular basis, and to do that the team needs an efficient and effective system that they trust. Clearing it out can be scary for teams that have been using the inbox as many individuals do, as their most trusted version of a to-do list. But leaving it all in the team inbox is basically requiring the team to prioritize their work using a brightly colored, categorized, and flagged bundle of stuff. That's not optimal. Daily is probably a minimum standard for clearing it out, but the rhythm mostly depends on stakeholder expectations. If you are interested in more detail, we've covered this more extensively in appendix 2.

STEP THREE: ORGANIZING AS TEAM— GETTING THE RIGHT LISTS IN THE RIGHT PLACE

CONTROL	FOCUS	PLANNING
Capture	Horizon 5: Purpose and Principles	Purpose and Principles
Clarify		
Organize	Horizon 4: Vision	Vision
	Horizon 3: Goals	Brainstorm
Reflect		
	Horizon 2: Areas of Focus	Organize
Engage		
		Next Actions
	Horizon 1: Projects	
	Ground: Next Actions	

One of the great challenges of a team is to find optimal ways of storing and reviewing what it has committed itself to. Far too often we've seen teams in overwhelm with no clear way of explaining why they are at a breaking point. Simple enhancements like an easily accessible team "Projects" list that is reviewed and updated consistently help to keep the team aligned on the right priorities and focused on getting the right things done.

For those already running a GTD system for themselves, one of the challenges is to define or navigate between the GTD definition of a project for an individual and what might be called a "project management" definition of a project for a team. These are two very different things. For individuals we believe it is worth tracking everything that will take more than one step but less than one year to complete on a GTD Projects list in their own system. (For more detail on why we suggest this way of doing it, please see appendix 1, or one of the earlier GTD books for details.)

Ideally, everyone on the team would have that kind of list for themselves, so reviewing everyone's Project lists to get a sense of what the team is engaged in would be doable. But practically speaking, getting through everyone's lists would make for a very long and slightly mind-numbing meeting.

Which raises a question that we hear regularly when working with teams. What does the team need to have on its radar versus what needs to be tracked in individual systems? One of our clients resolved this issue by developing a shorthand to differentiate personal GTD projects from team projects in their group discussions. They referred to small "p" projects, and big "P"—or capital "P"—projects. A project that was in an individual's system (using the GTD definition of a project) was a small "p" project. If it was a larger team project, it was a big "p" or a capital "P" project. The team would have the large-scale outcomes that require inputs from multiple members of the team on its big "P" projects list, while the small "p" projects would be tracked in individual systems. This allowed for an easy shorthand for discussing projects on the team, but also was a sorting mechanism that helped get them to the right place for review; some to individuals' systems, and some to the team projects list, which would be reviewed as a group in the weekly team meeting.

Wherever they end up, projects still get done one step at a time, so identifying next actions is useful if not imperative in a team forum. If clear ownership is established, those next actions can be left to the individuals concerned. Similarly, it would be overkill for the entire team to be kept up to date on what the next actions are for all ongoing projects across all the activities of the team.

The same holds for project support material. If multiple team members or stakeholders need access, then it only really makes sense to store project support materials in a manner that makes them easy to access and update by all team members. This can be handled with not only the very latest in collaborative software but also very simply. Many couples deal with this challenge by using a shared online document for common projects and a link to the document in their respective systems.

TEAM CALENDAR—WHAT MUST HAPPEN, WHEN?

Like the team Projects list, running a "master calendar" of events, milestones, and deliverables enables the team to get an overview of where they are with their commitments and the chronological relationships between them. If you want your team to hit critical deadlines, then a shared calendar that keeps them visible and is regularly reviewed will dramatically enhance the likelihood of them being delivered. Many co-located teams will still use a large whiteboard in their meeting room to present this kind of chronological clarity, but most others have now moved to a digital solution. The former has the advantage of constant visibility for those who work near it, and the latter permits asynchronous remote viewing and hybrid working.

TEAM REFERENCE

We have both had the experience of group software that was effectively used as a team reference, if the teams were familiar with the application, could easily see how things were organized, and had the freedom to access and input reference information on their own. At times it was also necessary to assign the management of a folder or subdatabase within the system to one person, who could then keep the information therein current and organized appropriately.

It's always tricky to come up with the optimal heuristics of how such systems are organized—i.e., what data goes under what heading(s) when there are multiple possibilities. That's why it's useful to have some regular review of how the system works, and for someone to refine or reorganize it as needed. It would be a mistake to assume that software out of the box will instantly let you know how best to use it. Often it may take weeks or even months to get it working smoothly for the team. That's also why it's a good idea to assign one person the role of "database manager," who can integrate suggested changes and updates as needed.

STEP FOUR: REFLECTING AS A TEAM— WHERE THE HECK ARE WE?

CONTROL	FOCUS	PLANNING
Capture	Horizon 5: Purpose and Principles	Purpose and Principles
Clarify		
Organize	Horizon 4: Vision	Vision
Reflect	Horizon 3: Goals	Brainstorm
Engage	Horizon 2: Areas of Focus	Organize
		Next Actions
	Horizon 1: Projects	
	Ground: Next Actions	

Taking the time to reflect as a team is a defining moment. It is when the team goes from lip service about the importance of learning as a principle to actually getting the benefits of it. We included "learning" as a must-have under the principles in the previous chapter because without it teams get stuck in a rut, fall behind their competition, and lose touch with their stakeholders. In Agile terms this time for reflection would be known as a retrospective, but as one of our clients observed, neither reflection nor retrospectives are simply about looking backward. There is an element of looking back to identify learning moments, but the exercise is actually designed to help move the team faster and with better focus and direction in the future.

There are numerous ways to reflect. Some include it as a brief part of every meeting, reserving five to ten minutes to contemplate not only on what was done in the meeting but how it got done. The reflection here is on "How did we work together as a team in this meeting?" Or perhaps more to the point, "How could we do this better next time?" Setting aside five to ten minutes of an hour-long meeting might feel like a lot, but the 8 to 16 percent of meeting time that it represents pays a huge return on time invested if the team uses it to surface and discuss the real obstacles that got in their way. This would be the time to pick up late starts, poor prep, or the nonadherence to any other agreed team standards.

At the other end of the spectrum, many teams will take a few hours at the end of the year to reflect on what happened in the year just past, both in terms of successes and "improvement opportunities." Most teams are pleasantly surprised to look back over the past months and observe just how much cool and useful stuff got done that they'd long since forgotten, as more recent projects and surprises covered previous achievements in a cloud of forgetting.

TEAM REVIEW MEETINGS—CRITICAL PULSE-TAKING

One of the most helpful frequencies for teams that do a lot of work with one another is weekly. We've seen it work with longer periods, and there are also times when rapidly changing circumstances dictate that daily stand-up reviews are needed to keep things on an even keel.

The content of a team meeting will be determined by the frequency of the get-together. Even the same people on the same team will have different perspectives in a meeting if it happens daily, weekly, monthly, quarterly, or annually, as they automatically generate thoughts at different horizons. A daily stand-up meeting would not be the place to talk about annual goals; a quarterly review session would not want to be dealing with operational details. We have often been in review meetings ourselves that we weren't sure were needed, but once there, we were often surprised by the unexpected rich content and interactions that took place.

We like to think of these reviews as an accelerator: not a time *cost* spent looking back at things past, but rather an *investment* in reviewing how things went to be able to do them better in the future. Where are we in each project? What needs doing next? Who is doing it? Critical for the success of a team weekly review is that the individuals on the team have done their own reviews. Without that, there will be too many gaps in information, too much, "I'll have to get back to you about that," with accompanying delays.

At a minimum, it will be useful to review the following about current team projects:

- Desired outcome

- Progress of the project, as perceived by the owner of the whole project (and eventual owners of any subprojects)

- Any milestones that have been reached or not yet attained and the current state of play with proposed next actions

Those will be a good starting point for a corporate team, but you really should refine them to fit your teams' specific needs. One of our colleagues did just that with her family. She and her husband started doing a weekly review of a shared Google calendar and found it helped them stay on top of their young children's sports activities, school performances, orthodontist appointments, etc. Though family life ran much more smoothly with just that review, they noticed a gap: the younger members of the family team were effectively "passengers," often unaware of what was coming at them in a given day. That sometimes led to unhelpful reactions, so the idea was to create a time for review, reflection, and planning, so the children would be well briefed—about their own schedules and those of their parents—so that predictable events like Mom's business trips were no longer a surprise, and unnecessarily tearful incidents were kept to a minimum.

The session takes place on a Sunday morning just after breakfast, next to a whiteboard in the hallway of their apartment. In roughly fifteen minutes they focus mostly on the coming week. The whiteboard is divided into columns from Monday to Sunday, and everyone enters the most important dates while giving a brief description to the others: e.g., "Project day at school," "7:30 in the office," "Clarinet lessons," "Aikido." Or also: "Birthday party for school friend Sophie."

Originally, the board was simply sorted by day, but after a few weeks the children suggested that everyone should have their own column inside of each day's column and a different color for each persons' entries, so they could understand it at a glance.

Once the bare bones of the week are clear, they ask some family-specific questions:

- Is there anything from last week that isn't finished yet?

- What do you need from us in this week? Money for Sophie's birthday present?

- Any communications or permissions from the school or sports clubs we have to see or sign?

- If there is an upcoming test, do we need to schedule time for learning? Do you need help with homework?

- Any special food requests?

- And last but not least: Who is doing which chores in the coming week?

This quick review feeds back into the parent's conversations about the week, as often the Sunday meeting reveals new challenges. Again, some quick questions are helpful:

- Do we have to adjust our plans because an important appointment for the children has been added?

- In light of changes to our schedules on a given day, do we have to organize child support?

Tickets, notes with signatures, and other support material are stuck with magnets directly on the board under the date on which they'll be needed so the children can take what they need on their own. Things change in the course of the week, of course, but the idea of a clear and up-to-date overview for everyone remains. Being on top of "predictable" surprises means they have more slack in the system to improvise with the truly unexpected: sick teachers, additional music tryouts, broken smartphones.

For some readers this may sound like too much formality for family management, but the family experience is one of reduced stress and much greater harmony. Not only do the children have a better understanding of how their plans fit in the wider picture, but they are also empowered to be more independent and self-reliant in their coming years.

As the whiteboard in the example demonstrates, where you keep all of this is not important if it is accessible to everyone on the team. We've seen everything from a spreadsheet on a shared drive to a relatively sophisticated filtering system in a piece of collaborative software. Many teams use such a document to support their reviews and update it in advance. Any standard other than "the document is complete and up to date ahead of each review meeting" would be a waste of everyone's time in the meeting.

The purpose of this is to keep the entire project landscape fresh for the team. To be transparent for the whole team about what is already on their plate, where they are on each project, and what—if any—issues are currently in the way. Here are some examples of questions that can be helpful for a more corporate team:

- If there are problems with priorities, can we start adjusting them?

- Does anyone on the team need help with something they are working on?

- How about the dependencies between projects?

- If one project can't go forward while waiting for the progress of another, does anything need to happen to manage expectations and minimize disruption elsewhere in the system?

- Is there an intersection of all these different projects that suggests we should bring them together so that we're not duplicating work?

- Can we harmonize and accelerate the deployment of these things that are going to be faster because we're much more coordinated than before?

It is in these meetings that the team Projects list (with a capital "P") demonstrates its true value. The reason it is so critical that a team and especially leadership have a team Projects list is to avoid the phenomenon of "work creep." If you think the amount of work that your team is doing is x, but it is actually $2x$ or $3x$ because of other commitments that members of the team have taken on without the team's knowledge, then it is no wonder that progress isn't being made on items that matter to you.

STEP FIVE: ENGAGING—PRIORITIZING AS A TEAM

CONTROL	FOCUS	PLANNING
Capture	Horizon 5: Purpose and Principles	Purpose and Principles
Clarify		
Organize	Horizon 4: Vision	Vision
Reflect	Horizon 3: Goals	Brainstorm
Engage	Horizon 2: Areas of Focus	Organize
		Next Actions
	Horizon 1: Projects	
	Ground: Next Actions	

GTD for individuals is (in)famous for suggesting that you prioritize using your intuition, basing your moment-to-moment decisions on an overview of complete lists and a calendar that is rigorously maintained. Some love this, but many complain that it is too loose a framework to meet their desire for certainty about the next choice they make.

But the model that David proposed in *Getting Things Done* isn't actually loose at all. If you've done the work of the first four steps in the model, then you've already done the heavy lifting of prioritizing. Provided you've taken the time to catalog all your commitments and have assessed them recently enough to feel confident you're not missing anything, you can enjoy the fruits of your labors. Because the right answer to "What should I do next?" is always subjective. There are models that can help make the call, but the calls need to be made in the moment, with full knowledge about any recent developments, and best available information about what lies ahead. Only then will you have the greatest likelihood of making the right choice.

> **Often greater risk is involved in postponement than in making a wrong decision.**
>
> —H. A. HOPF

Obviously, the specific nature of the team and its situation will determine how priorities are decided and acted upon. The team may have inherited a specific direction from upper management and must align with that. With other topics the team itself can figure out its operational strategy in a collaborative consensus style. In either case a complete overview of the team commitments will be required for the group to march forward in step together.

Various models exist to assist in team prioritizing, and might be useful in certain circumstances, such as "Harvey balls" and effort/impact matrices.

The former assesses the comparative progress of particular activities using ideogrammatic balls, partially or fully filled in to indicate their relative completion. An effort/impact matrix would place activities on a chart assessing the effort required to perform an

> Another flaw in the human character is that everybody wants to build and nobody wants to do maintenance.
>
> —KURT VONNEGUT

activity against the potential impact that activity would have. For instance, something that had high impact but low effort would be a sweet spot.

We say much more about methods for team prioritization in chapter 12.

Chapter 5

Horizon Five

PURPOSE AND PRINCIPLES

CONTROL	FOCUS	PLANNING
Capture	**Horizon 5: Purpose and Principles**	Purpose and Principles
Clarify	Horizon 4: Vision	Vision
Organize	Horizon 3: Goals	Brainstorm
Reflect	Horizon 2: Areas of Focus	Organize
Engage	Horizon 1: Projects	Next Actions
	Ground: Next Actions	

B y far the best-known framework in the GTD approach is the five-step model for getting control of your day-to-day life, which we covered in the previous chapter. It has been such a success that it completely overshadows what might qualify as its big brother: the "Horizons of Focus" model for clarifying focus and perspective over the longer term. In some ways it is the more important of the two. While the five steps of Capture, Clarify, Organize, Reflect, and Engage will help you to get control of what you currently have in play, the Horizons of Focus model clarifies *why* you are doing any of that stuff at all. Most come to GTD for its ability to help them get control of the day-to-day tasks and projects, but they stay to elaborate on their Purpose, Vision, and Goals, and the Roles that they have in their personal and professional lives.

What we notice is that once people have control over the detail of their lives, they hunger for meaning in their work. They don't want to just do the *same* work better and faster; they want to be sure that they are doing the *right* work. It is only by making conscious choices about the so-called higher horizons that people begin to use their enhanced ability to get things done on what really matters to them.

The same is true for teams. In this and the next three chapters we'll look at those higher horizons from the perspective of their utility for teams and offer thoughts on how best to flesh them out in ways that harness latent energy and motivation.

TYING IT ALL TOGETHER

There is a logic to the hierarchy of teamwork. Ideally, purpose, principles, vision, goals, projects, and actions are all aligned, but it is vanishingly rare that there is line of sight along all these elements on a team. Clarity at each horizon is best and most easily created at the team level. Individuals may work out how they all fit together on their own, but at huge expense in time, attention, and energy. Unfortunately, individuals are rarely offered the direction provided by clearly articulated purpose, vision, goals, and a concise summary of their role in delivering them. The conversation is not a complicated one. Ideally, everyone would have the following explained to them on day one in a new job, and then updated consistently over time:

This is why we're here. (Purpose)

This is how we play the game together. (Principles)

This is where we're going. (Vision)

Here are the milestones we'll pass on our way. (Goals)

And finally,

Here is your role in making that happen, and how you'll be judged and rewarded for your contribution. (Areas of Focus)

When a team gets all those points aligned—and consistently reinforces them over time—it has access to energy and motivation that is unimaginable without them in place.

That said, we are not suggesting that you need to have them all defined before you start doing anything. Many times the starting point is, and maybe should be, wherever there's a "fire in the belly." That could be a project that has already started, when someone realizes that the implications of what they are coming up with are far more important than they initially thought. Or it might be time to clarify "purpose," to see if the new project is really aligned with the bigger picture. Many entrepreneurs would struggle to articulate what their real purpose was in starting their business. They quickly got busy and haven't had time to reflect on it since. They may only want or need to get more clarity about their higher horizons when they are approached about a merger, or a buyout, or an acquisition. Or more dramatically, when life circumstances throw them a curve, such as a divorce or an unexpected and critical medical diagnosis.

In this and the next four chapters, we'll outline why we think it is worth taking the time to clarify each of the horizons on your team and make suggestions on how you can go about doing that. Exploring each of these horizons in any order will be fruitful. Though the order doesn't matter in terms of what has the team's attention, eventually the exploration will roll up to the question "Is this truly on purpose?" There is a hierarchy of priorities, and we'll start here from the top.

HORIZON 5: PURPOSE—WHY ARE WE DOING THIS ANYWAY?

CONTROL	FOCUS	PLANNING
Capture	**Horizon 5: Purpose** and Principles	Purpose and Principles
Clarify		
Organize	Horizon 4: Vision	Vision
Reflect	Horizon 3: Goals	Brainstorm
Engage	Horizon 2: Areas of Focus	Organize
		Next Actions
	Horizon 1: Projects	
	Ground: Next Actions	

WHY PURPOSE?

In the Korean War, captured American soldiers were subjected to a particularly pernicious form of brainwashing. For the first time in history, the relatively new science of psychology was weaponized in a systematic way. The soldiers' captors knew these were strong young men who would resist punishments and would close ranks to protect one another in the face of a common enemy. And yet within months some of the soldiers would simply lie down in a corner and die. What happened was subtle, but very effective.

Instead of attacking the inmates, their captors mostly left them alone. They were, however, offered small rewards—like cigarettes or extra food—for giving information about one another. If informing on others had led to punishments of the perpetrators, many of the informants would have resisted taking the rewards and stopped giving information. But this is where the approach was so cunning. Usually, the person who'd been snitched on got either no punishment or just a slap on the wrist. In those circumstances, why not inform on one another? The informer got rewards, and the person informed on didn't get badly punished. And so most people collaborated.

What this process ultimately led to was a complete isolation of each of the inmates, who could no longer trust anyone around them, and a complete breakdown in any belief that there was a purpose worth fighting for. If their own side was willing to inform on them for nearly no reward, what were they doing in the war in the first place? Over time most lost the will to fight, and many simply lost the will to live.

To be clear, we are not suggesting that anything so dramatic is taking place on your team. It may not be the best-run team in the world, but it is unlikely that there is a systematic campaign to have you lose hope and any sense of purpose at work. What is true is that many organizations are achieving exactly that result through benign neglect (what, after all, do the stats on disengagement at work really represent?), when being just a touch more conscious about articulating a clear purpose could be a significant lever for energizing the team.

We live in a time when—in developed countries at least—religious attendance is at an all-time low and is still dropping. Our trust in institutions (government, media, the legal system) is plumbing depths unknown in recent memory. Coming out of a global pandemic straight into a land war in Ukraine, with accompanying inflation, many began questioning why they were doing what they were doing. We all like to feel that our work and our lives have meaning, and events had begun making meaning difficult to discern.

The absence of purpose is felt day in and day out in teams around the world, with employees hired and—after the briefest of onboarding sessions—plopped in front of a freshly baked email account and given no context for their labor. Is it any wonder when the latest employee survey shows that the workforce isn't quite as engaged as leadership might hope?

Part of the challenge is that for many, the primary reason their organization exists is to enrich the owners. There may be some PR on the website about a commitment to all stakeholders, but actions speak louder than words. If the stated aims don't line up with what people feel they are rewarded for in the organization, then rewards take the day, not the statements. But we can still connect with—and have faith in—people we live and work more closely with at the level of the team.

To not harness the energy available from having a clear and inspirational purpose for your team is like trying to run your household appliances on AA batteries when a main power source is available. It might be doable, but it doesn't make much sense.

Looking at how this purpose has worked for individuals gives some sense of what kind of power is available. Without a purpose to guide and give meaning to their efforts, Nelson Mandela might have simply been an aging prisoner, and Martin Luther King Jr. just a Southern pastor who had a way with words. Against the backdrop of their respective purposes, their efforts changed the lives of millions.

A clear purpose lends meaning to work that is mundane but necessary for the fulfillment of the mission. The cathedral story illustrates it well. Over the years we've heard it set in Paris, Chartres, Cologne, Salisbury, and Rome, to name just a few. The location is irrelevant, but the tale itself is simple and revealing: a traveler headed for the city in question comes upon a group of stonemasons, chipping and chiseling away at some quarried stone. They are grimacing, swearing, and generally making an unhappy impression. "What are you doing?" asks the traveler. One of them lifts his head and says, "Making bricks."

A bit farther down the road our traveler comes upon a second group of masons, also shaping stones into bricks. This crowd is a bit less grumpy, and slightly more animated. He asks his question again. "Building a wall," their foreman replies.

A few steps farther, he sees another group, this one beaming and veritably whistling as they knock the stones into shape. He repeats his question, and one of the masons answers, "We're building a cathedral for the heart of that city on the horizon." No prizes for guessing the moral of the story: the why of what you do matters enormously to the motivation and energy levels available to do it.

We are no longer living in medieval Europe, of course, and cathedrals aren't as much of a motivational factor as they might once have been, but the point holds. Finding a "cathedral" in your business can be challenging, but it is usually doable. We've used that story to help businesses as varied as medical equipment suppliers through to corporate finance professionals. The cathedral in the former was a bit easier to find than for the latter, but even the team in finance were ultimately able to find a purpose in "helping owners realize the value in their businesses." Another client might have struggled, too, given that their team was charged with nothing more inspirational than recruiting for a train company. Instead, they found their inspiration in "enabling our corporate strategy." That might not seem terribly inspirational on first reading, but when set in the context of a corporate strategy that included huge investments to dramatically reduce the CO_2 emissions for an entire country, it took on real power. The team in question was set alight by the possibility of contributing to a cause they perceived as critical for the environment and the future of the species. Updating a spreadsheet to hire better people to have the trains run on time is one thing. Updating a spreadsheet to hire people to save the planet is another altogether.

Often it is best if your purpose is kept very simple. One of our recent favorites is from a company called BioLite. They produce cool camping cookers that will charge your phone while you cook with foraged leaves and sticks, and sell them at a fair price in markets that can afford them. With the proceeds they get similar tools to those who need them in the developing world. Their purpose?

"We are on a mission to empower people & protect our planet through access to renewable energy."

Note the use of "mission" instead of purpose. With a hat tip to Shakespeare, "A purpose by any other name would be just as motivational."

WAS "MEANINGFUL" EVEN CLEAR TO BEGIN WITH?

Many teams don't bother with purpose. If they pay it any attention at all, they adopt the purpose that has been hammered out for public consumption about their organization by the folks in marketing. This at least offers cosmetic justification for the efforts expended during most of their waking hours, but it seriously misses a trick. The purpose statement for a large organization is almost always too unfocused to be able to create energy and motivation for teams as disparate as a sales team and one focused on engineering, for instance. What is needed is clarity about the purpose of each team within an organization, and how that serves the organization's purpose.

The process of defining a team's purpose is challenging, but worth doing—even if it is never shared with anyone outside of the team. Apart from providing energy and direction to current team members, a clear and compelling purpose will serve as a recruiting tool. Anyone joining the team should ideally take a good look at the purpose of the team before they choose to take part. It's not that they need to sign it in blood before joining, but if the purpose is well crafted, it should serve to attract those who are inspired by it and deter those who are not. Once on board new members will be much clearer about the contribution of their work.

Being clear on purpose also opens possibilities. If we know we exist to solve a particular problem and keep clear of becoming attached to solving it in a particular way, we can avoid seeing new means of solving the problem as a threat. Knowing that David's company's purpose is to "enable all human beings to see a world with no problems, only projects" frees us from getting too attached to teaching GTD in a particular way. David could have stopped with writing *Getting Things Done,* but that was only one way of spreading the information into the world. For many years the "right" way to spread the message that later emerged in the book was via live coaching and seminars. Virtual delivery could have been seen as a threat to our traditional way of working, but our focus on purpose rather than means of delivery allowed us to develop virtual capability before we needed it. Without that, the pandemic could have been an existential moment. Instead, it was a quick switch to a new technology. Not without hassle, but not life-threatening.

[DAVID] In my years of management consulting that involved working with companies that were interested in making significant changes to be able to approach their future optimally, identifying the purpose of the organization was an obvious early step in the process.

What I found interesting was that in reexamining the purpose that had driven the enterprise to where it was, the results were never a change in the actual purpose—merely an understanding of it in a new way that would keep the organization viable.

For example, one client—the Institute for East-West Securities

Studies—had built a highly successful foreign policy advisory institute that was instrumental in creating collaborative research between NATO and Warsaw Pact senior people, to prevent anyone from "pushing the button" in the middle of the Cold War in the 1970s and 1980s. The revolutions of 1989 in one sense ended their immediate mission of preventing major global conflict. Was there a "next"? The founder couldn't stop—he knew that the tensions between the West and the Islamic world, and then later China, would eventually be critical factors to deal with. Preventing disastrous global conflict was core to the signature and DNA of the organization's work, and its initiatives have migrated elegantly to mitigate new threats.

Purpose also closes possibilities down, in a helpful way. In a world of too much choice, being clear on purpose simplifies focus. It's on purpose, or it is not. In or out. It is for lack of clear purpose that people continue to overload themselves with boatloads of work that look attractive in the absence of a sorting mechanism.

MULTIPLE PURPOSES MAY BE INVOLVED

[DAVID] I was trained by a mentor decades ago that when consulting with the founders, owners, and/or board of an organization about significant changes they considered making for a new, expanded direction, a critical first step had to be taken. The group (or individual) needed to clarify and express to peers their own personal primary purpose and vision for themselves that may (or may not, at times) align with the organization's. One person may want fame, another money, and still another to be of greater service. It's quite possible (and often was) that all three could be served by the company. However, if the key players were not conscious of one another's actual drivers, serious conflict could eventually arise in their decision-making and interactions. Peaceful coexistence of multiple purposes at the top level is paramount for going shoulder to shoulder downstream.

HOW TO DO PURPOSE

If you can see the utility of having a clearly articulated team purpose that everyone can sign up to, how do you go about creating one?

Location matters. You can do it anywhere, of course, but most find that taking their team away from the office to connect with what lights them up is a useful exercise. Asking people to contemplate deeply about purpose between tactical meetings in the office is unlikely to get the quality of thinking you want.

Once you have a group together in a useful spot with some time to talk and reflect, the exam question is "Why do we exist as a team?" Some find it more helpful to frame this in terms of problems solved, in which case the question is slightly different: "What problem do we solve in the world?" If there is an existing organizational purpose, it can be helpful to use that as a starting point. In that case the question would be "What is this team's contribution to the organizational purpose?" or "What problems does this team solve better than anyone else in the organization?"

If handled with input from and dialogue with the team itself, this can be a powerful connection both to the wider organizational purpose and between members of the team. This exercise doesn't need to take a long time, and it doesn't require anything like perfection to get at many of the benefits of an explicit team purpose.

It's worth knowing that there may be resistance to this exercise from some on the team. One of the reasons that teams struggle with purpose is because some of its members may never have landed on one for themselves. If you haven't faced the pain and uncertainty of attempting to articulate a purpose for yourself, then you can't know what energy is available once you do have one. And until you know what is in it for yourself, doing the exercise at the team level can feel very threatening indeed. But if you avoid the exercise as a team, you'll do the team equivalent of what individuals with no purpose do—stare at screens and eat ice cream to stay numb to an encroaching sense of meaninglessness.

From that place, cynicism is a standard reaction to any discussion of purpose. Pretty much every time we've run one of these sessions, someone will toss in what they hope is a hand grenade with a comment like, "Our purpose is to make money." But making money is not the purpose—it is a pleasant side effect of fulfilling the actual purpose better than any of the competition. In a bit of circular irony, having a clear purpose is one of the things that will help you do just that.

A common trap is pedantic word selection too early. In the first pass, the most important piece of this is not the wordsmithing. Too many teams get stuck battling over verbiage, as if a statement of purpose needs to be perfect the first time out. It isn't a matter of the word selection being perfect, but rather whether the words you do choose lend focus, energy, and motivation for now.

In both our respective companies we've reviewed and refreshed our initial purpose multiple times as we became clearer over time. The thrust of them didn't change, but what was long and slightly wordy in the beginning became ever more clear and focused with each revisit.

We suggest returning to the purpose periodically once it has been established to check whether it is still accurate, and whether the group can come up with a better formulation. The latter may be useful, but the real value of a brief review once or twice a year is to keep the purpose alive as part of the team conversation.

PRINCIPLES: **HOW WE PLAY TOGETHER**

CONTROL	FOCUS	PLANNING
Capture	**Horizon 5:** Purpose and **Principles**	Purpose and Principles
Clarify	Horizon 4: Vision	Vision
Organize	Horizon 3: Goals	Brainstorm
Reflect	Horizon 2: Areas of Focus	Organize
Engage		Next Actions
	Horizon 1: Projects	
	Ground: Next Actions	

We have grappled with the definition of "principles" for quite a while. Essentially, they mean the big "how" of how we get things done. But that can embrace (appropriately) everything from how often we service our bikes or brush our teeth to how we deal with conflict that arises in our team. A key aspect of engaging with your purpose is adding to the equation the agreed-upon behaviors you'll use as you go about doing that together. These are the considerations for what is acceptable as you work with one another. We see two different versions of this:

Principles—high-level guidance about the values, parameters, or guidelines of how you want to work together, and what is out of bounds.

Working standards—much more granular guidance about practices and processes that support making the principles a reality in day-to-day work on the team.

We'll handle the first of these with some examples below, and the working standards in the next chapter.

A way to think about your principles is to consider what you'd say to someone if you were delegating the running of the team to them and wanted them to succeed. What *must* they do to enhance the likelihood of success on the team, and what should they at all costs *avoid* as they run it? In the answers to those questions, you will have the raw materials for several guidelines for team interactions. Positive formulations of the desired behaviors are useful, so you may want to take the answer to the second piece of advice—here's what you should never do—and invert it to arrive at a formula that guides people in the right direction.

Some examples:

[DAVID] David Allen Company principles (a condensed list)

WE ROCK. That is, we hold excellence as a standard for our company and our culture.

We provide the world's best education, products, and services to achieve and maintain relaxed control and appropriate perspective.

We demonstrate the value we provide to the world (aka we do GTD).

We provide extraordinary service to our clients, colleagues, and ourselves.

We focus on the highest good for all concerned.

WE DO GOOD WORK. We consistently provide value to the world.

We do good work that makes a positive difference for our clients and improves people's lives.

We are good global citizens, providing significant value to the communities within which we operate.

WE MAKE MONEY. We ensure that our business is vital and viable.

We consistently focus on the best business practices, with an attitude of continuous improvement, paying attention and adjusting to feedback.

We hold ourselves accountable for optimal strategies that support our expansion and maximum return on our invested resources.

At every level we work to maintain an effective, appropriate focus of our money, time, and energy.

WE HAVE FUN. We sustain a rich, engaging culture.

We use a supportive, positive regard as our ultimate standard in our interactions with one another.

We pay active attention to one another and conditions in the company and take responsible and caring actions to directly address perceived concerns and opportunities.

We provide and encourage a relaxed, comfortable, healthy, and nurturing work environment.

We communicate honestly and directly, while respecting and listening to one another with openness and generosity of spirit.

We love having fun, laughing, and celebrating all wins.

We continuously challenge ourselves to grow, explore, and expand, personally and professionally.

We leverage the wisdom of the group.

We respect one another's unique gifts, strengths, and approaches.

That may seem like a lot, but it is important to remember that the above is the result of many years of thinking and refining to clarify and expand upon what was intended by the first, much less comprehensive, version. Don't feel you have to undertake something that comprehensive to get going. Below is a shorter version of the same exercise. Both have served our respective companies well over the years.

[ED] Next Action Associates—Company Purpose and Principles

Purpose: We change the world of work by embodying and sharing the life-changing art of stress-free productivity.

NAA PRINCIPLES

We:

Think outside of the box with ambition

Support working from anywhere

Provide regular opportunities to come together as a team; the better we know one another as people, the better we can operate as a team

Listen before diagnosing

Husband resources with prudence

Develop and leverage networks

Avoid triangulation or gossip

Encourage explicit conversations about capacity and prioritization when taking on new projects

Maintain a financial "buffer" to weather tough times

Are always clear about accountability

Encourage experimentation, creativity, and continuous learning

Keep a sense of humor

Maintain a canine-friendly environment

As you can see from the above examples, there is no correct form for these statements. Some will be shorter and more abstract, and some will be longer and more detailed. The form is a matter of taste, a useful output of what really matters: the discussions the team has about what is important to them. Documenting them preserves a clear record of those discussions, provides behavioral guardrails for the interactions on the team, and supplies a quick way to bring new members up to speed on what is expected from them.

As with the purpose of our respective companies, we've found it valuable to review these about once per year, using a variety of different exercises to keep the principles fresh in the minds of the team, and to uncover and discuss any areas where we have not been living up to our principles.

Chapter 6

Horizon Five—Principles Redux

HARNESSING THE POWER OF WORKING STANDARDS

CONTROL	FOCUS	PLANNING
Capture	Horizon 5: Purpose and **Principles**	Purpose and Principles
Clarify	Horizon 4: Vision	Vision
Organize	Horizon 3: Goals	Brainstorm
Reflect	Horizon 2: Areas of Focus	Organize
Engage		Next Actions
	Horizon 1: Projects	
	Ground: Next Actions	

[ED] It is five minutes to the hour, and I'm sitting at the boardroom table of a potential client in a leafy London suburb. Alone.

I'm here for a sales meeting with the CEO and his human resources head about bringing GTD to their top team and mid-level managers. They'd asked that I do a presentation, so I got to the room thirty minutes early to be sure there were no hitches in linking my computer to the in-house projector. It's a sales meeting between lockdowns during the pandemic, and I'm nervy. It would be good to make the sale.

The tech works easily for once, so I review my deck one last time. When finished, I check my watch. Three minutes to the appointed start time, and I'm still alone, with only a view of the car park out the boardroom windows for company. This is either a very tight ship, or a disastrously loose one.

At two minutes to the hour, someone finally appears, but it isn't either of the people I'm expecting to meet. Apparently more are coming to the meeting than I was led to believe. All good. That happens. I introduce myself and try to get a sense of who this person is. A member of the senior team, he tells me, just before he opens his laptop, puts his head down, and starts checking email.

Just before the planned start time I enquire about my hosts. My new friend looks up from his laptop, looks back to check the time, then burbles something about tracking them down as he heads for the door. The start time passes, and it's just me and the car park again.

A few minutes past the hour, my host—the CEO—rushes in, complaining about the absence of people he's invited to attend the meeting, whether physically or virtually. So it's a hybrid meeting. Got it. He opens his laptop, then a video conference platform to get the virtual participants onto the large screen at the other end of the room. But the conferencing software isn't connecting. He calls a tech person to fix it, then leaves again to assemble the missing physical participants. While he's gone, another person who I'm not expecting turns up, closely followed by the tech guy and my friend from earlier. We're getting there, but through the glass walls of the boardroom I can see my host is still doing laps of the office looking for the others.

It is now ten minutes past the hour, and I have two of what I've learned should be six meeting participants in the room with me, plus the tech guy. Given the comings and goings so far, I consider lassoing them with one of the extension leads beneath the table to keep from losing them again. The tech guy is sweating now and suggests a change of video platform. The CEO—now back in the room—sends an invite from the new platform, then calls each of the virtual participants on his cell phone to let them know of the change. One of them is driving; another claims no knowledge of the meeting but promises to drop off their other call to participate; and the third can't be found at all. I can't help glancing at my watch. We are fifteen minutes into the allotted time and have done precisely nothing of any use yet.

My initial nerves are gone. I know I can help these people. A lot. A few minutes later the video is up and running, and the driver is with us on a cell phone balanced on his lap, illegally, I think. Cue small talk and a bit of light passive-aggressive banter from the only person who turned up on time. Twenty minutes in, we're still waiting for the second virtual participant to join. I suggest we get going, in the spirit of having the start of the meeting take place before the planned end time. Time to shine.

A few minutes into my presentation, the last of the virtual participants joins. Ten minutes in—and a good thirty minutes after the planned start time—an older man enters the room without introducing himself. As he's too well dressed to be in maintenance, I have no idea why he is there. I'm in full flow, so I simply acknowledge him with my eyes and keep going. No one else in the room bats an eye as he sits at the table. Probably not the cleaner then.

I finish my presentation with twenty minutes left in our allotted hour and open up the meeting for questions. Our driver uses the pause to explain he's arrived at his destination and drops off the call. After handling a few questions and learning that the tardy mystery arrival is the founder of the business, we're down to our final five minutes. I suggest agreeing on some outputs from the meeting. A next action would be great, but at this point anything will do. Anything that would make the investment of nearly eight man-hours in this meeting seem like a halfway worthwhile investment. I flag the time constraint up, and the pace increases slightly, but not enough to finish on time.

We're past the hour now, and the energy shifts in the room. Everyone but me should already be in another meeting, and their urgency is palpable. Papers are collected, phones pocketed, and computers closed in that silent but firm way that indicates imminent departure. Three minutes past the nominal end time of the meeting we land on some agreements about next steps. Phew. Better than nothing, but I notice none of my hosts has made a note of them. The last I see of the CEO is over a quick handshake before he is out the door and off at a half trot. It seems there is another group waiting for him down the hallway. . . .

You might be wondering whether this meeting is a composite, pulled together to make a point. Unfortunately, not. It actually occurred as described, though certain details have been altered to protect the guilty. That it happened in the way that it did was wasteful, for sure, but the real tragedy was that all concerned were participating as if such behavior was normal. The group was irritated, but the irritation was at a level they took as customary for them.

"So what?" you might ask. A disorganized meeting with a tardy start in a suburb of London. What does that have to do with me? This meeting was unusually bad, but in its themes—unclear invites, appearing and disappearing participants, ill-prepared tech, late start, running over, and not capturing agreements—it was not unusual at all, and often daily fare for many of our clients.

These were not bad people. Smart enough to become mid-level managers in a growing concern, they were extraordinarily hardworking. As a team they were clearly getting enough of the right things done to stay in business. But they were hemorrhaging time and energy as they did so, and there were hints of the associated costs in the comments of the participants during the question-and-answer session. In that part of the meeting it became apparent that some of them were working so hard that they'd had their own brushes with burnout the year before. After just one hour I was in no position to judge the rest of their work, but in the context of that particular gathering, it was clear they were wasting time, energy, and a lot of goodwill by tolerating a remarkably low standard for how they set up and ran their meetings.

We think they can do better.

We think that with some relatively simple agreements on what we call working standards—a more granular approach to principles, describing what the team members expect from one another in terms of how they work together—would make an enormous difference to the effectiveness of the team. Some basic standards for how meetings get called and run would dramatically reduce the amount of stress in their team system and begin to build a culture that makes it much easier for the team to get its work done.

CHANGING STANDARDS TO CHANGE THE CULTURE

Much of what passes for culture change is far too complicated. The solutions proposed may be logical, often well planned, and appeal to our sense of cleverness, but often they are too clever by half. Huge programs are planned over the course of months and launched with great fanfare to achieve worthy cultural objectives. In our experience, though, the solutions do not need to be big or clever, they just need to work.

When we approach organizational cultural change in an organization, we keep it simple. We don't think it is helpful to attempt to improve behaviors by simply promoting abstract concepts like "trust" and "respect." They are desirable qualities on a team, to be sure, but what these concepts actually mean for day-to-day work is hard to grasp. No one perceives their relevance on Tuesday morning at ten thirty, for instance, when Tim from sales blows up all over one of his team members. Most culture changes fail because what they are trying to achieve remains too vague, and even supporters of change don't quite know what they can do on a daily basis to support it.

We believe that a useful definition of culture is "the way we do things around here." This means the way we do things when no one is watching, and what we normally expect from one another in how we interact on our team. It is a broad definition, but it allows for a richer discussion of the levers for making changes. Culture affects everything. According to Peter Drucker, it is so powerful that it eats strategy for breakfast. And if team culture is how you do things, then not clearly defining how you want to do things together is a form of negligence that impacts not only people's team performance but also their health. In our view one of the easily available levers that teams can pull to create culture change is by defining clear standards and processes that support individual performance and team collaboration.

There was a time when discipline and willpower were seen as the keys to making the consistent behavioral changes that would lead to great performance. Implicit in that belief was the idea that success was linked to inner strength—individuals' ability to get themselves to do things they didn't really want to do. And if they simply huffed enough willpower, and puffed enough discipline, any doors blocking the attainment of superior performance would eventually blow right over.

In recent years much of the research into change has pointed in a different direction. If you want to change your behavior—and performance—you'll want to pay less attention to your willpower, and much more attention to what your environment allows or encourages you to do consistently.

On one level this isn't complicated: we all know it's easier to go for a run when all our mates are heading off for one, just as it is almost impossible to not join in eating cupcakes if everyone else in the room is piling them down their throats. Similarly, the attitudes, habits, and standards of the people around us play a huge role in our own personal performance.

In his impenetrably titled—but seriously fascinating—paper "The Mundanity of Excellence: An Ethnographic Report on Stratification and Olympic Swimmers," Daniel Chambliss found that one of the key factors that drives excellence in competitive swimmers is quite simply the environment in which they found themselves:

> It is not by doing increasing amounts of work that one becomes excellent, but rather by changing the kinds of work. . . . Athletes move to the top ranks through *qualitative jumps*: noticeable changes in their techniques, discipline and attitude, accomplished usually through a change in settings, e.g. joining a new team with a new coach, new friends, etc., who work at a higher level.

He found that much more than "talent," monomaniacal focus, or working ever harder, it was the social and athletic standards of the environment in which athletes were—or chose to be in—that played a huge part in how they performed as individuals. This insight has implications both for the performance of individuals on your team and how they collaborate.

This book is about how people make themselves effective, or not, as a team. Changing what are considered normal team standards in the domain of execution provides an opportunity for a transformational shift in performance. For instance, is it normal in your organization to expect a twenty-four-hour response time on emails that you send, or is it normal to have to chase people several times about things you've asked for? Is it normal to start meetings on time, with a clear outcome, or do people consistently show up five to ten minutes late with no idea why they are in the room? These are simple matters. So simple that one might ask why anyone would concern themselves with them.

They may be simple, but they are not unimportant.

On an individual level, for instance, learning to touch-type seems beneath consideration for many who view it as a lower-order skill they don't have time to master, given the importance of their other work. It's no surprise, then, that they find it impossible to keep on top of the flow of communication coming at them, about all that important work. They can't keep up because they are hunting and pecking at their keyboard, which is like trying to sprint with a broken foot. Not smart.

Similarly, a lack of awareness about the cost of getting simple things wrong at a team level doesn't mean those costs don't exist. In fact, the organizational costs of poor email management and low standards for meeting attendance are incalculable. Part of the problem that you'll have in making these changes is that the scale of the problem—and its negative ramifications—may be unclear. Or, if the negative impacts are all too clear, they are considered normal, natural—just "the way we do things here." To get a sense of the scale of the waste, one needs to zoom out from a specific dysfunctional meeting and get a corporate, national, or international perspective. If one calculated the loaded payroll costs of the wasted time of the individuals involved, it would likely trigger some sort of additional reckoning of the actual price paid for such (sub)standards.

Before diving in to discuss the standards themselves, we need to clarify why you'd want to have standards at all. Or rather, we need to be clear that you actually don't have a choice about having standards. You already have them. It is only a question of whether you are aware of them, whether you've chosen them, and whether they support or undermine your team's ability to achieve its aims.

As evidenced by our meeting in suburban London, managing meetings optimally is low-hanging fruit to be picked. Some teams have a standard of starting all their meetings on time. Others say that it is perfectly normal to start meetings ten-ish minutes after the time in the invite. It isn't that the latter team has no standard. On the contrary, it has a very clear standard: it is okay to show up for meetings up to ten minutes late, apologize to the group, or not (the apology would be another standard—or not), and get rolling. There is nothing morally right or wrong about either of these standards, but one of them supports a more efficient use of the team's time.

If we were to define the standard our potential client at the beginning of this chapter currently holds for their meetings, it would be something like this: "We meet, eventually, talk over our laptops at those who bother to show up, keep no record of what we agreed, but hope something might happen as a result. Spot on. That's us."

It isn't just in meetings that standards are revealed. Your team has standards for everything from the channels in which they communicate, the response times that are expected of them, what's okay to wear to the office, and what it is acceptable to send out to a client when pitching for business.

That is the first reason for consciously choosing your standards. If you don't intentionally choose them, you'll still have them, but they are much more likely to be an unhelpful, ugly average of what each member of the team thinks is "normal." And that same lack of awareness means they will remain impossible to change.

STANDARDS ARE INFECTIOUS

Having low or no standards with regard to meetings is not an isolated occurrence. Not having standards, or not respecting them, leads to slippage in other areas as well. Conversely, simple standards that the team respects can have an outsize impact on completely unrelated areas. Like the "keystone habits" that Charles Duhigg wrote about for individuals in *The Power of Habit*, a small number of well-chosen team standards will lift engagement and performance in completely unrelated areas. Just as a consistent commitment to an exercise program begins to affect individual food choices, so, too, with team standards. Having everyone show up on time is not just a matter of efficiency and waste reduction. The energy generated by hitting that simple standard plays out through the entire meeting and beyond.

Another reason to choose standards is that in a world of increasing diversity and international work postings, intercultural and even interdepartmental expectations about how work should be done can vary widely. Everyone comes to the party with standards and expectations that they learned in their family, national culture, or previous places of employment. The gap between your expectations about how things should be done and theirs can be a source of completely unnecessary tension and resentment in a team. All that is needed to avoid it is clarity on how *this* team wants to work, independent of geography or function. If the team doesn't agree on or communicate those standards, then everyone lives happily in their own little standards bubble, thinking their way is the right way. That is almost a guarantee that some members are going to be upset and resentful about others not hitting undeclared standards, while others are left feeling as if there are things expected from them that they never agreed to.

For those who appreciate consistency, there is a lovely link back to the team principles we discussed in chapter 3. Any team that is willing to take the time to develop standards for itself is by definition engaging in **learning** (any standards will almost certainly be established in the context of a review of what works—and what doesn't—on the team). They'll also be taking the time to create **clarity** about expectations on the team, which will enhance the likelihood of those expectations being met, and contribute to building **sufficient trust**. If they take the time to communicate both the standards and the reason behind them, there will be **open communication** in play as well.

Once expectations have been created and agreed to by the team, they will tap into one of the most powerful forces in human change: the expectations of the group in which individuals operate. This insight was part of what moved one of our clients to recently take time out to consciously lift the shared working standards in their team. After several years of offering GTD seminars to individuals in the organization, they saw that there were unrealized team benefits available from the time and effort they'd invested in GTD. They had already put a critical mass of people through our initial and intermediate seminars, but they had not yet focused those newly acquired individual skills on a shared goal.

After learning the concepts and practices of GTD, they became—as a team—more aware of the gap between best practice and mediocrity in handling workflow, and had a shared desire to raise their collective game. They did so by establishing clear guidance on what was expected from individuals on the team and in interactions between team members.

Senior leadership in the organization took time out to reflect and decide on what they wanted in terms of working standards on the team. Here is a small selection of the kinds of proposals they came up with:

Email:

All email (received as "To:") is acknowledged within 48 hours.

Subject lines clearly describe the topic of the email. When the topic of an email string changes, change the subject line, rather than simply hitting reply or reply all.

Include only people in the "To:" field who have a direct action in the email, and use "Cc:" for those who just need to be kept informed.

Inboxes are clarified every 48 hours.

Meetings:

Meeting invites state the desired outcome of the meeting.

The start and end time of all meetings are honored.

Meetings should allow for transition time between meetings—default meeting times should be 50 minutes rather than 60, or 25 minutes instead of 30.

Identifying the desired standards is, of course, only the first step. They'll need to be communicated well, sold persuasively, and—most importantly—lived day to day by the leadership of the team.

No one would claim these efforts are rocket science (unless you work at Jet Propulsion Labs), but they don't have to be new and exciting to have a dramatic impact on team performance. From the research on athletic excellence by Daniel Chambliss again:

> Excellence is mundane. Superlative performance is really a confluence of dozens of small skills or activities, each one learned or stumbled upon, which have been carefully drilled into habit and then are fitted together in a synthesized whole. There is nothing extraordinary or superhuman in any one of those actions: only the fact that they are done consistently and correctly, and all together, produce excellence.

What our client saw was that achieving that kind of excellence happens in a similar way for a team as for an individual. Establishing and communicating some very simple standards—along with the skills to meet them—will contribute to an environment that supports individual excellence, which will in turn raise the standards higher, which will drive team excellence over time. A lovely virtuous circle.

THE EASY WAY TO KNOW WHAT YOUR STANDARDS ARE

Usually, you only become acutely aware of your own standards when someone violates them. To bring the need for standards into relief, it can be useful to look to an individual example of how standards can go wrong. When a couple first get together, there is no discussion of standards. They are in love, and famously blind. There is no need for common standards, or even much common language for the first six months or so. But once the honeymoon period has passed, differing standards begin to show up. Toothpaste tubes are left uncapped or squeezed in the middle, dishes are left on counters, accounts become overdrawn. Absent any discussion of the implicit standards of each of the participants, irritations, resentments, and squabbles are almost inevitable. What often happens is that the person with the stricter standard in a certain domain attempts to try to maintain it, but without the help of the partner. The person whose standard for cleaning dishes is "before dessert" starts feeling they're being used by the person with a standard of "there are still clean plates in the cupboard, all good." Before long, conversations about trivial things become nontrivial blocks to communicating effectively as a couple.

Checking each other's standards before a first date would be

> Discipline and freedom seem like opposites. In reality, they are partners. Discipline is not a lack of freedom, it is a harmonious relationship with time.
>
> —RICK RUBIN

overkill, but once things are rolling and intent is clear, many religions now counsel some form of marriage course to help a couple articulate their respective expectations. That articulation has two benefits: at least some of the standards are surfaced and discussed, and the conversation about them offers a template for discussing potentially contentious topics in the future as well.

We are not advocating overkill for teams, but believe that assuming everyone shares the same standards for how work gets done is a time and energy trap that is easy to avoid. The teams that get this right take it seriously and know it's not just a "nice to have." They know that it is core to containing friction in how they do what they do, so they pay careful attention during the setup, adoption, and the maintenance of their standards.

Standards can be developed in any area of team function, of course. Some will be more useful than others, given the context. The military, for instance, has incredibly detailed standards for the reflective capacity of shoe leather. Parents may expect what they consider vulgar speech to be forbidden to their children. In this chapter we are choosing to focus on areas where the opportunities for reducing friction and drag on a team are greatest. Just as GTD does not suggest overcapturing, constant clarifying, or obsessive organizing, we are not proposing to tie your team in knots with long lists of "have-tos."

A couple of examples will illustrate the cultural impact standards can have. The first is one that many of our clients have discovered is an extremely pleasant side effect of training a critical mass of their people in how to manage their workflow. When enough of their people have learned the value of outcome and action thinking, they've instituted a standard for closing out discussions of team topics. They consistently answer a couple of simple questions: first, "What is the desired outcome, and who owns it," and then "What is the next action?" In answering those two questions consistently, they found they had de facto moved their team to a proactive culture of accountability. The question about ownership gave them clarity on accountability, and the question about next actions got them a culture with a predisposition for action. No huge change program, just a couple of questions consistently asked at the end of team conversations about ongoing projects.

One of our favorite standards is the one that a client set for learning on her team. Given the speed of change in her industry, she was clear that without constant learning her team would not be able to compete in the market. Her solution? A standard for learning: two hours every week. She made it even easier for people to participate by authorizing two hours explicitly: Monday morning from eight until ten. No meetings, no calls, no nothing that wasn't about learning. With that in place, along with a menu of learning options from a learning academy created for a fast-growing team, a culture of learning became part of the background expectations for all who joined the team.

Choose as many as you need, but as few as you can. Each team must decide on its own standards to help it fulfill its purpose and vision. The challenge is to choose wisely. To start with, we'd suggest only a few of the highest-leverage ones, to allow you to keep enough focus on them to score some successes and build momentum and enthusiasm for adding other useful ones when the time is right.

We don't want to prescribe what is right for your team—we don't know your business well enough. That said, we believe there are simple standards that most teams will at least want to consider, as they are common across all organizations. When teams have reached agreement on how they want to run their meetings and defined the use of their communications channels, it has had a transformative impact.

MEETINGS

We've already identified some of the easy wins available with meetings, but let's assume that you're already onboard for starting and finishing on time. As an example of another factor you might want to consider, how about a standard that supports maintaining focus on the topic you're discussing? In just a couple of decades we've gone from having a laptop open in a meeting being a novelty—and mostly for the person presenting—to everyone in the group having a device at hand . . . and at *least* one. In one meeting we attended someone had four, so it was unclear how many simultaneous meetings they were actually attending. It's a sad fact that many so completely misunderstand the nature of the problem that they believe that part of the solution to their overwhelm lies in learning to master simultaneous and suboptimal attendance at multiple concurrent meetings.

The fact that having devices open in meetings has now become standard doesn't make it helpful. If the purpose of the meeting is to generate focus on a particular topic, or to get a decision on a topic using the expertise of all present, then it seems to us that anything that distracts focus is making your meetings less effective.

Some will rightly ask, "What if we need some piece of information that is on our computers to help move the meeting forward?" Great question, if we ignore that part of any meeting preparation should be . . . well, getting prepared for the meeting, so everyone doesn't need to be on a device to participate. That you *can* finish slides you'll later be presenting during a colleague's presentation doesn't mean that you should.

Your team needs to decide on what is right for its purposes. All devices closed will get you more focus. All devices open and available potentially offer more timely inputs of information. But it is long since clear that a lack of information is not the problem. The problem is that even smart, motivated people—who already know how much distracted participants negatively affect meeting outcomes—cannot resist something new moving on their screen. Like fresh muffins in the middle of the table for a motivated and well-educated dieter, a new email, a reminder, or a pop-up notification is effectively irresistible. Everyone glances down to see what just showed up. And in the few seconds they are "away," they are not hearing what is being said. Some estimate that it takes six minutes to get focused again, and others cite research that it takes twenty. Whatever the actual number, it's seriously suboptimal if you are trying to make decisions. Cue repetition, frustration, and poor meeting outcomes.

Hybrid meetings bring their own challenges, of course (which we address in appendix 3); but devices or no devices, we can offer some clear guidance for better meetings. Many have found these simple ideas transformative for their own lives. We think you can get huge improvements from three simple steps:

> Make sure everyone is clear on the purpose of the meeting—ideally before they agree to attend, but certainly at the start of every meeting.
>
> Be sure as you start that everyone knows what "done" looks like for that meeting, and by what time.
>
> Ensure that none of your meetings end without clarifying next actions and accountabilities so that the topics discussed in the meeting move forward once it is done.

There is more that you can do, but if all you did was move the needle on those three points, you'd already be having much better meetings. That would be great, but not if handling the topic in question didn't need a meeting at all.

FIVE REASONS FOR MEETINGS

There are essentially five reasons to hold a meeting. The first four we attribute to Andrew Grove's articulation of them in his *High Output Management* in the 1980s. We've added a fifth.

1. Give information. "We've brought you here to let you know . . ."

2. Get information. "We need input from you about . . ."

3. Develop options. "We're here to explore all the possible ways we could handle this . . ."

4. Make decisions. "In this meeting we'll finalize our decisions about how to proceed . . ."

5. Human connections. "We've brought you together so we can meet one another personally and put a more human touch on our interactions going forward."

Any meeting might have one or more of these objectives. It might have all five. "We're here to share some information, get some feedback, explore some possibilities, and make some decisions. Also, so you can get to know one another a bit more."

But if one attendee is there to simply get information, another just to make decisions, and a third who wants only to develop options, you'll have a problem.

A significant accelerator for team collaboration in a meeting is the visual identification of work. When everyone can see what all the participants are doing—or not doing—without having to ask, then vast amounts of otherwise necessary communication fall away, along with endless yawn-inducing "update" meetings. The entire team knowing who is doing what via an up-to-date team Project list means that redundancies can be identified and eliminated before they waste valuable team time and energy.

This working from a consistently updated common understanding of current reality is fundamentally different to the "status update" meetings of the past, where team members spent hours explaining the world to one another each week before they could move on to making new decisions.

COMMUNICATIONS CHANNELS AND RESPONSE TIMES

In the beginning, there was email. Well, in the *very* beginning there were smoke signals, papyrus, pigeons, memos, and faxes, and it is worth remembering that each of them was a solution to some of the problems of its predecessor.

Email has become so maligned that it is hard to remember now just how brilliant an innovation it was when it came into being. Virtually free once the software was purchased, it eliminated acres of paper and allowed for near instantaneous communication that enabled asynchronous working.

But once computers came off desktops—and eventually made their way into our pockets—the explosion of asynchronous communication became a burden for most. The success of the original *Getting Things Done* in the early part of the century was in part due to its impact on people's ability to master their email inboxes, often for the first time.

Not everyone took advantage of GTD, however, and for those who were not successfully coping with their inboxes, the ability to send longer messages via SMS showed up as a light in their tunnel. Having declared email "bankruptcy," they were pleased to discover there was a new "currency" in which to be out of control. More important, the direct reports of people who were no longer responding to their

> It is in self-limitation that a master first reveals himself.
>
> —GOETHE

email discovered—temporarily—that there was a new channel on which they had a better chance of getting answers from their managers. In a perverse piece of communications logic, people began sending texts—or calling each other—to highlight the presence of important emails. (If that doesn't strike you as perverse, what do you think repeated reminders about the same content does to efficiency on a team?)

When the SMS channel also became clogged, some felt relief might come from a new medium, whether a chat function, social media, or groupware. Each of these channels in turn offered brief windows for bankrupts in previous channels to get their heads back above water, but the lack of any systematic approach to communication meant they were soon simply drowning again in a new medium.

The problem got so bad that people began to complain about having to communicate and coordinate their work at all. If we had a dollar for every time someone has told us some version of, "I could get my real work done if only I didn't have to do email," we'd have long since retired to a tropical island. We'll confess we haven't been sympathetic listeners, as we believe that for most people, handling communications related to their team's work *is* their job.

The best of the best have recognized what is happening, and—like Goethe's masters—have revealed themselves through limitation. They have limited themselves by pruning the number of channels they use, and by defining the content and response times expected with each of them. That might seem like imposing too much structure, but on the other side of that actually limited structure is freedom from constantly checking an ever-expanding number of inboxes.

Let's take the culture development team of our client at Leroy Seafood Group, for example. They have identified from among many options four channels they will use to communicate: email, a collaborative software tool, texts, and calls. They have developed guidance on the kind of content that is most appropriate for each channel, and the response times that are expected for them.

MEDIUM	PURPOSE	RESPONSE TIME	COMMENT
Email	Used when a team collaboration tool is not possible—for example, in communication with people outside the department who do not have access to our relevant software.	Answered no later than the following working day.	Email **should not be** used for internal communication within the department. Team collaboration software is preferable for that.
Team collaboration software	Better information flow within the team.	Answered no later than the following working day.	Post to correct thread in appropriate channel, and only notify those who need to know. If in doubt create a new thread with a name that helps identify its content.*
SMS	Quick messages	Four hours	
Phone	If you must have input immediately.	Pick up the phone, or call back as soon as your circumstances permit.	You are not expected to be "on" all the time. Please call back if you have received an SMS asking for a timely response. If you call someone and they don't pick up, send a text message telling them why you called and whether you want them to call you back.

*See more details in appendix 2, on collaborative software.

This level of detail might be judged excessive, but it produces real-world results. The culture development team scored twenty to thirty points higher on "satisfaction" with their work in the annual employee engagement survey than similar teams doing similar work. Is that entirely due to their communications contract? Almost certainly not. Is their communications contract a contributor to greater levels of satisfaction on the team? According to the team, absolutely.

Why might that be? Like lines on a playing field, and rules for a game, their contract defines the boundaries of the game and supports the team to make it winnable. We'd be remiss if we didn't mention that the team members have all had some training in systematic handling of their own workflow. But even if they hadn't, they'd be better off playing a game in which the parameters for success have been defined, rather than one in which there are no rules and no clear path to winning. Being human, they like to win. The ability to do so, regularly—or at least occasionally—is almost certainly contributing to their sense of satisfaction with their work.

DOCUMENTING YOUR DECISIONS

Some will question the need for all of this to be captured and made accessible in that degree of detail. "We've agreed to it, it's working, we're good." Great. And the speed of change on teams today is such that many of the people who agreed to those standards may not be around in six months' or a year's time. Whose standards hold in that case? What happens when a new leader arrives?

Perhaps the best way to illustrate the value of having clearly documented standards is to consider what happens when a new team member joins. Until they learn anything different, they'll assume that the standards they bring from their old team or former organization are good enough. After all, they are an experienced professional, highly paid with years of experience. They naturally feel their standards are good enough. They've gotten where they are with them this far, haven't they? But let's assume for a moment that they are joining a team with higher working standards than they are used to. The new member will work out eventually, perhaps over the course of months, what the new standards are, and with luck, without too much damage to their reputation. In the meantime, however, the team has had some avoidable bumps, unmet expectations, and unnecessary tensions.

How much easier would it have been to be able to hand them a clearly documented set of standards when they consider joining the team? They can choose to join or not join, but once on the team they can't say, "I didn't know."

There are numerous ways to address team standards. A client of David's, a large pharmaceutical company, invited him to deliver a keynote presentation at a conference for their large legal team. As a group they were stressed because of a recent merger with another pharma company that was burdened with a number of lawsuits, which they now had inherited. The head of the legal department preceded David onstage, and his presentation was a situation update. At one point he put up a slide on-screen entitled "Here's what would piss me off." One example was a problem escalated to him that could have been handled by peer-to-peer communication and coordination at a lower level. David's point of view: that was quite a good example of standard-setting. It would have been nice, though, if the head guy also showed a list of "Here's what would inspire me."

CHOOSING YOUR STANDARDS

The example points the way to a solution for finding your standards. If you are still wondering which standards to choose, you might want to start a conversation on the team with the following questions: "What would bother you if we did it consistently?" Or, you could come at it from the opposite perspective: "What would excite you if we consistently got it right?" Other teams have gone historical, examining teams—good and bad—they've been on in the past and looking for the standards that made them what they were. With the good teams, it is simply a question of adapting previous best practices to the current team situation. For the bad ones, some analysis of what the bad standards were will precede turning them on their heads to look for the positive manifestation of the same.

You'll want to communicate not just the standards you've chosen, but the logic behind them. For the individuals who created them, this can seem a wasted effort. The logic is so clear in the moment of creation that there is a sense that "We know this. Why would we document it?" But it is the documentation of "why" that is critical for the understanding and acceptance of those who join the team months or years after the initial decisions were made. Apart from the likelihood that even those who created them might forget over time, there is a huge reduction in effort for all concerned in not having to cover the territory repeatedly with each new arrival. If you've ever looked at a poorly documented set of meeting minutes and tried to work out what got decided and how a given decision was reached, you'll know what we are speaking of. Providing a standard without the logic behind it runs the risk of its seeming to be just an arbitrary rule. And like all rules devoid of context, it will be as likely to generate pushback as buy-in from new arrivals. It is one thing to be told "no emails after 7 p.m." and quite another to be offered that standard in service of your own health and your team's ability to innovate consistently (because it isn't so overworked and overtired that it wouldn't know a creative thought if it smacked them in the head). There might still be discussion of the standard, but at least it will be rooted in a common understanding of what the standard is trying to achieve.

And it is in that context that any standards should be created. They can only ever make sense in the context of what the team is trying to achieve. Standards will be different on a team with the goal of going hell for leather toward an imminent IPO than on a team for whom part of its purpose is offering a sustainable way of working that attracts a particular kind of talent. To make sure the standards you develop are aligned with where you want to go as a team, you need to have agreement on where that is. Our next chapter is about getting aligned on a vision of the future.

Chapter 7

Horizon Four

VISION

CONTROL	FOCUS	PLANNING
Capture	Horizon 5: Purpose and Principles	Purpose and Principles
Clarify	**Horizon 4: Vision**	Vision
Organize	Horizon 3: Goals	Brainstorm
Reflect	Horizon 2: Areas of Focus	Organize
Engage	Horizon 1: Projects	Next Actions
	Ground: Next Actions	

WHY VISION?

Individuals and teams can have the same high-level purpose and yet have very different visions about what those purposes being fulfilled would look, sound, or feel like. A purpose might be "Serve the health and well-being of our community," and yet the visions to do that could range from "Establish viable alternatives to serve the homeless" to

> Fantasies are more than substitutes for unpleasant reality; they are also dress rehearsals, plans. All acts performed in the world begin in the imagination.
>
> —BARBARA GRIZZUTI HARRISON

"Put a practical, popular, and sustainable recycling program in place." Both are great, but not necessarily aligned in terms of resource allocation.

A team might agree on its purpose, such as "Optimally integrate our IT services," but what, exactly, would constitute "wild success" for this goal? "Great UI and UX on our desktops and mobile devices"? "Customers easily engaging with our interfaces, and appreciating them tremendously"? "Being considered 'leading edge' by the industry"? Or which of many others?

Taking the time to get aligned on what everyone is mutually committed to can have truly spectacular results, like the ones our client Nick delivered with his team as he set about scaling them to have a global footprint.

A BILLION-DOLLAR BABY

He was losing the room but didn't know why. It was the graveyard session after lunch on the first day of a two-day strategy off-site, and energy was flagging. Nick was trying to get his team aligned and pointed at something new, but they weren't onboard yet.

He'd been part of a fast-growing infrastructure advisory unit at one of the Big Four for a decade and, growing up in that business, had been a part of taking it from zero revenues to over $80 million a year. It was already a tremendous success, but, in his words, "It felt like being on a great journey with no real sense of what the destination was."

In a short break he scribbled some thoughts on a flip chart about where they might now head as a business, hoping to pull things together under the banner of "vision."

"The vision piece was very helpful," Nick recalled. "We loved what we were doing and were united by a sense that we were grappling with some of the great global challenges of our times. We knew we were doing excellent work for our clients, but the amount we were already doing only highlighted the scale of the opportunity we were missing. Taking the team and turning it into a global business seemed a logical next step."

What they came up with was the following:

- Infrastructure development is one of the great global challenges of the twenty-first century.

- We will be acknowledged as the leading financial adviser responding to this challenge.

- We will have a role on every significant infrastructure program worldwide. We will build a global advisory business earning US $1 billion globally.

- We will be the first call for governments and businesses on the basis of our independence, global reach and experience, and our deep sector knowledge and market insight.

- As a result, we will pioneer new markets and ideas, and will continue to attract the best people.

"The number wasn't the main focus of the vision, but I was confident there was a billion in turnover in it," Nick said. When he put that number on the flip chart at the end of day one, he found he was no longer fighting for anyone's attention.

A billion in revenue might not have been the driving priority, but it was extremely helpful in generating focus. The number had other advantages: it was easy to remember, and a great conversation starter with senior stakeholders. It also forced the team to think radically

> If you know what you want to do and you do it, that's the work of a craftsman. If you begin with a question and use it to guide an adventure of discovery, that's the work of the artist.
>
> —RICK RUBIN

differently about how they'd make it a reality. Just working 10 percent harder wasn't going to do it, and it was clear that the billion couldn't come out of existing infrastructure markets alone. To reach it the team would have to work out how to engage and partner with other countries, and with other areas of their own firm, in ways that hadn't been done before.

The next key moment came a couple months later, when these ideas were presented to a wider group in New York. At a certain point, someone on the team said, "*When* we are a billion-dollar business . . ." and no one laughed or left the room. On the contrary, the view was, "This is a once-in-a-lifetime opportunity and we ought to act on it." With the approval from the New York meeting, a strategy was created, and then condensed to fit on a single slide.

A couple months later the core of twenty people in New York became forty in London. The group from around the world came together in a hotel conference room where they found a large map of the world. Exceptionally large—ten feet high, and thirteen across.

The idea was to have everyone in the room see that the vision was not just pie in the sky by visualizing the components of the future business on the map. "No one really knew what a billion-dollar business looked like, so we thought if we can break that down into one hundred segments of $10 million, it would be easier to grasp it," Nick explained. "A few of those segments were already at $10 million, some definitely had the potential, and others . . . well, at that point they felt like crazy talk. But then so did the businesses we'd already created, back when we started."

Over the course of the next several days, they came up with 150 discrete business opportunities with $10 million potential and placed clearly labeled markers on the map to show their location. As each business went up on the map, they had a clearer and clearer picture of where the business growth was going to come from. At the end of the meeting, they pared the list back to a hundred opportunities and identified outcomes, accountabilities, and next actions for all of them. These plans, based on input from colleagues across the business and around the world, gave substance to the strategy.

This plan, underpinned by a clear and compelling vision, won the support of the global board. Less than a decade later, the business had blown through its original target of a billion dollars per year.

It wasn't just the number. "In presenting the vision, we tried to paint a picture of how the future business would look and feel," Nick observed. "One of the things we talked about was a global development center in India. Seven years later we found ourselves standing in front of a large team of incredibly smart people working there. The point is, when we looked back at the vision and the hundred businesses we brainstormed, we got way more right than wrong.

"And all of it came about because of capturing that thought on a flip chart early on. I sometimes wonder what would have happened if we hadn't captured the thought and done something about it. It likely wouldn't have happened and certainly would not have happened as quickly. It brought people together and motivated them to seize an opportunity."

YOUR TRACTOR BEAM INTO THE FUTURE

Stories like that are great illustrations of the power of vision. It is inspiring when someone takes a big idea and turns it into reality. The only potential downside to using such significant achievements to illustrate the catalytic impact of vision is that the examples used can make it seem like having a vision is something that has to be BIG and

IMPORTANT, and ... something that *other* people can manage to do. But getting a vision for a team is nothing more complicated than taking some time to work out what wild success looks like for the team on—roughly—a three-to-five-year time horizon.

The relevant time frame of a vision may depend on the particular nature of the project, company, and industry. How far out you should you be looking? It depends. A software vision might not be able to look beyond the next six months. An aerospace vision would need to stretch out to ten years or more. The leadership of a country will want to be looking twenty to twenty-five years out. For truly big changes, even that timeline might be too short. We once heard that if your personal vision was something you could complete in your lifetime, you weren't playing a big enough game.

People have visions all the time. About getting a new car, kitchen, or cottage. About planting a garden, or starting a charity, or building a company. If the word "vision" provokes an allergic reaction in you, pick your own term for it. The point is this: the *thought* of something new precedes its actual existence in the world. Always. If there's no thought, there's no existence. That's as true for a painting as it is for a public library. It doesn't even need to involve creation; the way to get out of a room is to have the thought about being in a different room. The way to catch a ball is to imagine how the ball can be caught. Once you have the "vision" of it, you don't need to calculate speed and trajectory and plan a sequence of muscle contractions to make that happen. Our bodies take care of the coordination below the level of conscious thought once we have the vision for it.

Despite millennia of using vision to change reality (pyramids, anyone?), this concept of vision remains divisive. Some love it, and some can't bear to even discuss the idea of it. It's just too airy-fairy. Too unrealistic.

Why focus on the future? After all, it never happens. It's always today, if you haven't noticed. But by giving ourselves permission to conceive of a better situation, be that a financial, organizational, or emotional one, it tunes our radar to perceive information and opportunities that would be missed otherwise. The value of a vision is not the future it describes, but the change in what we notice as we move toward it.

For those who remain skeptics about what George H. W. Bush called "the vision thing" (we're guessing that he wasn't a fan . . .), how about this: I'd be willing to bet you are reading this in a chair that was—at one point—nothing more than a vision in a designer's mind, in a building that was once just a fleeting image in an architect's mind. You may even be reading this on a device that was first imagined by an engineer, and—depending on whether you are reading it on a PC or an Apple device—formed part of either Bill Gates's vision to put a PC in every home and on every desk or Steve Jobs's vision to put beautiful, intuitive devices into the hands of his customers. So much for visions being "unrealistic."

Still think vision doesn't matter? Without the moon mission, NASA would have gone down in history as merely the most overfunded set of boys' toys in history. Seeing things that don't exist yet is the first step in how cool, new, and useful things get done in the world. We see things that aren't there, and—if they are more attractive than the currently available alternative— we get moving and find out how to make them happen.

> **If you don't see something done, you won't see how to do it.**
>
> —DAVID ALLEN

Why is vision so important on a team? Well, if your team only implements what GTD proposes at the level of next actions and projects, it will become more efficient. At that level we can turn the team into a machine, cranking out next actions and projects, but—at that level of detail—we still don't know whether the team is pointed anywhere good. The team could be doing all the right things very efficiently in a dead-end market. Examples are numerous, but perhaps one of the most obvious was Kodak dominating the market for film as digital images were taking off.

Even worse, the team has no reference point for where it wants to be heading, and can easily be working—again, very efficiently as individuals—at cross purposes. To be comfortable that the team's day-to-day actions are taking them somewhere they want to go *together*, the team needs a reference point on a longer time horizon. One of the key components of that is having a clear and attractive vision of what they want to *be*, *do*, and *have* in roughly three to five years. To get the team's energy focused and flowing in the same direction it needs a North Star around which to orient its activity. That North Star is the vision.

LIKE IT OR NOT, YOU CAN'T STOP VISIONING

The main reason to choose your vision consciously is that—as with the concepts we introduce in other chapters of this book—you can't *not* have one. Because humans are teleological—it is in our nature to move toward things as a principle—we always have some vision of what we want. Your team may or may not be aware of it, but it already has a vision. For many teams that haven't given vision any time or conscious thought, the vision is "Let's just not lose what we have." And that works, mostly. Year after year they produce pretty much the same results.

But here's the thing: there is an energy cost to just staying where you are. Going someplace better with the team will require a different quality of energy, for certain, but the momentum that comes from moving toward something the team wants—as opposed to simply defending territory—will more than compensate for any extra energy required.

Everyone has seen—and been inspired by—the power of vision in some context. Everyone is for vision when the vision becomes a reality. That some visions are realized while others die on the runway is not the fault of the visions themselves, but rather of a lack of commitment—and associated planning and new habits—which lead to the lack of success.

One of the reasons that people become cynical about implementing visions is that they have seen too many over time and been disappointed too often by a lack of follow-through. Again, this is not the fault of the vision but of the changing winds in corporate life. If you've put your heart and soul into making a vision happen, then find that it is abandoned when a new leader takes over, it takes some doing to get motivated to go over the top for the next leader's vision.

Sometimes they have simply lost faith in their own ability to execute things consistently enough to believe that they might be able to make the vision happen. Many have been overwhelmed for so long that the idea of taking on something new—and ambitious—provokes only a groundswell of despair.

HOW TO DO VISION

[ED] October 1975: ice hockey season is coming, and my twelve-year-old self is over the moon. I had grown like a weed through the summer, and my feet are bursting out of last year's skates, so we are off to get new ones to have me ready for the season.

I say "new," but as we didn't have a lot of money, each year I got a "pre-owned" pair. In my mind "new skates" actually meant "used skates, new to me," and after a few years of that, I didn't even think to want new skates anymore.

When creating a vision—for yourself or your team—one of the first challenges is likely to be simply allowing yourself to want what you want. Because that is the exam question here: What do we want?

Or, in the terms of the first *GTD* book, what does "wild success" look like on this team if we get this right?

Allowing yourself to want what you can probably get is easy; allowing yourself to want what you *really want* is much more challenging. What I ended up doing with my skates is what people often do with their visions. They stop wanting what they want and start only allowing themselves to want what they think they can get. There's a big difference. We do this as individuals, and as teams.

Young children do not have this problem. Before socialization they are exceptionally good at wanting exactly what they want, independent of the likelihood of getting it. As adults, after a few disappointments, we start to protect ourselves by negotiating with ourselves: "Well, I want x to the power of two, but given the global economic situation, politics in the organization, and my boss's mood, I'll settle for x plus 5 percent."

To protect us our subconscious has a helpful little hack: it simply stops us from wanting things that we don't think we can achieve. It keeps us from being disappointed, but it also keeps us from even imagining things that we have the potential to be, do, or have. That would be bad enough, but it also keeps us from playing the bigger game that our team, our families, and our communities need us to be playing.

There are a variety of ways of dealing with this challenge, but consciously developing an attractive, motivating vision is one of the best ways to turn your subconscious from a brake to a gas pedal on your potential, as an individual or a team.

The process of creating a vision for a team doesn't have to be difficult. It can take some time but doesn't have to be a huge, long exercise. For those who have enjoyed previous successes with it, conjuring up a vision of the future won't take long at all. If everyone simply answers the question "What do we want to be true on this team in three to five years?" and doesn't edit too heavily, then you'll have the raw material for your vision. Some like to take that a step further, and ask questions that evoke a sensory response: "What will we be seeing, hearing, feeling, etc., in three to five years' time?" A classic way to access this is to have team members write a fictitious article for a journal they hold in esteem, from the perspective of five years hence.

[DAVID] An exercise that has been repeatedly valuable for individuals or teams I've worked with is to have them write a *Wall Street Journal* or *Financial Times* article that describes in detail how insanely successful the team or project has been. It seemed hokey to some before they tried it, but everyone invariably got totally engaged and stoked about what they were writing, buying into the potential that they could make it happen.

With that done the main work for a team is aligning the raw material everyone brings to the table so that they are motivated to pull in the same direction. This can take time, but as with purpose, this discussion phase is extremely valuable. You want to surface and talk through divergences of opinion about direction and resource allocation and get aligned before problems surface on the road ahead.

One challenge you'll face is keeping the team from beginning to plan too early in the process. A good vision is one that you genuinely don't know how to make happen—yet. If you already know how to make it happen, it's not a vision, it's a plan, and you should just get moving on it. For a vision, all you need at this stage is to articulate a powerful desire for what the team wants. Simple in theory, but it can provoke negative reactions. The more the vision really *is* a vision, the more some of the team will start to say something like, "Wait a minute, this vision thing is all well and good, but how are we going to make this happen?" It's a great question, but one being asked at the wrong point in the process. One of the very few rules of a good vision session is that you need to keep people from being distracted by the "how" question at this early stage.

There is a reason that the question typically shows up. As mentioned earlier, wanting things can present a danger: the team might set a vision that it doesn't achieve. And? The potential downside risk of thinking big and not reaching your target is acceptable in light of the upside in energy and direction motivated by an inspiring vision.

At this stage of the visioning process, just capture what you really want as a team. It is only the first stage, where you allow desires to shape what becomes the final product. Everyone in the room has a brain, and they'll use it to be "realistic" once we get to the goal-setting and planning stage.

> A well-ordered life is like climbing a tower; the view halfway up is better than the view from the base, and it steadily becomes finer as the horizon expands.
>
> —WILLIAM LYON PHELPS

It won't happen exactly the way you envision it, in any case. If your vision is big enough, you'll never make it happen. That is not the point. The point is to get moving in the right direction. Once you do, the world may well change, and perhaps make the original vision redundant or ridiculous. So be it. More likely is that as things evolve around you, you should review the vision and make any useful adjustments. You can reroute once on the road if you need to, but the team still needs to know the direction in which to aim its collective efforts now.

In our experience, the vision often comes in two parts:

- A broad and global statement of where the team wants to be in three to five years

- A slightly more granular series of statements that describe distinct aspects (e.g., financial results, operational effectiveness, talent acquisition) of the business

To link back to the chapter on purpose, here's BioLite again:

Our Vision:

This planet's future will be shared by all of us—and we're here to make that future bright for everyone.

Our vision is to provide twenty million people with access to clean energy and to avoid three million tons of CO_2 by the year 2025.

BioLite's website hosts a running tally of lives it's touched, and that number is currently over seven million. Will they make twenty? Maybe not, but do the seven million who've gotten access to safe and cheap power really care?

A vision doesn't have to be "worthy" to be powerful. Here's a vision that drove spectacular success from a client in corporate finance:

We will be both the adviser of choice and employer of choice.

We will have fun and deliver £15 million revenue in our market.

We will:

- Dominate our market

- Hold many strong, deep relationships with our chosen clients

- Embrace sector or product specialists who can help get deals done

- Work across silos to fully contribute to our company's success

- Be seen as leaders in our offices, business communities, and in our industry

- Act with confidence, integrity, innovation, and creativity

The expression of "vision" could range from a few descriptive bulleted phrases (like the above) to a full-scale broadcast-quality video about the envisioned future.

ON KEEPING IT ALIVE

Vision only gets traction when the team stays in touch with it. It is only when the team vision is kept alive in regular conversation that it has the power to transform motivation, innovation, and results. This is not about an airy-fairy denial of reality. For the power of vision to really work, the team needs to be willing to consistently confront itself with the cold hard facts of reality. It is in experiencing the cognitive dissonance between what we *desire* as a team and what we currently *have* that we get the energy and motivation that the vision can provide. In these circumstances we—individuals and teams— always move in the direction of the image that is strongest for us. That is good, if we consistently reinforce the vision. That is not so good if we spend too much time focusing on the reality around us. ("This will never change.")

Again, many times the original vision is never achieved. It might have been either miscalculated or was premature for what then showed up along the way. But by identifying it to begin with, it puts us on a path that can lead to unexpected opportunities that only emerge if we're embarked on that journey. You have to be moving down the road to notice turnoffs that promise better paths, and establishing plans and milestones for the journey is what we'll cover in chapter 8.

Chapter 8

Horizon Three—Goals

CONTROL	FOCUS	PLANNING
Capture	Horizon 5: Purpose and Principles	Purpose and Principles
Clarify	Horizon 4: Vision	Vision
Organize	**Horizon 3: Goals**	Brainstorm
Reflect	Horizon 2: Areas of Focus	Organize
Engage	Horizon 1: Projects	Next Actions
	Ground: Next Actions	

W hile vision might remain stubbornly divisive or simply elusive, most people are comfortable with the idea of goals. They are closer timewise, less wild and crazy in terms of scope, and somehow more tangible. If purpose and vision are about generating motivation and energy, goals are about focusing and directing them at high-leverage targets. Also, most organizations are familiar with some sort of annual goal-setting exercise, framed as operational plans, strategies, budgeting, yearly objectives, and the like.

WHY GOALS?

Anyone who has bought into the value of delineating desired outcomes would naturally understand the reason to set goals. The old Cheshire cat saying that if you don't know where you're going, any road will do, is a bit of self-evident logic.

[ED] A few years into creating our UK franchise, we began to experience a "problem." Because of my relationships in Germany, Austria, and Switzerland, the turnover coming from those countries began to approach our UK turnover, even though we didn't have the franchise rights in those markets. The additional revenue was a nice problem to have, for sure, and it flagged up an opportunity. So as part of a visioning process I do annually, I set the vision of building a business in those countries that would impact ten times as many people and generate ten times our then revenues from those markets. Having allowed myself to want that outcome, a key aspect of the transformative power of vision kicked in: it became crystal clear that there was no way to achieve the vision by simply doing more of what we were then doing. Our existing level of success was dependent on my near-weekly travel to various parts of Europe. Without significant advances in cloning technology there was no way to get there ten times more often.

When shortly thereafter an opportunity presented itself to formalize our franchise in those markets, my partner and I began breaking down the vision into shorter-term goals. In light of the geographical realities—and our clone shortage—the only approach that made sense was to find local partners who could help grow the business. In minutes we went from a vision that felt inspiring—but quite big and scary (ten times!)—to something that felt doable with a bit of research and planning. Within months we'd identified local partners, and within a year a sister organization was up and running.

Eight years later, our organization in those markets was reaching dramatically more people and had grown by almost exactly ten times the original revenues that had prompted the initial vision.

There are similarities in the psychology of visioning and goal setting, but real differences in how they are created. When drafting a vision you want the team dreamers to keep the others from being too "realistic" and instead stay focused on what they collectively want. With vision you want to think big but not necessarily be super specific on details, or the plan for getting there. Setting a vision is like saying, "We'd like this outcome, and will keep our desire fresh to help guide our choices as we move toward it." With goals it is more a matter of, "We want this, and we will make a plan for getting it, and focus our energies to make it happen." When setting goals it is time for the team's more detail-oriented members—the accountants, engineers, and planners, perhaps—to take the lead.

> You have to believe in the long-term plan you have but you need the short-term goals to motivate and inspire you.
>
> —ROGER FEDERER

If we take a personal example, when envisioning your dream home you should think boldly about the features you want—number of rooms, open space, light, view, and maybe even the city or a neighborhood— but probably not get too attached to a specific address. Three to five years out it would be unhelpful to get that detailed. In our example from the billion-dollar-baby story in the previous chapter, a version of the original vision included opening a development center in Mumbai, but it actually came into being in Gurgaon, near Delhi. The important part of the vision was the existence of the development center, not the specific location. Getting hung up on doing a detailed plan for Mumbai would have been time wasted.

When you set goals, you ultimately do want to give your dream home an address, along with at least a good sketch of the map for getting there. Once Gurgaon had been identified, it was time for a detailed plan for creating the development center there.

We have seen teams succeed with a variety of different goal-setting approaches. SMART (Specific, Measurable, Achievable, Realistic, and Time-bound) goals were the reference point for many years, and many of those ideas are also found in more recent approaches, such as Must-Win Battles, or the current trend for OKRs (or objectives and key results). Explicitly or implicitly, many of the methodologies are based on principles identified by Edwin Locke and Gary Latham in the research that led to their seminal paper on goal-setting theory in 1990.

As far back as 1967, Locke discovered that as long as people had the requisite skills, hard and clear goals drove higher performance—much higher. Those with the hardest goals performed over 250 percent as well as those with the easiest goals. They also significantly outperformed people with more general targets, or who'd been simply told, "Do your best."

The value of getting specific about goals derives from a similar dynamic observed when agreeing on challenging working standards with one another; clear and hard goals define high performance in a way that allows team members to focus their efforts, use their existing skills, and prioritize appropriately to achieve them. All these things are less likely if the goals are vague or too easy to be motivating.

This is true in our experience, but there is a caveat for teams that have not been performing. Just as with young boxers who've had a setback, it is useful to restore self-belief and self-confidence with a few small wins before going for big ones. For a team that has gotten used to *not* achieving its goals, achieving them consistently—even with smaller goals—*is* a big goal. Like a young boxer who has lost a few fights after showing early promise, the team needs to rebuild a sense that it can get things done reliably.

One manager we worked with in a large global concern was charged with turning around a business unit that had been hemorrhaging money for years. His vision was to return it to being extremely profitable, but he knew that the team wasn't ready to take on that big a task yet. When setting goals with them, he made the first target simply to lose less money. For the team in question, that was already hard, and he made the target clear for them by agreeing on a smaller negative number for them to hit. Once they'd successfully accomplished that, he pointed them at getting just marginally into the black. It was only once they'd managed a small profit that he felt they were ready to take on the real goal. It took a couple of years, but with the team's confidence restored, he eventually got the unit back to being a significant source of profit for the business.

HOW TO DO GOALS

Just as the team's vision should contribute directly to the organizational vision, as we bring in the time horizon to one to two years, it is worth being a bit more granular about how progress needs to be made toward manifesting the vision. You are basically reverse engineering the vision by asking a simple question: "What, specifically, do we need to accomplish within the next twelve to twenty-four months, to have us feel we're on track to achieve our vision?"

If the team has recently done some assessment or review of what's recently happened prior to starting a goal-setting initiative, that exercise can serve as a critical tool to raise awareness of "current reality" before starting on thinking about the future. Questions like "What did we accomplish?" or "What didn't we, and why not?" and "What unexpected thing happened?" can all provide useful context for thinking about which goals to set.

Your goals are set in a particular context; just as you want the team's goals to drive toward the team vision, it is worth checking that they clearly support any organizational goals that have been communicated.

Traditionally, all of this has been done top-down from the leadership team, but as teams move toward a more agile approach, annual goals are often collected and selected from the bottom up. Although Locke and Latham's research has shown that assigned goals can work as well as self-generated ones (as long as the assigned goals are difficult and well explained), engaging the team in the process of setting the goals minimizes the time and effort to get commitment from those who will actually do the work.

One of our clients manages this elegantly despite having hundreds of employees. Topics for team improvement in the coming year are captured from anyone with an opinion and then prioritized democratically. Team members can then choose which priority projects they have the passion or skills for and sign themselves up to help drive them to completion. The result? A greater sense of autonomy in the team, and much stronger motivation to work on the projects chosen.

Ideally, the prioritization process clarifies something like three to seven initial high-leverage objectives. You can opt for more or fewer, but we suggest a small enough number that they could be put on a pocket card. One number-two executive in a global organization, when asked his key to success, pulled out a three-by-five card from his pocket. "It's my boss's priorities." The technology he uses to remind himself is irrelevant. The focus implied by the size of card is not.

The problem is that too often new goals are set without a ruthless discussion of what other projects the team will be pausing—or cutting entirely—to allow the time, space, and creativity to realize the new goals. Setting additional goals on top of an already undoable list of tasks is simply despair inducing. At a certain point more goal setting is simply experienced as a new round of punishment—more projects for the team to feel bad about. We'll come back to this point in more detail when we delve into team prioritization.

Goals are often expressed as rather hard-nosed results desired: profitability, volume of sales, new offices operational, etc. Those kinds of goals will get you the high performance we discussed in the introduction. What is often missed are the more "squishy" results that would enhance the health of the team's work together. If the team is not performing well as a team, then having a clear goal about how they work together would be a useful first step. If motivation is lagging, then something like "Our people are satisfied and inspired with the processes and accomplishments of the year" is one such goal. It will need to be made just as specific and achievable, with appropriate markers and processes put in place to gauge success.

For goals where progress is difficult to see initially, a further step can be useful. Sometimes setting "process" goals is a way to at least ensure that the right behaviors are taking place to enhance the probability of reaching the end-point goal. If you've set a goal to achieve 20 percent more sales in the coming year, and you've noticed that face-to-face coffee and conversation with clients seem to drive sales, then a process goal of five (or ten, or twenty) face-to-face meetings per week for each person on the sales team might be one intermediate goal to track as a means of enabling the achievement of the real target. Similarly, if you know that you need to be consistently adding new clients to grow the business, then a process goal might be to track the number of new contacts input to the team CRM on a monthly basis. The key here is to work backward from the end-point goal as a way to check whether there are obvious leading indicators that can support the achievement of it.

Then attention needs to be paid to the resulting list(s) of goals/

> An idealist believes the short run doesn't count. A cynic believes the long run doesn't matter. A realist believes that what is done or left undone in the short run determines the long run.
>
> —SYDNEY J. HARRIS

objectives on as regular a basis as is necessary to keep a team focused. Normally, if the goals were set from an annual viewpoint, a monthly or quarterly reassessment and recalibration are sufficient. But, again, the speed of change in the environment may require a more or less frequent recursion of the conversation and realignments. Whatever the decision about when and how to regroup at the goal level, it is a good idea to schedule those regular progress tracking meetings well ahead of time. Knowing they'll need to appear with an update will keep everyone focused on that content, and how they want to show up with what information when it takes place.

Our client from the example above chose to reassemble the team every other month for their review meetings, with each priority project getting its own one-to-two-hour session on different days of the week. In a spirit of enabling clarity and transparency across the teams—or among different teams—these virtual review meetings are open to anyone who wants to listen in. Hundreds do, with the result that information flows easily across the team, and more brains are focused on solutions for any roadblocks.

What we've described here applies for most corporate teams, but setting goals for a team does not have to be a major undertaking. It can be as formal as an off-site retreat setting for the group or as informal as a relaxed conversation with a life partner.

[DAVID] My wife and I do a process at the end of each year, in which we make a list of all the things we accomplished or experienced during the previous year, and what we'd like to have on that list at the end of the coming one. It takes just a few minutes. Works for us.

GOALS GONE WRONG

When goals don't work out, we see a few recurring themes: an insufficient number of ideas presented to be able to select enough good

ones; unclear accountabilities; goals not defined clearly enough to engage interest; allowing personal enthusiasms and stakeholder
politics to inflate—and make undoable—the
team's list of projects; and inconsistent follow-
ups lacking in rigor.

To prevent those outcomes you could use
one of the approaches mentioned earlier in
this chapter, but really anything that helps diverge (capture lots of ideas about how to realize the vision), converge (prioritize those raw
ideas down to a few high-leverage first targets),
plan (in sufficient detail to get going), and follow up (with consistency
to track execution over time) will do the trick. If you want to keep it
simple, that could look like doing a team mind sweep to externalize
everything that has the team's attention, reading chapter 12 to remind
yourself why you need to radically cut that back to succeed, then check
out chapter 10 to get started on planning the selected goals. You'll
very quickly start looking for people to take charge of different workstreams that contribute to the achievement of the goals, so the next
chapter is about nailing down accountability—who'll take care of what
along the way to making the goals a reality.

> **Everybody sets out to do something, and everybody does something, but no one does what he sets out to do.**
>
> —GEORGE MOORE

Chapter 9

Horizon Two

AREAS OF FOCUS
AND RESPONSIBILITY

CONTROL	FOCUS	PLANNING
Capture	Horizon 5: Purpose and Principles	Purpose and Principles
Clarify	Horizon 4: Vision	Vision
Organize	Horizon 3: Goals	Brainstorm
Reflect	**Horizon 2: Areas of Focus**	Organize
Engage		Next Actions
	Horizon 1: Projects	
	Ground: Next Actions	

WHY ROLES?

This horizon connects the more abstract levels with the operational aspects of life and work. Most people and teams have some sort of to-do list and calendar to manage day-to-day activity, and some people and teams have goals, objectives, or visions that keep them focused on more strategic priorities. What is often missed in team and self-management is clarity about the roles that need to be fulfilled to be sure that both upper and lower horizons are linked up. When this clarity is taken for granted and instead left abstract and vague (too often), issues inevitably show up that produce stress, frustration, and block forward progress.

Like not maintaining our health, having an unclear accountability on a team is fine for a while, but eventually creates at least minor chaos. Not being clear about who's tracking team commitments, or who's responsible for the team calendar, or who's responsible for reporting to upper management, can create a significant drag on personal and organizational productivity.

For any team or organization, role clarity is critical. That's why organization charts were drawn up, attempting to define the various aspects of the business that needed to be maintained—customer service, finance, human resources, sales, marketing, operations, etc. Those delineations do not of themselves indicate what specifically needs to be done in each of them—they simply point to an area that should be maintained at a sufficient level or standard to support the goals and vision. If the team's work is suffering because of problems in a particular area, then it requires identifying projects and action decisions to get things moving. That is most clearly handled by someone "in charge" of that area.

The clarity about roles also gives clarity to the parameters and membership of the team. In a world where few people seem to be able to say who is actually on their team, clarifying who you can count on is a key piece of achieving joint aims.

A solo entrepreneur works within their own total organization chart. They have to party with potential clients (marketing), manage the money (finance), make sure the product is delivered (operations), and deal with complaints (customer service). If they are successful and want to grow, they will usually hire an assistant to help with a bit of that. Then perhaps an operational manager, or a finance person— whichever they want to offload as an area of responsibility first.

Then . . . and then . . . and then—an organization with "silos" builds up to handle each of these functions. That process seems logical and probably still is for many more traditional organizations. However, as we've alluded to in other chapters, the nature of work and the teams and organizations that perform that work have shifted rapidly. The old silos don't really function well as such anymore. There is a need for much more fluidity, cross-silo interdependence, and clarity about who's handling what, on an almost day-to-day basis.

This certainly pertains to the team level. It should be driven by the purpose of the team, and its accountability to any larger body. Once a team is clear on what the goal is—launch the new IT application for workflow, have a motivated workforce, publish this book, etc.—the component areas required to be handled need to be delineated and their respective expected results clarified. This then provides the criteria for communicating about how to assess critical aspects of the team workflow efficiently.

"Jose, how's it going with your area?" "Susan, anything you need from any of us with your projects?" Etc.

This may sound like obvious common sense, and we're sure there are teams functioning quite well in this regard. However, in our experience most teams could use a more rigorous examination of their members' roles and associated accountabilities, even in some of the smallest projects and initiatives. "Were you going to handle this, or me?" is unfortunately a rather common fly in the ointment.

And as the environment shifts (sometimes rapidly), the team needs to reassess and recalibrate the various responsibilities. "We've just had our budget cut 40 percent. How are we going to manage our resource allocations now?"

[DAVID] This is a story about how I learned about the power of role clarification.

My first real mentor in the management consulting world,

Dean Acheson (not the former secretary of state under Truman), took me under his wing to learn the organizational-change model he had developed over the course of years. It was profound, highly successful when applied, and trained me in much of my own professional and intellectual property development in the 1980s. Aside from learning the value of capturing and clarifying "open loops" in the organization to clear the decks for changes needed, one of the more critical pieces of the model was creating a new organization chart. Traditionally, such structures were built on bubbles reporting to bubbles that bubbled to the top, but this novel one started at the bottom. "Bottom" did not mean lesser, but more foundational. What was the final output of the organization—its "valuable final product"? "Well-designed products that are sold to delighted customers for a profit." Once that was clarified, the question was: What are the component outputs that produce that? "Well-managed assets" (finance), "people interested in what we do" (marketing/PR), "signed contracts" (sales), "viable, expanding company" (executive), etc. This was prior to deciding anything about specific people filling these roles. Then we did a rigorous inventory of every single activity that took place in the company. Everything from "take money to the bank" to "clean the coffee room" to "report financials to the board." We then examined that list and distributed each discrete activity in columns on an org chart based upon what outcome was most supported by that activity.

Once that chart was signed off by the top management, we then assigned people to be accountable for those columned outputs. Not surprisingly, the top members of the organization found themselves spread across the org chart. They (and their reports) had "sort of been" responsible for those areas, but because a specific person had not really been given clear accountability over a particular outcome or area, everything rose to the top for decision-making. That was a formula for burnout of those at the top, and a potential drag on speed of action because of ambiguity about authority to move things forward without some top-level sign-off.

So, as well as witnessing the value of implementing this process for my small-business consulting clients, for decades we managed our own small company with role-based org charts. It enabled us to navigate occasional rough waters with sufficient clarity and minimal stress.

Then, when I discovered the Holacracy model, it became evident that this could be taken to a whole new level of detailed clarity and effectiveness. Every single activity required to run the company was to be put into a context of role, purpose, and accountability of that role, with a person assigned to it. The relief of pressure on me, plus the exponentially enhanced clarity and freedom of decision-making it provided to all involved in our work, has been phenomenal.

HOW TO DO ROLES

Role clarification on a team doesn't need to be a major event. It can simply be signaled by something showing up for the team that hasn't been addressed yet and getting clear about how it should be dealt with, and who would do that. And, additionally, if similar things may show up in the future, would/could that person continue to be accountable for it.

Another key positive factor in defining roles, and who has them, is the prevention of confusion when someone on the team or in the organization leaves. What's left? If it's unclear and undocumented what they were

If everybody minded their own business," the Duchess said, in a hoarse growl, "the world would go around a great deal faster than it does.

—LEWIS CARROLL

accountable for, it's often a messy scramble to address any gaps that have been left when they go. When the roles and accountabilities are clear and logged, handing jobs off to others becomes a much easier and more seamless affair.

The chief learning officer of a Fortune 500 global company told us he really knew the value of GTD practices when a senior-level direct report passed on her job to someone new. The two people did not know each other but both had been through GTD training. In their handoff meeting, both pulled out their complete projects lists and role accountabilities, and in a matter of an hour or so, accomplished what would have normally taken days—if not longer—to ensure a seamless transition of roles.

In our years of one-on-one coaching, this horizon has often been the most significant in determining our client's priorities. Once our clients feel they have a grasp on their projects and attendant actions, an overview of their areas of responsibility invariably surfaces larger but more subtle things that have their attention. One newly appointed CEO in a major financial firm was pretty clear about his professional day-to-day organization and focus, because it had already been relatively hard-baked into the system. The staff, the committees, the meetings—all pretty much on cruise control. But we ended up spending an entire half day focused on his personal life—investments, properties, children, vacations, etc.—which only came to the fore when he was led through the discussion of his major areas of focus.

Most people have one job for which they get paid but fulfill various roles for that salary. With a bit of thought, they could usually identify four to seven things they would be held accountable for doing well. It's the same for teams, and the delineation and complete description of roles would represent a team's job description, as a team. Identifying them and detailing them is guaranteed to be a fertile discussion.

Sample organization chart:

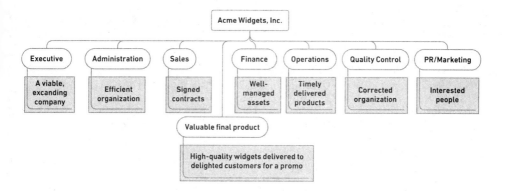

At its most basic level, this is a template to identify an organization's roles (admin, sales, etc.) with their discrete accountabilities identified. A sole entrepreneur would wear all of these hats; and a large organization would distribute multiple subroles within each division.

Drilling down a level, under Operations, the following section provides an example of what we mean.

ROLE: CUSTOMER SERVICE

Purpose—Brand-enhancing, customer-delighting, profitable customer service

Accountabilities:

Providing customer service for products sold to individual consumers, including digital products and online memberships

Defining and updating client response templates

Training customer service backup resources

The example remains high level in terms of detail, but as part of a larger team exercise to clarify boundaries between roles it served its purpose: to act as a way to resolve confusion or conflict about who is responsible for what. Many teams choose to clarify the role in much more detail over time, as questionable situations arise and are clarified. This increased detail helps prevent recurrence of the confusion and is also particularly helpful during handovers to those picking up responsibility for a given role.

[ED] For the past few decades I've been involved in running a retreat just south of London that is held twice each year. During that time we've had dozens of volunteers come and go from the organizing committee. That could have produced untold problems when there were handoffs to be done, but one of the things we got right early on was to have each person write up in considerable detail what their role's responsibilities were, along with a reasonably precise chronology of what needed to happen before, during, and after each retreat. Once that was in place, it has been a matter of occasional light maintenance to keep everything up to date. Before handing the role on to their successor, each person in a particular role updates their document to take account of any enhancements they've made.

Using that simple approach, we have been able to integrate new members of the committee incredibly quickly, and have them perform at a good level with next to no hand-holding—or mishaps in the organization of each event. It also has meant that we have fewer challenges in recruiting new people (as everyone can get a good understanding of exactly what they are committing to), and the "puzzle pieces" of the retreat fit together in a way that minimizes the effort for each person who helps. The whole thing runs successfully on just two one-hour team meetings per year, in which we debrief the previous event and coordinate the next one.

As a side note, having all of the organizing documents for each role documented in this way has meant that several other retreats have been quickly and easily started using the same model. When someone comes to our retreat and wants to undertake something similar for themselves and their community back in their part of the world, we give them our pack of documents. They just need to find bodies to fill the roles. If they all do a halfway decent job of using the checklists and descriptions we've provided, their event goes off successfully, too. To date there are four such offshoots operating in different parts of the United Kingdom, and now even in different countries.

Over the course of the previous five chapters, we've done our best to give a sense of the potential benefits of spending time to bring each horizon into better focus for your team. We hope you've taken away that there's no "right" way to engage with all this thinking and decision-making, other than what's needed to have all the players feeling appropriately engaged with their endeavors. What's true is that a team needs to feel comfortable with focusing on any of these horizons when needed. If there's an allergy to action decision-making or rethinking vision, purpose, or goals, then there will be an invariable bump in the road, if not something more severe.

> **If a decision-making process is flawed and dysfunctional, decisions will go awry.**
>
> —CARLY FIORINA

It doesn't much matter where you start—getting clarity at the next action level, or with your purpose—but we notice that when a team gets control of their day-to-day and breaks free from the tyranny of the urgent in their work, it often unearths a desire to get clear on what all the busyness is about.

One of our clients offered the fundamentals of GTD to his team, and several months later the desire to clarify purpose and vision spontaneously came from the team itself. "They came to me and said, 'We have all these projects, but we don't really get how they fit together, and where that is leading.'" After a couple of days off-site, doing the work we've outlined in this chapter and elsewhere in this book, they felt they had the big picture for why they were doing what they were doing. What is interesting is that they only became aware of the need for the off-site once they got clear on the number and variety of projects that they had underway and once they had created enough brain space with a new way of working to have the thought that "We don't know how all of this fits together, and it would be better if we did." For many people, constantly losing the battle just to stay current means that they don't have time to even think about the context for their work.

Not only that, but the team has ready-made criteria for decision-making and prioritization. If you know why the team exists, and you know that the thing in front of you doesn't help you achieve that, then you are a lot closer to a decision on "let's do it" or "let's not." If you know where the team wants to go in terms of its vision and goals, but the thing in front of you doesn't get you closer, ditto. And finally, if you know what your role is, and the thing in front of you is not related, then you really want to think hard before you take it on or shift it to the person who has that responsibility on the team.

A minority of teams get as far as doing the work to get clarity at all these levels. An even smaller number then use that information in a way that supports them over time. Because having done the work of getting clarity is only the first step. And keeping the horizons alive for the team is a process, not an event.

When an organization treats these higher-level-thinking and decision-making processes as a tick-box exercise, the horizons usually die of neglect: "We did it, we published it, let's get back to work." That is a bit like saying, "I showered last year, so I'm good for a while, right?"

Unfortunately, that is precisely where many teams go wrong with the work they do on their higher horizons. Average teams do all the work at an off-site and come back and publicize the work they've done. Then the work ends up in a drawer. Slightly better ones at least get the information onto posters. Good teams come back and do the same, but then go on to reinforce the purpose, vision, and goals on a regular basis in official channels. The best teams do all of that, too, but they do something more: they link day-to-day decision-making to whether each decision will get them closer to fulfilling their purpose or achieving their vision. In their world, purpose and vision aren't merely material for office decoration, they are business tools to help them make better decisions about how to stay focused and out of overwhelm.

CONTROL	FOCUS	PLANNING
Capture	Horizon 5: Purpose and Principles	Purpose and Principles
Clarify		
Organize	Horizon 4: Vision	Vision
Reflect	Horizon 3: Goals	Brainstorm
Engage	Horizon 2: Areas of Focus	Organize
		Next Actions
	Horizon 1: Projects	
	Ground: Next Actions	

These horizons represent where "the rubber hits the road." We addressed handling team projects under "Organize" in chapter 4, and we suggest leaving the tracking of next actions to the individuals responsible for specific projects. Consistent tracking of next actions on all projects by the team would quickly overwhelm even the

> You've got to think about big things while you're doing small things, so that all the small things go in the right direction.
>
> —ALVIN TOFFLER

most motivated and detail oriented, though occasional updates from the individuals concerned will serve to build confidence that things are on track across the breadth of the team's activity. We mention these levels here for completeness, as they must be addressed as we deal with the implementation of decisions made at higher horizons.

Are all the team projects targeted to the larger, longer-term outcomes? Are the actions people have identified aligned with the right things? These are eternal poke-points that must remain regularly addressed in team discussions.

Chapter 10

Planning (and Replanning) in a Complex, Fast-Moving World

CONTROL	FOCUS	PLANNING
Capture	Horizon 5: Purpose and Principles	**Purpose and Principles**
Clarify		
	Horizon 4: Vision	**Vision**
Organize		
	Horizon 3: Goals	**Brainstorm**
Reflect		
	Horizon 2: Areas of Focus	**Organize**
Engage		
		Next Actions
	Horizon 1: Projects	
	Ground: Next Actions	

As we noted earlier in this section, *Getting Things Done* became famous for its five-step model for systematically gaining back a sense of control over individual workflow. With earlier chapters in this section we've shown how both that model and the Horizons of Focus framework can be useful for teams, too. Now we turn our attention to the third key tool from the original *Getting Things Done* book, the Natural Planning Model®. Though probably the least well known to a broader public, for its fans it has proven its value as a go-to resource for planning anything from a family vacation to an organizational-change project.

There are many ways to get planning wrong. If you've worked in a large organization this scenario may be familiar to you: a few months after a change in leadership, a new strategic initiative drops from on high with a request for immediate action. A meeting is called, in which plans for implementing the strategy are discussed. Time is too short to complete a decent plan in the meeting, so a planning committee is formed and tasked with bringing a detailed plan back to the full team in a subsequent gathering. The committee goes to work and does what good planners do: produce lists and mind maps, sequences, workstreams, spreadsheets, and Gantt charts, sometimes even for multiple scenarios. In the next large team meeting the plan is discussed and—with a fair tailwind—signed off. At this point the team can roll into action and take the first steps outlined in the plan—and discover that reality has rendered much of the plan unusable because of unrealistic expectations and changing conditions. Once they start acting on the plan, they face the earthly reality identified by former heavyweight champion Mike Tyson: "Everyone has a plan until they get punched in the face."

If that scenario hasn't crossed your path yet, how about this one: the annual planning cycle. The top team decides targets for the organization, and those are broken down and cascaded to the division level, which cascades to the department level, which cascades to the team level. Teams are tasked with planning and budgeting for the coming year, and these plans and budgets are aggregated at each level on the way back up to the top. This exercise can occupy as much as a month per year, with much of the organization tied up in planning (budgeting) meetings.

So much effort goes into the planning that in the end there's a sense of, "Well, we've spent all this time planning it, so this is how it's going to be, dammit!" The whole thing can become a bit of a modern-day rain dance. "If we collect clean data, crunch the right numbers, and detail a great plan, somehow it will happen like we planned it." It is a form of magical thinking. Unfortunately, just because it's been planned down to three decimal points in a spreadsheet won't make it happen.

The intensity and regularity of this ritual means that the folly of it now largely escapes the participants. Like migration for geese, it is just what happens each year in September, or when a new leader shows up. But planning like this simply makes no sense in the context of the volatile, uncertain, complex, and ambiguous (VUCA) world we mentioned earlier. To underline the point about how fast things are changing, what has happened to that concept is informative. Before most people had heard of it—much less understood the implications for their business planning—the world aligned on a newer concept. Many now think we are living in a BANI world: brittle, anxious, non-linear, and incomprehensible. Whichever kind of world it is, it certainly is moving faster than any static plans can account for.

It might be easier if we simply admitted we'd all like a lot more control over what is happening in our environment, but that no one really has much. Not in the grand scheme of things. And basically no one knows anything about the future.

The overplanning approach clearly doesn't work, but organizations still struggle to abandon it. Part of the difficulty in letting it go is that there is a certain safety in planning, which gives a sense of control while playing with formulae in spreadsheets, getting dates to line up in a calendar, and making the bars on a Gantt chart align just so. A bit like retirement planning, it all makes sense on paper, where no reality intrudes and wreaks havoc on the careful planning. But any planning exercise is attractive for the same reasons that a chess game is. The variables may be myriad in a game of chess, but the game is winnable. It is much different than real life, where reality is poised to give all the long-term planning a good hard punch in the face. We need to understand what's in our control and what isn't in our control, then how to adapt to what is changing around us.

Another reason it is hard to let this way of planning go is that it used to work better than it does today, in a world that was moving much more slowly than it does now. Plans drawn up over a couple of weeks might still be relevant by the time a team got moving on them. No longer. The world—and your clients and competitors—are simply moving too fast.

Finally, companies hang on to old-school planning because of the financial commitments of large and complex projects. Companies need estimates of how much things are going to cost, and when they'll be finished. Even if both of those estimates are way wide of the mark, someone, somewhere, ultimately has to green-light the project, and wants to be able to show that they did their due diligence in the event it all goes wrong. In publicly quoted companies there is a finance-driven requirement that a number is committed to Wall Street or the City every year. Much of the effort in the annual planning cycle has nothing to do with the activity of the company in question, but rather with building a coherent story that keeps investors reassured.

Unfortunately, not planning also doesn't work. As mentioned in the chapter on New Work, there have been some who've gone completely overboard with the idea of "agile" working. Our client's not planning and prebooking seminar rooms ahead of time simply resulted in a lot of firefighting as they scrambled to find rooms at the last minute. So you need a plan, but it would be more honest if everyone concerned was a bit clearer that it is nothing other than a lot of collective guesswork.

Faced with the folly of overplanning, and the lunacy of not planning at all, how should we navigate? If you have read this far into the book, you already know we are fans of purpose, vision, and goals. The challenge is to balance the structure and direction of purpose and vision with nimble responses to what is happening around you, day to day, week to week, year to year.

It's another example of an opportunity to leverage the tension between two ideas that seem like opposites: the need for a strong commitment to a structural skeleton of purpose and a vision of where you want to go, but maintaining adaptive soft tissue around them that allows you to cope with shifting terrain that means you're not restricted to a straight and predictable path. When new information shows up, and the path forward is clearly blocked, or a gap opens between what is happening and what is in the plan, you need to be able to respond quickly with a new plan to get things back on track or to go in a new direction.

In the continuous chaotic evolution of the world in which we now live, there is a need for a way of planning that is dynamic and responsive to the pace of change. In an atmosphere that can feel brittle, anxious, nonlinear, and incomprehensible, how can a team plan quickly, easily, and dynamically so that they can move forward with at least a modicum of confidence?

In our experience, a big part of the solution is in the Natural Planning Model, which became part of the GTD toolkit because it's the way that humans do planning and execution most naturally and easily. The Natural Planning Model (NPM) very quickly made the leap from individual to team use because it so clearly articulated the way we plan when we get it right. It allows fast and dynamic planning so teams can get moving quickly and with confidence in their first actions. It helps reduce fear and procrastination on projects that at first seem too big and scary, because it encourages enough planning to feel comfortable taking the first steps in the project without committing to weeks or months of planning. That allows movement that generates momentum, which in turn opens possibilities for serendipity that can only appear once things are moving.

For most teams the longer, more detailed planning approaches like PRINCE2 are simply irrelevant because of the speed and nature of their work. That is not to suggest that there is no place for detailed long-term planning. The NPM was never intended as a replacement for more elaborate methodologies like PRINCE2 but as a complement to them. If you are building a bridge, a boat, or a nuclear power station, please use one of those approaches to be sure that everything fits tightly when assembled. But even in projects as complex as those, there is scope for using the Natural Planning Model for shorter-cycle planning. Huge projects with massively detailed plans have a rich history of sliding over in terms of time and budget, and huge amounts of time are wasted in replanning things that will simply need to be replanned again. It is far better to use a planning approach that is quick and flexible—using a larger and more detailed project plan as reference for completeness—and to get back to moving things forward rather than wasting time in replanning it all just one more time. Longer term, the only thing that makes sense is a broad-brush approach to a long-term plan, combined with consistently updating relevant parts of that plan as new information and events shape what is possible.

One of our clients described it as dropping a magnifying glass onto different parts of his long-term plan as he moved toward them chronologically. The long-term plan was never accurate or detailed enough, but it provided rough guardrails for the project. As his team moved forward in time, they'd put a metaphorical magnifying glass over the next couple of months of the project and plan using the Natural Planning Model. This shorter-term, magnified version of the plan got much more traction, because it was more real. Three to six months out, the plan meant little to the team. But the next hours, days, and weeks were very present and drove a completely different level of engagement, motivation, and collaboration.

WHAT IS THE NATURAL PLANNING MODEL?

Situational focus—the Natural Planning Model

Using this model is the key practice for getting any situation or project under control and appropriately focused. Whereas the Horizons of Focus model described in previous chapters is primarily a current but static descriptor of the realities of the different horizons, and useful for ensuring an overall context for prioritizing, this model is more focused on generating action in the realities of the moment. It has similarities to the horizons model but is more focused on intentional activity: How should we be thinking about our wedding? What key position are we missing on the team? Should we organize an off-site meeting? Etc.

There are five separate stages in the NPM:

1. Purpose and principles

2. Vision

3. Brainstorm

4. Organize

5. Next actions

Purpose and principles

Why are we doing this project? What has our attention in this situation? And what are our rules of engagement in doing this?

Vision

What would success look, sound, and feel like? What's the desired end result? How will we know when this is satisfactorily achieved?

Brainstorm

What are any and all of the potentially relevant details that we should consider about this?

Organize

How should we structure our thinking about the emergent key components, priorities, and sequences? What are the key parts that need to get done to get to our desired end state? Who needs to be responsible for each? How should we structure our go-forward process?

Next actions

What are the next actions on the current moving parts, and who's got them?

WHY CALL IT "NATURAL PLANNING"?

As mentioned earlier we're effectively planning all the time, whether getting dressed, making dinner, or even just getting out of a room. We want to accomplish something (purpose), have a picture of what it would/should look like (vision), consider multiple options (brainstorm), decide the pieces that need to happen (organize), and start moving on it (next action).

If everyone involved is equally comfortable and confident that all the next actions and people doing them are the right ones, then there is no need to explore the model any further until that situation changes. That is seldom the reality, however, and projects either need more purpose/vision/outcome focusing or more operational implementation detail. And many need both.

WHY IT WORKS FOR TEAMS

The model is helpful for teams for several different reasons. Point by point, here are some thoughts on how the model supports teams specifically:

CONTROL	FOCUS	PLANNING
Capture	Horizon 5: Purpose and Principles	**Purpose and Principles**
Clarify	Horizon 4: Vision	Vision
Organize	Horizon 3: Goals	Brainstorm
Reflect	Horizon 2: Areas of Focus	Organize
Engage	Horizon 1: Projects	Next Actions
	Ground: Next Actions	

Purpose

When an individual plans a project using the Natural Planning Model, it may be challenging to come up with the purpose for the project, but once clarified there is rarely any confusion about what it is about, as they defined it for themselves. On a team, conversations are often needed to align on why the team is doing the project in question. Having those discussions up front can save time and conflict further into the project. Getting clear on purpose also opens possibilities for how the problem (that the project is supposed to resolve) gets fixed. If profitability is the issue, the sales team may think it is the job of management to reduce costs, while management might think it is a project to increase sales. It's not uncommon for all invested parties to come to a mutual agreement about a novel way to handle the situation, solving everyone's wished-for outcome, once the purpose is clear and they have the freedom to go "outside the box" for a solution.

The NPM supports getting clear on purpose and outcomes before charging into action. This is important for any project, but even more so for the kind of work that teams of knowledge workers are faced with each day. At least in manufacturing there will be a reality brake if things are not on track. Something will bump into something else or won't be where it is supposed to be when it is needed. It will be immediately clear that there is a problem.

With digital or knowledge work projects where progress is less visible, such as in marketing/social media or design, unless things are very tightly defined, it can take far longer to determine that they have gone off track.

Principles

Previous team agreements will hold (see chapter 5, Purpose and Principles), but it is useful to have any project-specific parameters clearly identified for the project in question. Clarifying as a team what the nonnegotiable boundaries are and how we want to play together makes clear what is in and out in terms of how we want to carry out the project. Particularly if the project is being delegated to others, it is critical to give them the benefit of any experience on the team about what has or hasn't worked with this kind of effort in the past. Deadlines, budgets, reporting requirements, and stakeholders who must be consulted (or avoided) should all be made very clear to those about to do the work.

These "rules of engagement" conversations can be inspirational. How important is "having fun together" on the project? It really is, for many teams, but seldom acknowledged. How about "using this project to advance how well we work together as a team" or "using each of our individual engagements with this project to further our own personal development"? Those kinds of up-front recognitions of potential value of involvement, when understood and agreed to by the team, can really enrich the experience for everyone. Also, in case the project is delayed or even canceled midstream (not an unusual circumstance), it can still be a win for the players to play.

Vision

CONTROL	FOCUS	PLANNING
Capture	Horizon 5: Purpose and Principles	Purpose and Principles
Clarify		
Organize	Horizon 4: Vision	**Vision**
Reflect	Horizon 3: Goals	Brainstorm
Engage	Horizon 2: Areas of Focus	Organize
		Next Actions
	Horizon 1: Projects	
	Ground: Next Actions	

Vision expands thinking by doing that expansively in terms of the very best possible outcome(s) for the project. As earlier in the chapter on vision, letting go of what is currently considered possible so that the team can think about what it really wants as an outcome for the project starts to add some motivational juice to the cocktail needed for completion.

On a practical and operational level, clearly defining a team definition of what "done" means on a project is useful in ensuring that there are no pieces left hanging at the end. For instance, if a project for the team is to "hire an expert in X technology," when is that "done"? When they've simply found the right person, or when an employment agreement has been signed, or when that person has been appropriately integrated into the team and system and their involvement is cruising smoothly? Those diverse outcomes would generate different regular status reporting and different criteria for completion.

Brainstorm

CONTROL	FOCUS	PLANNING
Capture	Horizon 5: Purpose and Principles	Purpose and Principles
Clarify	Horizon 4: Vision	Vision
Organize	Horizon 3: Goals	**Brainstorm**
Reflect	Horizon 2: Areas of Focus	Organize
Engage		Next Actions
	Horizon 1: Projects	
	Ground: Next Actions	

At this point what the team needs is ideas, lots of them. The NPM enables a team to diverge massively to get a large volume of ideas out on the table. Anything—good, bad, and mad ideas—that might serve the purpose and could move the team toward wild success is acceptable at this point. In our experience this brainstorming phase is many times more creative for a team than for an individual. When the team is truly brainstorming, not censoring ideas but building on good and bad suggestions alike, is when the magic can really happen. The key is to get them all out and visible for the entire team to consider.

Especially in relation to the GTD methodology, externally capturing potentially relevant ideas saves our minds from having to try to remember them. And it frees up our limited cognitive space for more ideas.

Many times a team will brainstorm as the first step on a new project, instead of first clarifying the above. That certainly might have some value. But if this is done absent of clarity on the purpose or vision for the project, it can lead to so many divergent points of view about relevant details that it can undermine the collaborative creativity for which brainstorming is highly regarded.

Organize

CONTROL	FOCUS	PLANNING
Capture	Horizon 5: Purpose and Principles	Purpose and Principles
Clarify		
Organize	Horizon 4: Vision	Vision
	Horizon 3: Goals	Brainstorm
Reflect		
Engage	Horizon 2: Areas of Focus	**Organize**
		Next Actions
	Horizon 1: Projects	
	Ground: Next Actions	

After opening things up to get lots of ideas while brainstorming, the organizing phase requires sorting good ideas from bad ones, and then organizing and prioritizing the good ones within specific workstreams.

Once purpose and vision are clear, and sufficient brainstorming of potentially relevant details have been identified, this phase ordinarily requires the most time and detailed thinking and structuring. Purpose, principles, and vision decisions, plus brainstorming, can often happen in a few hours (or even minutes!). Getting a complex project sufficiently organized, however, can often take a full day or more.

Starting with a rich brainstorming mind map or at least lists of things to consider, one would naturally tend to sort the thinking into major components, priorities, and/or sequences of events. Usually, all three will come into play. "Here are the five major things we need to handle; here are the top two; and we need to address them in this order."

This step often invites usage of the various organizing tools—any and everything from sticky notes on a page to spreadsheets to intricately designed templates for such products as an airplane or a new pharma drug.

This phase is not simply a static organizing of previous thinking. Invariably, much additional and important creative thinking emerges here. "Oh, wow, in order to get this going, we need these other people and resources . . ." etc. Organizing is usually more of a creative process than it's given credit for.

Of course, as is true of the previous steps, if team planning begins here ("Let's get organized about this!") without sufficient purpose and vision clarity and sufficient brainstorming, the outline will be missing key pieces, and as such will be too abstract and operationally handicapped. The plan winds up in the drawer, too divorced from reality.

Next actions

CONTROL	FOCUS	PLANNING
Capture	Horizon 5: Purpose and Principles	Purpose and Principles
Clarify	Horizon 4: Vision	Vision
Organize	Horizon 3: Goals	Brainstorm
Reflect	Horizon 2: Areas of Focus	Organize
Engage	Horizon 1: Projects	**Next Actions**
	Ground: Next Actions	

With all that work done, getting to next actions is a relatively simple affair. It is merely to identify what moving parts of the plan can be currently actionable, to determine the next actions on them, and to ensure they are tracked and assigned appropriately.

So, too, with accountability. Because the team has participated in the shaping of the project plan, there is much more buy-in for picking up the various workstreams when it comes time to find bodies to do the doing.

The model is not only useful for planning a project first time out but also as a diagnostic when a project has become stuck. In that case it involves reviewing the above framework alongside what is happening on the project and asking what is missing.

We worked with one person in a global investment firm whose job was to manage the annual summer conference for new associates, which was coming up in a few months. She had inherited the job from someone who had attempted to manage it previously, and the legacy included significant burnout of everyone involved in producing it.

There had been multiple last-minute crises—the whole thing had a reputation internally of being no fun at all. When asked about a plan she might have, she produced a large chart with all the components of the project laid out in a formal timeline. We asked her to identify all those components that could have a next action that could be done now, to prep ahead of time. There were dozens. But they were not on the plan, because she hadn't yet identified them. She'd likely have caught them, but probably only once deadlines approached. Crises prevented.

If you think this planning model is simply for the corporate/professional world, we've seen it being used for some of the smallest and most personal projects and situations, especially when doing them with other people, to great benefit.

[DAVID] When my wife and I decided to get married (several decades ago), we thought it might be interesting to apply the Natural Planning Model to our wedding. What was the purpose of our wedding? Great question. Our answers were objectives like "give our friends the opportunity to share their supportive thoughts and congratulations" and "manage that efficiently in one event instead of dribbling it out over time." We then came up with two important principles: (1) Only invite people whose feelings would not be hurt if they weren't invited. We had a large network of friends we wouldn't have room for in our venue, and we wanted folks who offered that kind of unconditional support. (2) We must have fun doing this. Too often these major events create more stress than needed, so we agreed we'd blow the whistle on ourselves if that became the case. We brainstormed and organized rather easily, with the next actions allocated to each of us as needed.

HOW TO USE THIS MODEL FOR TEAMS—TIMING

There are six steps, but they don't all need the same amount of time. In workshops, when we have our participants plan several of their projects in just twelve minutes, here is a formula that seems to optimize the time:

- Purpose: 45 seconds

- Principles: 45 seconds

- Vision: 2 minutes, 30 seconds

- Brainstorm: 3 minutes

- Organize: 4 minutes

- Next actions: 1 minute

Is that the perfect timing? Who knows? It's a good start, gets things moving, and gets someone all the way through the model so they have a drafty draft of a plan in minutes rather than hours or days. It optimizes the value from extremely limited planning time to create what is almost always the first iteration of a plan that will need several iterations to grow into something more robust. At this stage what you want is something that is easy to draw up on the back of a napkin. You don't need a perfect plan to get started; you need enough of a plan to have some confidence that your next action is the right one. Is it a complete project plan after twelve minutes? No way. Is it good enough to have confidence about what to do next to get started? Absolutely. The beauty of it is in how it saves time if this first iteration is put in front of the team rather than just some vague idea like, "We should do something about X." It enables a team to move quickly, and iterate and improve the plan, without wasting time.

You can usefully extrapolate from that shorter version to the timing for an hour-long group session:

- Purpose: 4 minutes

- Principles: 4 minutes

- Vision: 12 minutes

- Brainstorm: 15 minutes

- Organize: 20 minutes

- Next actions: 5 minutes

Is that perfect timing? Not the point. The point is to get out of stasis and a desire to immediately draw up a perfect plan, and into action. Both proposed timings above fail miserably at the first objective (perfect plan) but knock it out of the park on the second (enhancing the likelihood of action and momentum).

EXAMPLES OF USING THE NPM

Those two sample timings are on the shorter end of the spectrum, but the NPM is not just for quick and dirty work. It can be used for much more detailed planning as well. One of us once used the Natural Planning Model as a structured process for setting up a new team in two days, completely from scratch. We were working with a team leader who was a big fan of the motivating power of purpose and vision and asked for help with getting his new team pointed at something that they could focus their energy on.

The two-day format offered scope for robust conversations at each step of the way through the model, and even some useful iteration of certain parts. How did we do it? On the morning of day one, after an opening from the team leaders and some context setting, we launched straight into a conversation about the purpose of the team, and—with a bit of support from us as facilitators—we had a workable draft of the team's thoughts on why they existed by midway through the first session. It was too early for a break, so we moved directly to a discussion of principles—how they wanted to play the game together—along with some basic working standards for the team at the beginning of session two. Then it was time to work on vision.

By breaking the group into subgroups and letting each of them create independent visions for the organization, there might have been a risk of ending up with radically different ideas when we reassembled. But despite minor variations, they all wanted to go to a similar place. After some discussion and refining, by the end of session three we had a decent draft of a unified team vision. All the key ideas were there, and it was plenty good enough to use in the next step.

The final session of day one was spent in Brainstorm mode. The team externalized anything and everything that would help them reach their vision first as individuals, and then shared with all the team's members. They simultaneously organized their ideas into clusters before the end of the day.

At the beginning of day two, we returned to the outputs of the first day. Having slept on them overnight, we got the benefit of a bit of subconscious marinating, and got next-iteration drafts of Purpose, team standards, and Vision up on the walls.

With those as reference points, the team broke up to continue the organizing they'd started the day before. By and large the clusters of ideas were broad-stroke versions of projects or workstreams. Subteams each went to work on detailing one of those plans in a longer session and then rotated through the work of other subteams more quickly to get all eyes on every project and enhance the original plans with the expertise of the entire group. The afternoon of day two was spent exclusively identifying the "capital P" team projects and "small p" individual GTD projects, and we were able to give everyone time to identify next actions for what they'd be reporting back to the group in the next team review meeting.

It took just two days to go from nothing planned to clarity on the team's higher horizons and accountabilities, decided on with rough project plans and clear next actions defined for all project owners. No one on the team was ever aware that all of this had been created using the Natural Planning Model, but everyone was mightily pleased with the results.

Don't have two days? No problem, for as we demonstrated above, we've taught hundreds of thousands of seminar participants how to plan a project in as little as twelve minutes.

What we see most often is that team leaders will opt for something that looks more like the twelve-minute version than the two-day version and use that to kick off an hour-long session with their teams to revise and enhance the scrappy version they brought to the meeting.

One of the things that makes this approach so successful is that it is so easy to use that very little skill is required to make it work. One client took his team through it with no experience with the model at all. He simply followed the process by reading aloud what was on the card he'd received in his materials pack during a seminar with us. Despite his inexperience and the clumsiness of his facilitation, the team used the planning process to significantly improve their performance and become one of the highest-performing teams in a well-known tech giant.

One of us used the model to help a senior leader organize disparate ideas into robust planning of a campaign strategy for getting the top job in his organization. Using this model, by the end of an hour he had looked broadly and deeply enough at the project to know that it was doable, and he left with a dozen projects to do or delegate, and some next actions he could crank through in the hours following the meeting. Again, something that seemed extremely big and potentially out of control was reduced to a series of outcomes and discrete next actions, and he was able to drive the projects to successful completion and get the job he wanted.

We've also facilitated a daylong meeting for a senior team in aerospace using this approach. The people involved were rocket scientists and the discussion was . . . well, rocket science. But without understanding more than a few words of what was said, we were able to take them through the process in the sequence we describe above. Our job was to simply capture what they said in response to the questions and prompts inherent in the model. Not only did they think the day was a huge success, but the facilitator was considered a key contributor, despite never really understanding a word of what went on.

[ED] Perhaps the most financially valuable work I've done so far was the hour-long meetings I took with two separate colleagues to run a couple key accounts through this process. Each account was already generating substantial annual revenues but was slightly stuck in terms of growth. With an hour of planning time on each account—and regular review sessions—we were able to double and then triple the annual revenues from those accounts inside of a couple of years.

Of course, we'd not have much credibility as authors if we hadn't planned this entire book using exactly this approach. The original idea for *Team* was fleshed out and turned into a book proposal using the model, and the first iteration of each of the chapters was planned in fifteen minutes once the proposal was accepted. A second, longer pass turned them into more robust plans. Were those plans complete?

Not even a little. Were they sufficient to clarify enough about purpose and direction, and to externalize the best and worst of our thinking on each chapter? Absolutely. Thanks to this approach, we were never staring at a blank page at any stage of this process.

Another context in which we've seen this method used effectively is as a support for delegation of chunky projects. Some of our clients employ this framework for delegating either inside or outside their own departments. They work through the framework with the person who is inheriting the project in something like an hour and use the time to pass along all of their best thinking to be sure that the new head has the maximum chance of succeeding with it. Once this is installed as a standard on the team, either party can bring a first iteration of the plan to a first meeting, which together they can turn into a robust handover document.

One of our colleagues has installed something similar with his team; if people have changes they want to make in the organization, they use the Natural Planning Model to rough out their initial thinking. They won't raise it in a team meeting until they have a decent draft of a project plan so the whole team doesn't waste time at meetings starting from scratch with every initiative.

One of our clients was making the transition from being a traditional, linear broadcast organization into one that is much more customer-centric with a direct-to-consumer operation—a fundamental change of business model in an attempt to keep others from eating their lunch in the streaming wars. As part of that transformation there were huge projects that at first blush seemed so big as to be almost insurmountable. Where to start, when everything needed changing? The leader resolved it by bringing the Natural Planning Model into their team toolkit. Breaking it down into different projects and running them through this process got them quickly to next actions so things got moving. Instead of being stymied by the fear and angst of "How are we going to accomplish all of this?" they were able to start by moving one little piece at a time. The projects got momentum, and things began to accelerate. In the end it simply became part of the operating rhythm of how they moved things forward. It was employed in how they planned for interacting with stakeholders and how they thought about articulating the overall team strategy, mission, and purpose. That combination of purpose and the vision of wild success was incredibly helpful when they got stuck in the weeds. When it came to prioritizing, it was relatively easy for the entire team to look at potential options and make a call on which one would get them closest to the wild success they'd envisioned.

Over the course of the preceding seven chapters we've looked at how the three major frameworks of "classic" GTD can be used to support the work of a team. In the next section we want to build on those frameworks by expanding on some ideas that were implicit in earlier books, but that will benefit from a deeper dive in the context of a team.

MANAGING A TEAM

Chapter 11

The Structures of Leadership

eadership is perhaps the most researched and discussed theme in all organizational literature. It has been estimated that there are close to two thousand books produced each year that have the word "leadership" in the title in the United States alone. With so many brains pointed at the topic over so many years, it is hard to imagine any remaining doubts about how to do it well, and yet there remains a perceived lack of leadership in most organizations—political, military, corporate, or otherwise.

Our own experience has been that, while there is a billion-dollar industry teaching "leadership," there is much less focus on the basics of what leaders can do in concrete terms to help their teams to succeed.

In writing this book, we did not set out to add to the pile of leadership literature. But the further we delved into the topic of team effectiveness, the more it became clear that the quality of leadership on a team makes a huge difference, given the wide variations in how people actually lead.

One of the ideas that has produced the most smiles from our students over the years is David's concept of a "crazy maker," someone with a bright vision who is very clear on where they and the team should be going, but with no plan or consistency to provide a sense of control over the day-to-day movement toward that goal.

This kind of leadership is characterized by exhorting people to buy into a compelling vision, so they'll have more energy to take on so-called BHAGs (big hairy audacious goals) and deliver superhuman results as they do. It's about ACTION! and ACHIEVEMENT! The problem with this scenario is that they are often attempting to hit stretch goals while neglecting the fundamentals of how those goals will be achieved. Many of the models offered for better leadership point aspiring leaders at becoming great and charismatic leaders but often ignore the practical basics.

THE NUTS AND BOLTS OF LEADERSHIP

What we want to focus on here is more mundane: the nuts and bolts of leadership, the leading by example on skills and standards that support team functioning, and making sure the team is more than a collection of talented individuals by paying attention to the actual mechanics of the team. Doing so means that when you develop a grand vision for your team, they will have the tools, structures, and processes to execute on it. Without those simple elements in place, declaring a challenging vision for the team is like John Kennedy declaring his moon shot for NASA with no wrenches on hand.

What we'll not be discussing in detail here—as these aspects of leadership have been so well covered elsewhere—are the "softer" aspects of leadership: charisma, personal impact, inspirational communication, etc. It's not that they don't matter. But they are most effective when used as a complement to some leadership fundamentals, like creating a team structure that works, clarity on roles and responsibilities, and establishing clear standards for being part of the team.

As we see it, the "soft" stuff is the most difficult to get right. And it is even more difficult if you aren't getting the easier stuff done well—or at all. Having skimped on the fundamentals—the crawling and walking of leadership—you'll find you don't have the technique to run fast with the hard stuff. We see people trying to make great strides with the truly difficult aspects of leadership while failing at the fundamentals. Hamstrung by petty emergencies, they miss opportunities to make progress with important relationships and vital strategic work.

We're not saying that inspiring leadership is unnecessary, just that it is only one part of a much larger picture. Because it is the sexiest bit of the leadership role, it gets outsize attention, while some of the more prosaic parts are given almost no attention at all. Aspiring leaders are encouraged to choose "leadership" over "management" in some strange hierarchy where management is the poor stepsister. The fact is you don't get to choose. You must do both.

There are simple standards and processes that—if ignored—can torpedo the grandest vision. If your vision is to go to the moon (or whatever that is for your team), but everyone is tangled in unread e-messages or block-booked in ineffective meetings, good luck with getting your lunar lander off the launch pad.

A GREAT VS. AN EFFECTIVE LEADER

Great leadership is not a matter of individual heroics. Individual leaders do not lead a team to success by being ever more wonderful themselves, or by whipping their team on to ever greater performance. For one thing this very visible kind of leadership is useful in a vanishingly small proportion of the roles where leadership is required. It also involves a narrative where people are striving ever upward in some imaginary hierarchy, gaining more power and influence as they progress. It can seem like this is the standard view of leadership because these battles over power and influence are played up in the media, which—in a desire to sell advertising—has to construct it for their readers like a real-world Marvel multiverse of competing forces.

There is a place for high-profile and highly directive leadership, but in most situations what is needed is a lot more *good* leadership, and a lot less people striving to be *great* leaders. As the past few years have shown, "great" leadership can create tremendous polarization and paralysis. Too often these outsize personalities themselves become the story, rather than how they are actually resolving the issues of the day.

So-called great leaders are rare, and often seriously flawed. We need fewer "great" leaders, and a lot more "ordinary" people willing to step up to lead. We believe that everyone can be a leader—and probably is, in some context already—and that everyone can certainly improve their skills as a leader.

WHAT DO WE MEAN BY LEADERSHIP?

We should define our terms. We believe it opens the door to much more genuine leadership action if we move away from the idea that leaders come into the world destined to lead, high-impact geniuses who give rousing speeches in moments of crisis. We're more interested in the people who take care of things in a way that means there will be no crises at all. Our desire is to open the concept up to include more people. People who don't feel like "great" leaders but who want to make things happen on projects they believe will make the world a better place. Many individuals have no desire to be leaders at all but do want to solve big problems. They want to help those around them to perform above and beyond what they believe they are capable of as individuals, by removing friction and noise from the functioning of the team so that it can deliver dramatically more than the sum of its parts might suggest.

One definition of a leader is "someone who gets things done through other people." If that is so, then it makes sense to turn the standard leadership dynamic on its head. It isn't the leader who needs attention from their people, but the inverse. There is no leader without a team to lead, and the leader needs to focus on the needs of the team as its members will be the ones doing most of the work. It is the team that needs someone to provide air cover but also make sure that the runways are kept clear, to keep them moving forward in difficult situations.

When trying to find a way to describe the kind of leadership we feel is missing, we tried on various metaphors. At first we went with "mechanic," as much of what we see makes a difference is quite mechanical. But a team is alive, not a machine, so we kept looking. We're suggesting something that is more like what has been described as "servant" leadership but might also be described as a team "plumber." That might seem like a humble or even unattractive metaphor, but you only need think briefly about what our world would look like without great plumbing to know just how important that work is. And still, as a descriptor it wasn't quite right.

LEADER AS GARDENER

The job of the leader is to set the vision, nourish a culture that enables the vision to become reality, and then coordinate action on and around the team to facilitate that. It is in the development and maintenance of a constructive culture that another analogy is perhaps the best fit: the leader as gardener, working with a living system. A gardener doesn't actually grow plants or make flowers bloom, of course; they simply tend the soil, make sure that trellises are in place, and that weeds don't choke healthy development. Similarly, a leader can't do or control the work of the team. But by doing the mundane maintenance of the structures and working standards of the team they keep day-to-day emergencies to a minimum and allow space for the energy of the team to flourish.

For instance, good leaders find ways to keep themselves from becoming the bottleneck on action and decision-making on the team. They do this by being responsive to incoming communication, but also by not allowing a culture to develop where every decision drifts up to their level. Good gardeners don't encourage plants to get permission before they grow. The folly of that is easy to understand. But if team roles have not been sufficiently defined and empowered so that individual members feel they can get on with doing their jobs, and only bring real exceptional circumstances to the leader for their input, the team will be stymied and the leader will drown in decision-making.

Easy wins come from clarifying who can make what decisions at what level. We've touched on that in chapter 9, on the roles—or Areas of Focus—on a team, but allocating and monitoring these roles is another area that is usefully done by our leadership gardener.

On any team there are things that can be done by pretty much any member, and a set of things that only the leader of the team can do. Scanning the horizon for changing trends, and maintaining heterogeneous relationships both in your organization and inside and outside your specific industry, are the kinds of responsibilities that can easily get lost when the leader is too busy resolving tactical emergencies that the team could handle.

Which brings us to delegation. We'll go into it in much more detail in chapter 13, but in a chapter on leadership we can't step around it. To succeed as a leader there is no way around the responsibility of delegating quickly and effectively, then tracking and coordinating the tasks that have been delegated to different parts of the team. Everyone on the team can do their job relatively successfully with a partial picture of what is going on, but the team needs at least one person to stay on top of how it all fits together. This is another job that is often ignored by visionary leaders, who don't like to "get bogged down in details" but then overcorrect and don't pay appropriate attention to them. It's why so many of those in leadership roles get such huge bang for their buck from maintaining up-to-date Agenda and Waiting For lists; with minimal effort they can track and follow up on the detail of the commitment matrix that they are at the center of.

ROLE-MODELING IS LEADING

In our work with leaders we have been consistently surprised at how little appreciation they have for their ability to improve conditions by the power of their own example. Because of the stress and strain they are under, they can go blind to just how much others are looking to them as a reference point for how to behave. Their willingness to do the simple work of walking their talk has an outsize impact on both the performance and the morale of the team they lead.

This is simultaneously one of the biggest levers for affecting the culture of the team, and one of the greatest leadership challenges. Leading by example is powerful not just because it sets a tone and improves team morale, but because of what it changes in leaders, who come to trust themselves to do what they say they'll do. It is only with that degree of confidence in themselves that they feel comfortable asking others to do the same.

Whatever the standards on a team, everyone can hold them for themselves, of course. Like with the original GTD steps, no one needs the boss to be getting it right all the time to be able to behave better themselves. But the example set by someone in a leadership position does set the tone for a culture that either encourages or discourages the behaviors that lead to healthy high performance. It is very difficult to insist on great meeting hygiene when your manager's meetings start late and are run like a three-ring circus.

Another area where a leader can have an outsize influence is in modeling a more effective way of thinking about work. For instance, it is easier to protect time for thinking, reviewing, and learning—getting strategic about your work and life—when you can see someone demonstrating that it is possible, even when they are buried. And especially when they are buried. If they don't, what example is the team to take from that?

We've seen individuals use GTD to succeed on teams with both great and god-awful leadership, but for a team to get the full benefits available from the principles of the methodology, it helps if there is a wholehearted endorsement of the principles of GTD from the person or persons leading the team.

The idea of culture that we proposed in chapter 6 on working standards is one of clearly defined standards for action and behaviors, and as such is much more concrete and easier to envision. Making it more visible increases leadership leverage when trying to drive culture change in an organization, which is why it is so important that the leader—or leaders—on a team demonstrate the behaviors and standards they want for the team.

When a leader pays attention to team standards—and the culture they support—it provides a structure in which individuals can gauge their own performance and begin to hold themselves and their colleagues to account. In this chapter—and others that follow—we'll outline some relatively simple things leaders can do to communicate their intent about the new way of working, and how they can offer support (and challenge) for others to hit agreed-upon standards. For example, if every meeting a leader attends starts with being clear on the desired outcome for that meeting, a new tone is set for all future ones. If the leader consistently insists that all meetings end with a wrap-up on agreed next actions, then accountability starts to be cooked into the structure of how the team operates daily. This would be a small win, tactically, but culturally, over time, huge in terms of its impact. To not get this kind of win—given that it comes at pretty much zero cost to the team—seems wasteful to the point of negligence. Getting those small things right around agreements that the team makes with itself about how it wants to work together are what enables the team to get the bigger ones done.

We believe that clear standards are the backbone of high-performance culture. You don't have to like someone personally to be able to do good work together. More important is agreement on how you engage with one another.

ENCOURAGING ACCOUNTABILITY AND RESPONSIVENESS ON YOUR TEAM

In our observation the leader is almost always the greatest threat to team efforts to upgrade their way of working. There is nothing more corrosive for a team than feeling that there is "one standard for us, and another for them." Any situation with that kind of inconsistency allowed will corrode goodwill.

But it is an error to set yourself up as the police officer for whatever behaviors the team agrees on for itself. You may need to take the lead on setting the standards, but the only way they have a chance of being maintained over time is if they get buy-in from the team—and are maintained by the team. If there is a sense that they exist to embody the leader's standards but not their own, a feeling of resistance and resentment begins brewing that will undermine whatever performance gains the new standards could produce. But it can't be the job of the leader to hold everyone on the team to account for what they have promised. That only leads to a "mommy" or "daddy" dynamic on the team that won't serve the leader or allow the team to unfold its true potential. The job of our leader as gardener is to nourish a culture within which holding to account is normal, almost reflexive. There are two parts to that: you need to be able to consistently hold people accountable for things they've promised to you, and you need to create the circumstances where people can hold one another to account for promises made to one another and to the team. If the standards are developed by the team, it takes pressure off any one individual to enforce them. It moves it away from the individuals concerned and puts the focus on what the team agreed was right for the team's performance. You must take care, however, that this is not implemented in a judgmental way, but rather as an objective expression of the team's own ideas about what will help them to work best.

In all of this, your not-so-secret weapon is capture. A leader who does not capture agreements as they occur is basically turning accountability on the team into a lottery. As the volume and complexity of topics increase, so, too, does the likelihood that you'll lose at that lottery.

WHAT, SPECIFICALLY, CAN YOU DO AS A LEADER TO HELP DRIVE A CULTURE OF HEALTHY HIGH PERFORMANCE ON YOUR TEAM?

Many people in leadership roles find that they are already doing much of what was proposed in the earlier GTD books, at least in some form. They had experimented enough to have found an effective way of working that allowed them to attempt to organize something larger than themselves. For many of them what the frameworks of GTD offer are a way to understand how their existing practices fit together into a coherent system. Once they do so, they can get to work on repeating them, expanding them to other areas, improving the processes, and then speeding them up.

It isn't necessary for a leader to be a black belt in all the aspects of GTD to succeed with what we are proposing in this book, but using—and demonstrating—some of them will certainly help. As a leader you cast the longest shadow in terms of working culture, and people will notice and copy what they see.

Whether you lead a large or small team, here are some relatively simple things you can do to communicate your intent about the new way of working, and to maximize your investment in offering GTD to your team:

- Bring paper or some other means of capturing commitments to every meeting and demonstrate capturing them as they are made.

- Protect thinking time. More than anyone on the team, the leader needs time to think and decide. If the leader—who is responsible for being the eyes and ears of the team with senior leadership and the outside world—is stuck in tactical meetings all day, then they have no chance to do the critical thinking and reflection on the wider picture that allows the team to become more strategic with its efforts. To keep their calendars from being overwhelmed by meeting requests, some leaders find it useful to protect some time in each day for thinking about and making decisions on new topics. Some executives we have coached have made a policy of no meetings for their first hour in the office. Others request that their PA plan in a couple thirty-minute blocks for clarifying their work each day and let them know they can move them as necessary but never completely remove them. The nature of organizational life—with conferences, all-day meetings, and occasional emergencies—means that there will be days when you simply get no time for thinking about new stuff, but those thirty-minute blocks can be rearranged into a subsequent day to give you some welcome protected time to catch up.

- Maintain complete Agenda and Waiting For lists for when you meet with members of your team individually. Not only will this make meetings with your directs more effective, but it also allows for ad hoc catch-ups between scheduled meetings when time permits.

- Maintain an overview of what the team is up to. To do that you must have clear and complete dashboards that let you know exactly what has been committed to and when the deadlines are. Without external support there is simply no way for your brain to handle the sheer volume. You don't need a larger, more colorful screen, a more powerful computer chip, or a better piece of collaborative software. All you need are up-to-date lists that you consult when needed.

- As an extension of that Agenda list idea, use a "company town hall" list for all of the topics you want to communicate publicly in wider forums, or several "meeting with client X" lists so that you have a place where you can organize ideas when they occur, giving you a head start on preparing for those meetings.

- If you have an assistant, schedule five to fifteen minutes every day to go through your Agenda and Waiting For items for them and—perhaps more important—theirs for you. By giving them small amounts of time consistently through the week to answer their questions, you remove yourself as the bottleneck and enable them to help you more effectively.

- Give your team twenty-four-hour response times on emails you receive. Sometimes that might only mean an "I'll get back to you," but it will indicate that you are serious about people staying on top of their inboxes. A non-negligible side benefit of this kind of responsiveness was identified by Duncan Watts and his colleagues in an analysis of leaders' email response times and team satisfaction. In a large-scale analysis of email activity, organizational charts, and employee satisfaction surveys, they found that leaders' responding more quickly was predictive of higher team satisfaction scores.

- As a leadership gardener you should also be aware that the same study identified that after-hours emails were associated with lower satisfaction about work-life balance. Whatever standards the team develops, you'll want to respect them. Independent of that you'll want to give a bit of thought to when you are sending communications. In our observation, even when a leader feels they've been clear that, "I'm sending them over the weekend/in the evening, but don't expect you to respond then," most people are unable to keep themselves from checking and responding if they are receiving mails from their boss after-hours. Work when you want, but think hard about what cultural signals you are sending—and what implicit standards you are proposing if you are seen to be working at 2:00 a.m. on a regular basis. There is no right or wrong here, but if only from a personal brand perspective, this is a double-edged sword. You might get an admiring, "Wow, what an animal" response, but you might also simply become the object of pity or resentment, as someone who can't get on top of their work without working through the night.

- Integrate useful GTD ideas and terminology into team discussions. For instance, take the first few minutes of each meeting to clarify what the desired outcome is, and the last ten minutes to get clear on who has the projects and/or next action. After delegating tasks, you can also let people know that you have a waiting for or a project delegated record. That language can be helpful to signal that this is a new way of working.

- Consistently underline what current priorities are. A senior manager and major champion of the GTD methodology in a well-known high-tech firm told us that in his weekly staff meetings, he puts his own personal mind map of his current work situation—especially his projects and initiatives—up on the screen for all to see. All of them. He uses that to update his team about his priorities. He said it clarifies much about what's now most important and why he's making his decisions during the rest of the week. It makes it much easier for his people to then recalibrate their own sense of priorities and their ability to support him.

- Do a weekly review. Many leaders complain that the tactical detail of their team's work is not allowing them to be strategic with their efforts, or with the energy of the team. They can't quite believe it when we tell them just how simple it is to be strategic. By setting aside about an hour a week for reviewing and updating their dashboards and getting the overview on progress on their projects, they are already being more strategic than 95 percent of the leaders in the world.

- Be visible with your weekly review. You can't force people to do their own, but we've seen clients encourage it by suggesting something like, "From 2:00 to 3:00 p.m. on Friday, I'd like all of us to give one another the space to do a weekly review. You don't have to do it at that time if you don't want to, but please don't disturb others who are doing it." It'll be critical that you be seen to do it yourself at that time (or some reasonably consistent time, at least when you are in the office). The main point is that you do it at all, as that will keep you on top of things in a way that enhances the responsiveness of the team.

- When people are working in the office, offer them different spaces for thinking and reflection, if possible, and be encouraging with permission to use them. Some clients have provided a quiet room with desks for staff to pull away from their own spaces and undertake their weekly review away from the distractions of drive-bys or calls. (This is especially important in open office environments.)

- Suggest, negotiate, and adhere to some simple standards for team interactions. We covered this in greater detail in the chapter on working standards, but it bears mentioning here as it will most often be down to the leader to initiate them. As an exercise it will perhaps take more time and energy than many of the above recommendations but will also likely provide the biggest payoff.

One thing that we have not covered here but is a huge part of a leader's role is to support their team with prioritizing and managing the sheer volume of possible things they could get up to. It is so important that we've devoted the entire next chapter to it.

Chapter 12

If You Don't Have a No, Your Yes Means Nothing

The chapter title is provocative, perhaps, but in our work, we constantly encounter people who are so far underwater with their commitments that they can no longer see the surface. Worse, they have no idea in which direction to swim to catch their breath. Still, they'll happily say yes to one more deliverable. And then to another, and then just one more, rather than feel the discomfort of saying no.

Just as there is a limit to how much an individual can take on without blowing up, the same is true for a team when it faces the stress of having too much opportunity. Potential new clients, products, and markets all sing a siren song that leads to overcommitment, and there is only so much incompletion and lack of progress that a team can take before it starts struggling.

Most teams seem to try to ignore the problem and continue drowning in a sea of overwhelm as a result. The operative fantasy seems to be that "if we just work hard for a bit longer, that light on the horizon in our calendar a

> When water covers the head, a hundred fathoms are as one.
>
> —PERSIAN PROVERB

month out will appear and save our bacon." But of course that light only dims with each passing day as the team moves toward it and new urgencies intrude. By the time four weeks have passed, what looked like clear space in the team calendar a month earlier now looks like a game of Tetris gone wrong again.

We know that one of the biggest challenges to team effectiveness is a lack of focus, and the biggest challenge to team focus is allowing attention and energy to be spread too thinly by saying yes to too many things. In this sea of "Yes!" your team needs to create islands of "No!" in service of prioritizing what is truly important. This chapter is all about just that: how to support your team with consistently saying a powerful no to enhance the impact of what they say yes to.

Saying no was addressed in the earlier GTD books as well, of course. When clarifying incoming stuff fully half of your options are to take no action at all. Later, when reflecting and reviewing, there is clear guidance to rationalize and focus your lists when you see things that are no longer relevant. While the concept was clearly outlined in previous books, we see a need here to go deeper. We believe that the ability of a team to say no is a critical component of producing healthy high performance, and very few teams are saying it nearly enough.

Very often we see that the busiest teams are the ones that are doing the most work that they don't need to be doing. They are reporting on things that nobody looks at anymore, for instance, but no one has bothered to query the process for a few years. One of our colleagues reported that a woman with whom he was working felt that half of what she was doing was superstition. "Nobody knows why we do it," she said. "But

> Besides the noble art of getting things done, there is the noble art of leaving things undone. The wisdom of life consists in the elimination of nonessentials.
>
> —LIN YUTANG

we're all concerned that if we don't do it, something bad is going to happen." What exactly, no one seemed to know, but it would be bad, for sure. Particularly in organizations that have been around for a while, administrivia crud gets laid down in layers in the cogs of the organization. Processes aren't mapped and reviewed, or there is simply no process for questioning why things are being done at all.

WHY YOUR TEAM NEEDS TO SAY NO MORE

If you want to know if a team has a "no" problem, just look at their calendars. If you can find no evidence of spaces to eat, sleep, play, or occasionally respond when nature calls, they might not be quite getting the balance right.

This is easy to get wrong, as we are blind to the opportunity cost we incur when we accept too often. We feel we are clear on what we are saying yes to, but—because we don't yet know our future options—we can't know what we don't *get* to say yes to (or even think of) because we are so busy with existing commitments. Even worse, many of the projects you say yes to are "pregnant" with other projects and subprojects. But you won't know that until you get started. Your only prophylactic against adopting all the eventual subproject offspring is to say no in the first place.

We also can't see the reputational damage we are doing to ourselves or the team by delivering late—or not at all. Sometimes people chase us, and more rarely they'll complain directly about it. Much more often they complain to someone else, or simply stop wanting to have us on their projects.

> You don't have a time management problem, you have a "yes" management problem.
>
> —PAULA BOYLE

The other cost we can't evaluate is the reactivity that comes from not creating enough space to see the patterns in the problems that keep reappearing, and to look for solutions for root causes rather than repetitively just treating symptoms. In our work we almost never see teams that protect time for a consistent practice of review of both *what* got done and *how* it got done (how the team functioned while delivering). Without that review time the team will at best struggle to raise its game over time; at worst, they're stuck repeating the same old errors.

As David has said elsewhere, you don't need *time* to find those solutions, but you do need *space*. Not physical space, but enough space between thoughts that you can imagine something new. Having a great idea doesn't take time, but it is nearly impossible to have new and creative thoughts when your collective heads are on fire because of how overcommitted you are.

The knock-on impacts on other parts of the organization are also never costed out, so overcommitting and underdelivering seem like venial sins rather than the cardinal sin they actually are. It seems as if they only affect the person or team that is overwhelmed, but as our colleague Bruce Faulkner was quick to point out when we were discussing the issue with him, it is much, much worse than that. In the financial crisis it wasn't just one bank that went down when it had overcommitted. Each bank had obligations with many other financial institutions, and if one fell, it put many others potentially at risk as well. So, too, with teams. When one team is overwhelmed and begins missing deliverables for which others are waiting, many in the organization are affected in their commitments as well.

Faulkner is a keen student of how "queuing theory" plays out in a knowledge work system—how beyond a certain point, individual and team workflow don't *slow down* with more inputs, they *break down*. If you've ever wondered why everyone is so damned busy, queuing theory has at least part of the answer. Queuing theory is an arcane specialization that analyzes why and how production systems clog up and stop working efficiently.

Queues—or places where things wait before being processed—are visible all around us in the real world. In manufacturing, in retail, even at your local coffee shop. A classic example would be if you have a freeway with four lanes, and you close one lane for repair and traffic backs up. A logical—but faulty—calculation would predict that it will take 25 percent more time to get cars through the bottleneck. If you've ever sat in miles of traffic trying to get past a blocked lane you know the reality of queuing theory means that it can take 2 to 300 percent more time to clear the resulting traffic jam.

So much for queues you can see. The queues in knowledge work are harder to spot. They still exist, but you can't see them. Every individual has their own queue (of messages to respond to, meetings to book or attend, reports to write, etc.), whether they are a secretary or a CEO. In a best-case scenario the queue of work in progress on a team is on a list somewhere, but usually most of it is stuck in people's inboxes or in between their ears. That is bad enough.

What makes it worse is when leaders attempt to manage workers using an idea that is useful in manufacturing but is very unhelpful with knowledge work. In manufacturing, the thing that needs doing—and the amount of time to do it—is clear. The frequency of those things arriving is also clear, or at least relatively predictable. In those circumstances, you can try to push utilization to 80 percent or more and still have the system function. Not so with knowledge work. With knowledge work, the nature of what needs doing—and the time needed to do it—is endlessly variable, and the timing of each task's arrival is also often unpredictable. So when a firm sets a goal of having 80 percent billable time, for instance, they effectively have moved everyone to at least 100 percent utilization. And that is before they run into the standard-issue predictable unpredictability of life.

This is why things have become so crazy busy. If you are 100 percent utilized, and so is everyone else around you, then booking a meeting with a few colleagues becomes a multimessage (and sometimes multiday) ordeal that eventually results in one of two things: a meeting in six weeks' time, or sooner—at 6:00 a.m. Because of the timely nature of the decisions necessary, the latter is often the solution. People who continue to say yes to new projects in a situation where people are already that stretched are simply not helping.

Finally, when teams become overwhelmed and begin losing track of commitments and missing deadlines, the pain of not fulfilling is only part of the cost. They also begin to corrode their self-respect and their self-efficacy—their belief about what they are capable of. While less obviously painful, this may be the bigger price to pay over time.

The fundamental problem is in misunderstanding what a sustainable workload is. Sustainable capacity isn't 100 percent—not for individuals, and certainly not for teams. This is one of the great misperceptions about modern work. It often stems from someone noticing that in extremis, teams can go far above and beyond their normal capacity. Like a mother lifting a car off her child after an accident, we are all capable of superhuman feats when necessary. What we can't do is continue to do them, day in and day out, without serious consequences for our physical, mental, and relationship health, and for our most important projects. Fortunately, with rigorous prioritization there is a way through, as the following story relates.

FROM LATE AND OVER BUDGET TO EARLY DELIVERY

It was a big ask. The project was already estimated to be running nine months late and was seriously over budget. In his role as head of strategic projects at a major UK bank, Stuart Corrigan was tasked with getting things back on track.

After spending some time assessing the situation, he concluded that the problem was not the quality of the people on the team, but rather how they were spending their time. His first move was to have everyone write down what they were currently working on. Together they went through the resulting lists item by item and pruned everything that didn't directly move the project forward. In the end, after a few hard conversations, they managed to cut the original lists by 80 percent and stuck everything else into backlog.

It was clear to Stuart that some on the team weren't happy about the effort: "There was a bit of complaining about the exercise, but what some people were effectively saying was, 'Okay, I see that you want us to focus on that project, but I don't want to work on that all the time. I want to work on the things I like to work on.' But that's why so many teams don't deliver what they could. They spend too much of their time on tasks they enjoy rather than on ones they need to stay focused on to move priority projects forward."

If the team wasn't happy about the process, they liked the results. Once they got truly focused on the priority project, they ended up delivering it way ahead of expectations. "The results were nothing short of spectacular. By making sure that people were working on the right thing at the right time, we ended up delivering it a month early from its original due date." They saved millions in the process.

"Beyond that, when we surveyed the people on the team with a proper psychological survey tool, motivation had gone up by 30 to 40 percent on average. When we asked why they were so much more motivated, people credited that they had achieved the unachievable on that project, but also that they had so much more clarity on what they were doing."

The same process had a similar impact on other projects as well. "By trimming the list of things right back, then using the GTD technology to get everyone clear on the big things we wanted to deliver, we got way more things done than I ever thought possible. And some of them were really complex things to deliver.

"Consciously moving all of the nonessential work to a back burner forced us to face the reality that as human beings we are susceptible to being pulled off track by the work equivalent of coffee and donuts;

> What lies in our power to do, it lies in our power not to do.
>
> —ARISTOTLE

things we like to do but are not really on task. To stay focused, a culture of 'Let's get it off the list' is critical."

Stuart's success is not unique, of course, but it is rare enough to be a useful illustration of the power of taking a *team perspective* when saying no to generate the focus and momentum necessary to complete key projects.

THE PROBLEM IS TOO BIG FOR EVERYONE TO SOLVE ON THEIR OWN

A quick metaphor: it has become clear that—in the developed world, at least—you don't have to make a special effort to become obese. Just eat what is easily available, drive to work, sit in front of a computer all day, drive home, watch a movie, sleep, repeat. You'll be big as a house in no time.

This isn't a failure of individual willpower or discipline. If 10 percent of the population is struggling with their weight, that might be an issue related to insufficient individual willpower. When 60 to 70 percent of the population in the United States and the United Kingdom are overweight or obese, we really need to start looking elsewhere for the cause. It is not that individuals have no power to deal with the problem, but the deck is seriously stacked against them. There is something going on with the system—the food environment—in which they live.

The same is true with the sense of overwhelm that people are feeling. If 10 percent of the people in our society were feeling stressed or overwhelmed, that would probably be their problem. But when the Gallup survey we mentioned earlier revealed that 79 percent of those workers questioned are disengaged, and other surveys consistently report people feeling overbusy, in overwhelm, or trending to burnout, that is a systemic issue. As a society we have treated stress and burn-out as an individual issue, but we believe that is only a piece of this puzzle. The individuals affected are simply the canaries in our collectively overworked coal mine.

Even if it were accurate that the problem was mostly due to an individual's failure to prioritize well, it's simply not helpful to put the responsibility on the individual, when it is clear that the majority simply are not capable of saying no enough to keep themselves from overwhelm. The social and financial forces arrayed against them are vast, and each individual is relatively weak in the face of them.

We now have the challenge of living and working in a world that doesn't stop. And staying 24/7 attuned to that world—a seeming necessity for some and/or an addiction to the buzz for others—runs counter to what we now know about the human psyche. It needs rest. Cognitive science has proven that our brains need "archiving time" to digest the complexities of our days, and the collective brain of a team is no exception.

Continuing to suggest the individual only needs to work harder, or smarter, might best be described as pernicious prescribing—saying, "Here is a solution," when we know from experience that most people can't actually implement it. And that prescription—just keep doing more—is an easy sell, as many live in what a well-known writer and cultural critic from the University of Chicago, Professor Lauren Berlant, called "cruel optimism." One of the most prevalent versions of cruel optimism is the belief that if we just work a bit harder we'll get what we want, and be happy. But the working harder—and harder, and harder again—is actually a block to happiness. An old personal-growth idiom is relevant here: you can't get enough of what you don't really need.

To return to our metaphor, the people who do manage to lose weight—and keep it off—do so because they accept that they can't outrun their mouths—physically or calorically. They have to change the quality and reduce the amount of food they are consuming to succeed. So they build structures that make it easier for them to say no to unhealthy food than to say yes. Those structures either take decisions away (don't have unhealthy foods in the house) or make it dramatically easier for them to say no when faced with a poor food choice (finding a community that is fitter and healthier than they are and is consistently making better choices).

Similarly with saying no to tasks. Individuals struggle to deal with overwhelm unless the structures around them change. It's not that the individuals are completely impotent, but dealing with at least part of this problem at the team level will make things easier for all concerned. Both individuals and teams need to say no a lot more than they are currently doing, and this is simply much more likely to happen if the team structure and team processes support it.

The team that says no to protect focus and avoid multitasking creates space for individuals to do their work. Individuals are much less likely to get to important strategic work if they are consistently saying yes to things that feel urgent in their inbox. One simple example of how decisions at the team level can help is when a team agrees it's okay to say no to email (or other communications channels) for parts of the day in order to be able to do strategic work. Otherwise, the cost of constant context switching will kill both productivity and motivation on the team, and stall progress on important projects.

> **The less we are able to refuse, the more automated we become.**
>
> —GAVIN FLOOD

Another way the team can help individuals was covered in chapter 9. Great role clarity bakes in a host of nos by establishing clean interfaces between the roles. Team members know that if something comes to them that isn't part of their responsibility, their job is to move it to where it belongs or escalate for clarity.

PRUNING TEAM PROJECTS

Anyone who deals with roses, bonsai, or landscape trees knows that to optimize the plants' health and beauty they can't be left to develop with the random sprouts and limbs that naturally show up as they mature. Those suck energy that should be channeled elsewhere in the plant to produce elegant balance and form. Pruning is an art, and it's just as important for team activities as it is for the garden.

Cutting the team projects list way back is just good strategy. Whenever things change in or for an organization, it invariably creates new projects. Seldom, though, are existing projects appropriately curated, and very quickly there are more things for the team to do than can be easily dealt with. Just as healthy lakes have an ingress and egress of water, so, too, with commitments. Lakes without egress quickly become bogs—water comes in when it rains, but nothing flows out. The history of such bodies of water is not great. Perhaps the best known is the Dead Sea.

Healthy systems have a balance of flow through them, not a preponderance of inflows over outflows. Projects should be consistently completed to support that equilibrium, but commitments should also be consistently pruned.

Saying yes to too much "cool" will bury you alive and render you a B-player, even if you have A-player skills. To develop your edge initially, you learn to set priorities; to maintain your edge, you need to defend against the priorities of others.

—TIM FERRISS

HOW TO GENERATE A POWERFUL COLLECTIVE NO

As we intimated earlier, the busiest and most frustrated teams are often ones that are doing the greatest amount of work that contributes nothing to the achievement of their purpose and vision. If you have a team full of people saying yes to ad hoc incoming requests from the team's stakeholders, and there is no central—or even distributed—inventory of what the team is doing collectively, there is no way to know how much work the team already has on its plate. The only way out of that particular mess is to get clear on the team's capacity and on how much it has promised to deliver.

Not being aware of all you have to do is much like having a credit card for which you don't know the balance or the limit—it's a lot easier to be irresponsible.

—DAVID ALLEN

The foundation for good prioritization is maintaining consistent oversight of all current commitments. Whether on a whiteboard, a digital or wall-mounted Kanban board, or a simple spreadsheet, prioritization is easiest if the team can consider all their obligations in one place.

Once they are all visible, the team can discuss the list. The questions in such sessions aren't complicated: Where are we? What is the status? Where are there challenges? What needs more resources? Bearing in mind what the organization is trying to accomplish, what is significant, and what can we deprioritize? What are we going to let go of, at least for now? What can we get rid of entirely? Just asking "Which of these things gets us to where we want to go?" is not enough.

That question needs to be further refined to "Which of these things gets us there fastest?" or "Which of these possibilities moves the needle the most, and unlocks the largest strategic chunks for us?"

In team reviews the group has to look at the big picture and consistently check that the promises that have been made remain doable. Once everyone is clear on who is currently doing what, the conversations can get challenging. "Why are you working on this when we need to be working on that?" or, more diplomatically perhaps, "What's the relevance of the projects that you're working on, relative to where we want to get to?" When priorities get decided collectively, it creates visibility of what everyone is working on and how it relates to the larger outcomes.

Collectively defining the prioritization also makes for less possibility of conflict. There is no longer a mismatch between person A who thinks *this* is a priority and person B who thinks *that* is a priority. Having had those conversations collectively, the team will also be much stronger than any individual in its ability to say no—and hold the line when challenged. The joint decision will provide resilience in a case where an individual might cave.

We are not suggesting that the team review all of the work-related small "p" projects of every individual (though that would also be very revealing), but that the team certainly review all of its big "P" projects. We aren't concerned here with how you do that technologically, but we are very concerned that these reviews happen regularly in some form. This exercise may or may not actually be able to *remove* work from the team in each review, but it certainly acts as a brake on taking on new projects, or offers the clarity required to renegotiate timelines on existing ones. As noted above, a critical question for the team to ask themselves when considering assuming additional projects is, "If we are taking this on, what are we letting go of to give us space to get it done?"

What is wanted is consistent pruning of the team's project list as part of the culture of the team, and not only as an emergency measure. Doing the exercise consistently over time will build the team's sense for what sustainable healthy capacity actually feels like.

When doing prioritization as a team, it will sometimes make sense to use different approaches than the ones we suggest for individuals. If the team is meeting often enough, any reasonably transparent process will work as long as it moves things off the list and into Someday/ Maybe, and prioritizes what's left, but here are some other possibilities.

SOME USEFUL MODELS FOR PRIORITIZING AS A TEAM

The "Eisenhower Matrix"

This is a four-box model, with "Importance" on one axis and "Urgency" on the other. The idea is that if you plot all your commitments into boxes labeled "High Importance, Low Urgency" or "Low Importance, High Urgency," for example, you'll be able to prioritize more effectively. Although you must pay immediate attention to the topics that

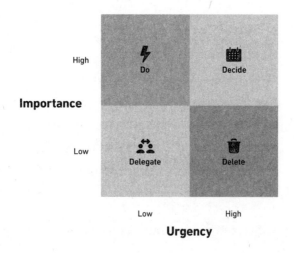

are "High Importance, High Urgency," the way to reduce the number of fires in your system is to pay more timely attention to the topics that are "High Importance, Low Urgency." It is there that the team can begin to move out of reaction and into driving its own agenda.

This way of prioritizing works better in theory than in practice for day-to-day use, but it has significant merits for longer-cycle planning. Taking time once per month or once per quarter to consider which projects are going to get attention, and which will be dropped or incubated, allows the team to focus its energy and attention on things that matter most and move the team quickest toward fulfilling its purpose and vision.

Model: Impact vs. Effort

This is a simple but effective model for identifying where to start on a new project. If projects, subprojects, and eventual next actions are plotted onto a graph using "Impact" as the x-axis, and "Effort" as the y-axis, then overlaid with a two-by-two box, it becomes very apparent where one should begin. Tasks that have "High Impact" but "Low

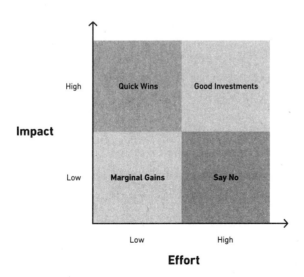

Effort" are your "quick wins." They can be helpful for getting momentum and generating buzz around an initiative. Things that are "High Effort" and "Low Impact" might still be important once the project is well launched, but should be put into Someday/Maybe for now.

Model: Doing it, not doing it

Even easier still, one of our clients in a global media firm used a simple prioritization system to help their team manage its efforts: focus on this, maybe focus on this later, drop this entirely. Using only these categories, they managed to cull 25 percent of projects from the team project list in one sitting.

Team support for individual prioritization

Part of the reason individuals struggle to have confidence in what they choose to do at any given moment is the absence of clear priorities from their team leadership. And in a world of de-layered, hybrid, and asynchronous New Work, hyperclarity on real priorities is even more important, because there is less structure and oversight to help people make decisions quickly on the fly.

Making those calls requires clarity on priorities, which is why clearly articulated and communicated purpose, vision, and goals are so important. They have the impact of preloading plenty of nos, because the team has decided at a higher level what it is committed to. If something shows up that doesn't contribute to them, the team isn't doing it. Without the clarity provided by those filters, it is simply too easy to say yes to random new stuff.

Not only do these things need to *be* the criteria for decision-making, but also they need to be *seen* to be the criteria for decision-making. This is another area where the leader has an outsize impact. If the leader is not referring to the higher horizons consistently, then the team might even be better off without a purpose and vision. Doing the work to clarify them but then ignoring the results is worse for morale than not having them at all. Ideally someone needs to ask a version of the question "Does this get us closer to or further away from our vision?" whenever significant decisions are being made. If that takes place in public forums, then individuals will be much more likely to make it an intuitive part of their own prioritization as well.

> What's essential is to do less better.
>
> —MARCUS AURELIUS

Another way leaders can support individuals in saying no is during one-to-one conversations with their direct reports. Good leaders have always intervened when they notice someone on the team is overloaded, but there is no need to wait for someone to be lightly toasted before helping them reprioritize. Apart from discussing priority items on the projects list of their directs, leaders can look at the totality of the individual's list and consider whether one human can realistically deliver everything on it.

For both leader and team member, this is one of the places where a complete Projects list shows its true power. Coming to a meeting with your boss and simply telling them you are feeling overwhelmed definitely risks a blank stare in response. Chances are good that your boss is feeling that way, too, and a report on your emotional state may make it difficult for them to help you. If you show up at that meeting with a list of the eighty-seven projects you believe they are expecting you to complete, you'll have a better basis to check if there are any that can be deprioritized, or to request support

> It's not always the actual work that is the hardest part of a job and success— it's the decisions, compromises, and choices that need to be made.
>
> —BARBARA ABRAMS MINTZER

with ones that are stuck. Without that clarity it is incredibly difficult to have an effective conversation at all.

The other way in which the leader is critical to effective prioritization is in offering air cover to the team from new and irrelevant incoming. Once they have prioritized the list, the team lead ideally gives the team members authorization to say no to any other requests coming from outside the team. This often breaks down when the leader says yes in a meeting with their peers without checking the capacity of their own team to take on a new project.

If the team lead continues to say yes to look good with their peers or higher-ups, then the whole initiative to stay focused on priority work will amount to nothing. In fact, it will amount to worse than nothing, because the team will be both cynical *and* overwhelmed. We suggest not making any in-the-moment commitments to deadlines until you are very clear about the current capacity of your team.

Until a team is saying no often enough that its members are confident that—at least some of the time—their life is manageable, sustainable, and fun, then throwing another piece of collaborative software, a mindfulness course, or a yoga session into the mix is simply wellness-washing. Those initiatives are not wrong per se, but they are not a solution. They are a bandage. It's like saying, "Just keep going hard until you get sick, and then hey, here's something to recover with." The real solution is in focusing—and protecting—our energy and attention.

Chapter 13

Delegation That Works

ave you ever wondered why so many teams seem to work in a state of permanent stress, constantly reacting to the latest urgency? In the previous chapter we addressed how it might be that they are simply taking on way too much stuff, but in our view another potential culprit for this pattern is poorly executed delegation. Consider the following scenario.

A mid-level leader gets an email from on high, requesting a presentation for the following month's senior leadership team meeting on a topic for which his team is responsible. It's an important deliverable, but not currently urgent. The leader has a system for such tasks: he flags the mail and gets on with more pressing requests, saving the new one for later.

For the next several days he notices the flagged mail numerous times as he scans his inbox, but it never feels as if there's enough time to do anything about it. Eventually, he stops seeing it, even when looking right at it. It's become just another flag in the pile on the screen, part of the wallpaper of a busy life. When it slides from the first screen of flagged mails to the second, then third, it is effectively lost from sight entirely. A barely perceptible flutter of butterflies when scanning his calendar a few weeks out means some part of him can never quite forget the task completely, but it's not enough to penetrate the cloud of urgency in which he consistently works.

So it's an unwelcome surprise when the chief of staff to the CEO forwards their original mail the week before the meeting to assemble the pre-read and any visuals for the presentation. The impending deadline occasions a shot of adrenaline, which finally provides the focus to think clearly about the presentation. "What do I need here . . . ? Some slides would be good. Right. Not good with slides . . . Who can do this?" And so it comes to pass that one of his direct reports—who handles the topic day to day on the team—gets a three-line email late on Thursday evening requesting a deck ahead of the presentation the following Tuesday. The report doesn't have much slack in her calendar between now and then either, but wants to be a good team player, so replies that she'll get it done. With a day of meetings already planned for that Friday, there is no other option than to take the assignment into the weekend. Between previously booked engagements with her friends and family, a deck is drafted over the weekend and delivered first thing Monday. As there's been no clear conversation about what the team leader specifically wants, it's decent, but much too long and detailed. There's no time to send it back to have it reworked, so our leader spends much of Monday afternoon cleaning it up and cutting it back to get it ready. The slides go out late to the chief of staff and are absent from the pre-read that went out on Friday. At the leadership team meeting, he manages a competent but slightly sweaty presentation, turning to the screen with each slide change, eager to find out what he is about to say next.

End result? A frayed relationship between the team leader and his direct report, another contribution to stress on the team, and another tiny ding in its reputation with stakeholders. All of which could have been avoided by more timely and clear delegation.

Like leadership, delegation is a distinct skill that is rarely taught and almost never given the attention it deserves when new leaders are first given people management responsibilities. The assumption seems to be that if you give someone an assistant or some direct reports, they'll intuitively know how to use the extra capacity effectively. But that is rarely true, because delegating large numbers of tasks to others is an entirely new skill set.

In *Getting Things Done*, delegation large and small was a significant part of the solution proposed for handling personal workflow. It is clearly signposted as one of three options for handling things that require action when clarifying daily workflow.

To remain focused on the flow of work through an individual's world, that first book was restrained in its treatment of the mechanics of delegation, simply suggesting that all handoffs be tracked on a waiting for or projects delegated list. This was no small thing. For many of our clients, that simple idea filled the single largest hole in their existing system: things they were waiting for from others. And beginning to track those things on lists outside of their heads led to not only a decrease of stress for the person running the list but also to many fewer ad hoc interruptions in the system around them as they chased tasks they had delegated. Without a trusted list to track them, tasks and projects that had been delegated had to be followed up when the delegator thought of them, because otherwise they might be forgotten again.

But there was little detail offered in *Getting Things Done* on the why, the what, and the how of delegation itself. Our focus here has shifted to the team level, and in this chapter we'll build on the clear guidance of that book to flesh out the principles of great delegation.

Laziness or incompetence aside, the single biggest career killer is an unwillingness—or inability—to delegate effectively as the world rewards your successes with increased responsibility. If you do it well, you can expand your reach almost exponentially. If you don't, you end up stuck in overwhelm, attending to details that keep you from doing the strategic work that will dramatically increase your own impact. And still, most days we work with clients who have stuff on their lists that they clearly should no longer be doing themselves.

In our work with leaders, we see many reasons that they get overwhelmed in their jobs; the sheer volume of things coming at them is certainly one, but a hidden problem is often a subconscious resistance to delegating. On one level this makes no sense. If someone could get work off their plate surely they would want to, right? But even those with many possibilities to delegate don't always use them. We've both seen people who had many opportunities to delegate, but whose need for control meant that on some level they were more comfortable being a bottleneck instead. Even when some were willing to delegate, if they didn't take the time to think about what they wanted in terms of outcomes, they simply couldn't use the resources at their disposal effectively. Put another way, by not taking a few minutes early on to get clear themselves, they couldn't enable their assistants and direct reports to help. This will be as true for AI assistants as it is for human ones. Without clear prompts, they'll either idle in neutral for lack of direction or boil the ocean trying to be helpful.

The seeds of this problem are sown very early in our careers. When you enter the workforce, someone else is usually doing the deciding about what gets done, and the actual work is being done by you and your peer group. You are judged on the quantity and quality of what you achieve, and any extra effort you put in has a direct impact on how much you produce. One of the ways that you can distinguish yourself is to work harder than those around you, and if you work 10 percent or 20 percent more than others, this can often be easily observed in the results.

When you are rewarded for all that additional effort by being promoted—and given your first team to lead—an odd thing happens:

your theoretical reach is dramatically extended, but your personal ability to impact the total output of the team is often radically diminished. Let's say you now have nine people working for you. The sum of their collective efforts is potentially nine times greater than your individual effort, but your potential contribution as an individual to the total output of a ten-person team is much smaller. Instead of getting 10 percent more output when you increase your own work rate by 10 percent, you now have a 1 percent impact on the results of the team. And ironically it is the team's output—not your own—that is the new measure of your effectiveness in the organization.

It is a hypothetical example, and the math is meant to be representative, not precise. But if you accept the broad-strokes calculation, you can see that you could work twice as hard—100 percent more—and still only have your team increase its output by 10 percent.

Let's say you haven't blown up your health in that effort, and get promoted again. You now have an even bigger team—ninety-nine souls you can employ to achieve team objectives. In theory the new team has dramatically expanded your reach. But now, if anxiety about your promotion drives you to simply increase your own work rate by 20 percent, you will only impact the productivity of the new team by a whopping 0.2 percent. Given that the total team would double its productivity if each member only did 1 percent more than they are currently doing, 0.2 percent is a meager return for all your extra work.

Even if you have no aspiration to be promoted into a larger role, we hope it is clear from our speculative mathematical exercise that working harder each time you take on more responsibility is a fool's errand. A leader's incremental efforts—even if it means giving up sleeping entirely—are not going to be what moves the needle in the performance of a larger number of staff. But still we see people start to get up earlier, stay up later, and work through the weekends rather than think more carefully about how they leverage their team through effective delegation.

The only way to get the best results from a larger team is in letting go of the perceived need to stay busy, busy, busy as an individual, and instead using the time to think more strategically about the efforts of the team. Thinking through how best to leverage team resources is the very essence of knowledge work for whoever is leading the team.

Easy to say, but much more challenging to do, of course. But fighting for the time to think and delegate strategically is a more worthy challenge than simply giving in and mindlessly working ever harder.

For successful delegation, here is what we suggest you think carefully about:

- What to delegate

- How to delegate (the mechanics of the agreement)

- Personal power (how credible you are when making your request)

WHAT TO DELEGATE

[ED] When coaching executives who are underdelegating, one of the interventions I have found most helpful to break the pattern is a phrase that came to me early in my career, when dealing with a senior leader who was struggling with overwhelm: "Only do what only you can do."

This is not an admonition to laziness. On the contrary, it is asking someone to step up and away from what they are comfortable with, so they can do what they are uniquely placed to do for the team. Leaders at all levels are often promoted for being good at their previous jobs, and their tendency is to want to keep doing that same job. They have proven that they are good at it—often the best in their organization—which is why they got promoted. And not only is there an emotional pull back to what they know how to do well, but there is often real discomfort with the entirely new skill set required by the new position.

"Only do what only you can do" is not intended as a hard rule, but as a useful filter for what you elect to put on your own plate. If something can be done by someone else, you should hand it over to them, even if you are convinced that they won't do it as well as you. For instance, if you are promoted to lead a team you were formerly a part of, it is critical that you let the person who took your job make it theirs. Your dipping back down into the detail of their work can only disempower them and keep you overbusy with things that are no longer a good use of your time and energy. A big part of the reason you got so good is that you had plenty of practice, and they'll need those opportunities—and your coaching—to get as good as you have become. Your job is no longer to continue what you've already achieved, but to work out who should now undertake tasks, give them a clear brief and adequate resources, then coach them to completion, and—occasionally—clean up when they make mistakes.

The other part of the new job of leading the team is to keep busy with doing the things that other people on the team simply cannot do. Your people can't go to your boss or people higher up in a client organization to get support for their work, for instance. They need you to keep yourself free enough to be able to do those things.

> Never tell people how to do things. Tell them what you want to achieve and they will surprise you with their ingenuity.
>
> —GEORGE S. PATTON

As we covered in greater detail in the chapters on purpose, vision, working standards, and leadership, a leader's critical responsibilities include the following:

- Leading on creating the purpose, vision, and working standards

- Communicating those values consistently by using them as a tool for day-to-day decision-making

- Establishing and nourishing the culture the team has decided it wants for itself

- Clarifying what needs doing, and delegating to those who will do it

- Coordinating and tracking who is doing what by when

- Defusing conflicts and offering air cover to those who are doing the work

These are the kinds of things that only the leader can handle, and—if that list doesn't already make it apparent—it is a full-time job. Without timely delegation it is often an impossible one. It's for that reason that many of our clients in leadership roles change the order of the questions David proposed for clarifying work in *Getting Things Done*. Instead of first asking, "What is the next action?" before checking whether they can delegate it, they first ask, "*Can* I delegate this?" If they decide they can, they then try to delegate the largest discrete chunk of responsibility possible. Rather than handing off next actions, they seek to hand off whole projects—and sometimes even entire Areas of Focus for which they've been responsible.

[DAVID]: In my consulting days in the early pre-digital 1980s, I spent countless hours with mid- to senior-level professionals, desk-side, walking them through the Capture and Clarify stages of what became the GTD process. As they began going through the plethora of stuff we had collected in their in-baskets, I had them decide the next actions desired or required for each item. Once the action had been decided, if it couldn't be finished immediately (the two-minute rule), my next question was "Can this be delegated?" not "Would you *like* to delegate this?" If the answer was yes, I had a paper-based delegation form for them to fill out immediately and place in their out-basket. Their assistant was coached to pick up the out-basket contents and distribute as appropriate. The second day of my work with the executive/manager, a phenomenal outcome occurred: they were getting responses in their in-basket reflecting the immediate progress being made on what they had delegated. Most were amazed that good work was getting done before it was in emergency mode.

HOW TO DELEGATE

As with workflow itself there is a sequence of necessary steps in a delegation process. These can be done poorly, not at all, or using best practices. If you know the sequence, and use more best practices than worst, you will produce more successful outcomes with your delegation.

We refer here to the work of Fernando Flores, who spent many years identifying how something we do every day—speaking—can be employed more consciously and with more precision to enhance the likelihood that we produce the results we want when working with others. Perhaps the most practical application of his work was with respect to delegation.

In effect Flores did for delegation what David did for workflow. Both identified the component parts of activities in which we're so immersed that we often can't clearly see what is actually happening.

By clarifying and putting in order the component parts—for work-flow in GTD, and delegation in Flores's model—both David and Flores highlighted how to get better results and build more effective working relationships.

As with GTD Flores didn't see delegation as being an exclusively top-down dynamic. It might be a leader delegating to a direct report, but the inverse was also true. Often a leader gets requests from those below them, and ideally they are handled with the same degree of clarity.

To get the full benefit of Flores's work would require more time and attention than we can give it here, but there are extremely useful ideas that we can pass along in a brief summary. To go deeper, start with his book *Conversations for Action and Collected Essays*. What follows is a resume of the most easily integrated ideas from his model for delegation in that work:

Phase 1: Preparation—Take at least a few moments to prepare for the conversation with the person you'll be handing off to. Think carefully about your desired outcome, when you want it, and any resources that the person can access as they do the work.

Phase 2: Negotiation—Best practice is to actually speak to the person about what you want, versus just firing off an email or chat message. It pays to think about the delegation as a conversation to negotiate—or "co-design"—the deliverable. That collaborative dynamic runs right through this process. For instance, where most people being asked to do something see their only option as simply saying yes, Flores identifies four other options. The first one is obvious—saying no—but the others are less so:

- The person being approached might ask for more information, or for more clarity on why the project is important.

- They could commit to respond later, and give themselves some breathing space to check their capacity.

- They might even make a counteroffer if they see that there is either a better outcome possible or some better way to achieve it.

If the project in question is going to go ahead, establish what Flores calls the "conditions of satisfaction"—a list of details that both parties agree represents successful completion and by when, along with the resources available to the performer and how they'll stay in touch about progress. In our experience, not taking the minimal time necessary to be clear—and aligned—on these points is the single greatest source of frustration in delegations that go wrong.

Phase 3: Delivery/Completion—Here the person who has accepted the task of delivering the project goes to work and provides updates, if those were part of the agreement. If circumstances change so dramatically that delivery becomes impossible, they'd communicate that immediately and perhaps offer an alternative solution. Similarly, if the world moves on, and the person who has done the delegating no longer needs the project completed, they would communicate that quickly. Truly successful delegation is a partnership in which both parties are invested in not only a successful outcome but a respectful use of each other's time and energy. When the person doing the work believes they are done, they'll say so, ideally on or before the due date.

Phase 4: Satisfaction (or not)—Once they've looked over what has been delivered, the person who delegated the work is either satisfied, or not: if satisfied, everyone is happy; if not, they might request further work. Either way, they would offer thanks for the effort expended.

Variations on the elements described are implicit in every delegation, large or small, even if they are not necessarily acknowledged or used each time. Knowledge of them—and the sequence in which they occur—offers more possibilities as you delegate and dramatically enhances your chances of getting successful results. This is true whether you are delegating or being delegated to. If you are delegating something, it will be more likely to get you what you want; if you are being delegated to, it will make it more likely that you hit the target first time out, rather than needing several attempts to satisfy the person for whom you are doing the work.

If we go back to our scenario from the beginning of the chapter, here is how it might have played out differently:

Our leader gets a request to present at the senior leadership team meeting. The next day while clarifying his inbox, and with a good working knowledge of other commitments for the coming weeks, he realizes this is a commitment too far. While thinking through how to get it done, it occurs to him that while it is important that a good presentation gets made for senior leadership, it is not important that it gets made by him. One of his direct reports has been doing a great job covering that brief on the team, and it would be good to reward her with a bit more senior exposure. With a bit of coaching, the entire project—including the presentation—can be handed off to her. At their next scheduled one-to-one meeting, the leader spends five minutes talking through his own desires and expectations about length, format, and tone. His direct report—who is pretty slammed herself—doesn't just say "sure" immediately but asks some clarifying questions to get a sense of how this project fits with the other priorities for which she's accountable. After a brief discussion she agrees to respond within twenty-four hours. The following afternoon she makes a counteroffer: she'll take on the project, as long as she can pause or pass on to others a couple of other projects with similar due dates. Between them they then agree on the elements of a successful presentation, due dates for the finished deck, and when to deliver its first iteration for review. Over the course of the next weeks, the leader spends a total of twenty-five minutes reviewing drafts of a deck, and another half hour coaching a run-through. Deck and pre-read are submitted a week ahead of time, the direct does a great job on the presentation, and our leader uses the time in that meeting to focus on the reactions of senior leadership to the presentation, and on making notes for coaching his direct in their next one-to-one.

In this scenario the overall impact on the team in terms of urgency is minimal, the relationship between manager and managed is likely improved, and both the quality of the presentation and the identity of the team are enhanced. It's an ideal scenario, certainly, but also one that's easily emulated. It's more challenging than simply saying yes to everything, but also more likely to produce rewarding results.

[ED] In debriefing failed projects—or simply ones generating more than the usual amount of frustration for all concerned—having this simple model facilitates a systematic review and often makes it clear that the trouble has arisen because the people involved have mishandled a particular step in the sequence, or left it out altogether. Sometimes the problem comes from simply having too many people involved, which means that expectations and accountabilities are not fully aligned. Much of the mischief is generated in rushing through the negotiation phase with no real negotiation taking place. People in a hurry often try to shortcut the process and attempt to hand off a project without taking the time to detail exactly what success would look like, and available resources for getting it done. Egregious failures are almost guaranteed when the "negotiation" consists of a brief forwarded email.

One of the things we suggest you always negotiate is "by when" delivery is expected. Counterintuitively, this will create more space for the person taking on the work than if the delivery date is left open, or simply expected "as soon as possible." Though being loose about due dates can seem as if it will empower those doing the work, it often adds more pressure. If leaders don't specify when they need something back, it can have two equally unhelpful effects: people assume it is more urgent than it actually is, or that it isn't as important as other urgent matters and give it less attention than needed. Not giving that clarity is lazy delegation, and when a number of tasks pile up without clarity on deadlines, it makes it more difficult for a team to prioritize well.

PERSONAL POWER

Knowing the theory of why to delegate more, and the mechanics of how to do it well are key, but we want to acknowledge that there is another element that is in play as well here. Your eye contact, tone of voice, willingness to tolerate the discomfort of holding someone to account, and whether you manage your own commitments well will all play a role in how your requests are handled by those to whom you are delegating. It is not the focus of this book, but your own behavior as you delegate and follow up will have a dramatic impact on the success of your handoffs. If you want to explore this point further, the work of Dr. Richard Strozzi-Heckler on leadership and the body would be a useful starting point.

Because it can dramatically reduce misunderstanding and disappointment on a team, learning to delegate well is a critical skill. But it is the freedom it creates to look up and around at the wider context in which the team operates where it can make an even bigger difference. For the good of the team,

I am all for the petty success. A glorious failure leads to nothing; a petty success may lead to a success that is not petty.

—ARNOLD BENNETT

someone needs to be standing apart like a meerkat on a mound, listening and looking for patterns in what is coming in across the business. If the team is busy doing its piece of the whole, it needs someone to be looking up at the horizon, identifying opportunities and risks, and maintaining important relationships before they become apparent down on the ground. This can feel uncomfortable; it doesn't feel like "work," at least not like the work done early in a career, but it is a key activity on a team that—when left undone—can lead to tremendous inefficiency and an enhanced probability of strategic error. Too often the leader doesn't get to these more strategic things—that only they can do—because they are too stuck in the details that someone else could and should be handling. For the success of the team, those must be delegated.

Chapter 14

So What? Now What?

In our preface we suggested treating the book as a menu, with some dishes that are more to your taste than others. Much of what we've written applies to larger and more complex team situations. We may have even lost some of you there in your reading because you didn't feel you were playing at that level of game. The principles and best practices discussed, however, are applicable at any level of even more informal groupings and events—your parent-teacher committee, family outing, or townhouse owners' management board. (Boy, that can be a doozy!) Our editor, on first read of our draft of the book, called it (positively) "lean." It truly is, in that any single sentence or two, anywhere in the book, may hold a key for you. If you are involved in any way with others to get things done, in any framework, just pick a paragraph at random, and it will likely hold something valuable for you, to either identify best practices, or help improve your current ones.

Please relax about choosing where to start, or in which order you want to move through the material. We've put suggestions in some of the chapters about possible steps to take, but if you've gotten this far, we trust you've already had some important and at least interesting ideas to be working with.

You won't want to eat everything on this menu the first time around. Choose whatever you feel is most relevant for your team right now, have a go, and then come back for more once those concepts are firmly embedded. Much like David's *Getting Things Done* has proven a valuable reread for thousands, we think this will live in the same category.

What we don't suggest you do is simply put the book down and put a tick on your reading list. Some say knowledge is power, but in our experience, what some call knowledge can be one of the great barriers to real learning. As teachers and coaches we're regularly confronted with learners who respond to a learning opportunity with some version of "Nothing new in that, I know that already." They seem to experience a sense of disappointment that they didn't find enough shiny new toys for their frontal cortex to play with. The thing is, if we did our jobs well, then there is much that you've read that you will recognize. You'll recognize it because it matches your own experience, which is as it should be if we've truly captured the principles of working on a team.

> For the things we have to learn before we can do them, we learn by doing them.
>
> —ARISTOTLE

So perhaps you "know" this material. Good. That is the start. What many people mean when they say they know something is that they know *about* the subject in question. But that is radically different from knowing how to use the knowledge effectively. Real knowledge (or real learning) is being able to use what you know, consistently, even in unfamiliar and difficult circumstances. The former can be picked up from a book or an article; the latter can only be attained by practicing until the "head learning" is put into consistent use in the real world.

Take, for example, a professor of anatomy and physiology who knows everything there is to know about how muscle is built in the body but isn't currently engaged in a program of exercise. Their knowledge is of very little use to them in terms of keeping themselveshealthy. Understanding how muscle gets built is great, but if we are picking sides for a game of football with our team from the introduction, we'll definitely be picking the people doing wind sprints and practicing free kicks, not the anatomy and physiology expert. Similarly, knowing about things you could do with and for your team is beneficial, of course, but to know about it and not use it is getting an inside line on the booby prize. In terms of benefits from the investment of your time, you'd almost be better off not knowing what to do, because if knowing isn't accompanied by doing, most people simply use that gap to beat themselves up. It is only in doing the real-world work of implementation that you'll gain the real prizes.

What we've proposed is not complicated, and getting great results doesn't necessarily mean making radical changes: small changes, practiced over time, can have a dramatic impact on your results.

It's worth taking a moment to consider what you are trying to accomplish in working with others. In other words, what is the problem that you are trying to solve with a team? Or, perhaps more positively, what is the desired end state you have in mind for the team? What are you trying to enable on the team? Better organization? More trust? More speed? Less waste? More role clarity? Improving responsiveness in communication? Better knowledge management, so the team can find what it already knows quickly and by anyone who is looking?

It's important to know. All the challenges listed above can be handled, but they can't all be handled at the same time. You'll have to prioritize, of course (see chapter 12, on saying no . . .).

Any and all of this is easier if there is a committed core team to drive things forward. If you don't have that already, that may well be your first project.

AND, FINALLY . . .

Both of us are inspired and enthused to have created a working manual that has been requested and is clearly needed in so many important sectors of our world. And we would be thrilled for you to share in that with us, utilizing any of this material to improve the conditions around you. We may have overwhelmed you with the volume of nitty-gritty stuff about teams that we have dived into in this book, but it has been with the best intentions of sharing what we have seen and learned—good and bad—that might help.

We're all in this, together.

Acknowledgments

We'd like to say a huge thanks to the countless people we have trained, coached, and connected with doing this work over the years, who have provided us the experience of learning what really works and resonates to improve conditions in our lives. Thanks, too, to all the people who've asked what the book is about and then—upon learning of the topic—have said some version of, "Oh, please get that written quickly—my team needs that." It is good to learn that the problem you've set out to solve is a big one.

Profound thanks to all of the team leaders, team members, and subject matter experts who offered their time and expertise to answer questions about what works on teams in the real world: Sebastian Luge, Bruce Faulkner, Simon Collins, Nick Chism, Sarah von Nordheim, Kerstin Wagner, Annamaria Dahlmann, Alexander Gisdakis, Clemens Dachs, Frode Odegard, Jan Arve Haugan, Marion Horstmann, Martin Murgas, Nicolas von Rosty, Randal Fulhart, Robert Peake, Stefan Graff-Lonnevig, Thomas Leubner, Max D'Huc, Craig Jennings, Matthias Reuter, Tobias Winkler, Stu Foster, Annamaria Dahlmann, Marx Acosta-Rubio, Robert Hendriksen, Pete Hamill, Andrew Ward, Kevin Wilde, Michael Stenberg, Scott Joslin, Spencer Hanlon, Aksel Van der Wal, Andreas Helget, Tim Sismey, Judy Goldberg, Konstantin Wiethaus, Jonas Langeteig, Stuart Corrigan, Lawton Harper, Andy Denne, Wilhelm Lange, Dan Haygeman, Morton Rovik, Paul Vahur, Peter Yaholkovsky, Eric Mack, Stefan Pista Godo, Peter Byrom, Viacheslav Sukhomlynov, and Imran Rehman. A special mention to Robert Peake and Moni Danner for their contributions to the appendix on collaborative software. Special thanks to our tireless editor and great friend, Rick Kot, at Penguin, for his patience, book savviness, and encouragements; to our new editor Laura Tisdel and the PR and marketing team at Penguin; and to our accomplished agent,

Doe Coover, who's managed the business side of getting GTD in all its forms into print, and who has championed and shepherded this book from initial idea through to publication.

[DAVID] I have additionally so many people to thank, but here are the main ones:

Ed, such a dear friend and colleague, who did the yeoman's task of most of the text and overall framing, and his dedication to the methods we've described in the book and its articulation has been an inspiration to me.

Kathryn, my life partner, for her insights along the way, and who's tolerated my own ambient anxiety about getting this book right.

[ED] This book could not have happened without the help of the incredible group of people who've offered their time and energy to support its creation. In addition to all the above, I'd also like to thank the following:

David, friend, mentor, and coauthor, for being open to new interpretations of his original ideas, and his ability to build on them in service of the project. Linda Roser, who helped structure and protect my time, and was quick and resourceful in finding research material when needed. My partner Todd Brown and my colleagues in Next Action Associates, for bearing with me as I dialed back other activities to focus on this work. Soenke Ahrens, for his book *How to Take Smart Notes*, and his support and coaching in structuring the vast quantity of information and interviews that risked sinking the project before it got off the ground. The Monks of Worth Abbey, for providing a quiet place to crank out a draft, and to patient friends, who've waited supportively as I said no to way more things than I wanted to so I could stay focused on this project.

Finally, to my partner, Paula, for tolerating long absences, putting up with my misery when at home and things were stuck, and for proofing bad drafts and making them better when the words were flowing.

Appendix 1

What the Heck Is GTD, Anyway?

Because we have referred to various aspects of Getting Things Done in the previous pages, it can be useful to know what we've been talking about if you're not already aware of its basic principles. To understand it fully is not overly critical, as the content in the previous chapters has plenty of standalone merit. But some awareness of GTD ingredients can enhance your experience of the book.

GTD IN A NUTSHELL

There are two essential elements of stress-free productivity: control and focus. They are tightly woven together. Without control we lose focus. Without focus we lose control. However, achieving control and achieving focus requires separate and discrete practices.

A bottom line is that this methodology describes the best practices to be clear and confident about what you're doing—as an individual (described in David's previous books) and as a team (in this one). As straightforward as that may seem, it has taken several books to unpack all the variables that need to be considered to feel confident about how you are engaging with the world.

The three powerful GTD models that address these are:

The five steps of achieving control

The six Horizons of Focus

The Natural Planning Model

These practices require no specific technology to implement and can be used by anyone at any level of personal or professional engagement. While they can invoke necessary and very sophisticated thinking and decision-making when applied, they do not normally show up automatically in needed situations. They can and need to be learned and practiced, in appropriate contexts, even (and often especially) by their most accomplished users.

They are not difficult to understand and incorporate. They represent universal principles and practices about matters everyone deals with, much like gravity. A child deals with gravity to make their ball bounce; a Formula One race driver relates with it in their sharp turns. We have found no situation in which any of these models is not applicable for increased effectiveness.

THE FIVE STEPS OF ACHIEVING CONTROL

When we get a situation more "under control," as in riding a bicycle, piloting a sailboat, cooking a big dinner, or managing a team, there are five distinct stages we put into play:

Capturing

Clarifying

Organizing

Reflecting

Engaging

We'll illustrate this using a hypothetical, but maybe typical, out-of-control situation:

You're having guests come for dinner. But you don't arrive home until late in the afternoon, and your kitchen looks as if a hurricane has hit it.

Capturing

This critical first step is identifying what has our attention in the situation. Ninety-nine percent of the time that reflects something that is "off," unusual, or ringing some internal bell about it—something is not on cruise control, not part of the normal scheme of things (yet). It could be off in the sense of something wrong; it could be something unexpected that shows up—good or bad; or it could be something we become aware of that could use more attention or action.

What you immediately notice in your kitchen is all the stuff that's not the way it should be or where it should be. The place is a mess—not everything, but there is a lot there that is off. Dishes are in the sink, condiments are on the counter, and there are some items in the fridge with sell-by dates that need checking.

Clarifying

To further get control, you need to make some decisions about what has your attention. Is it something that needs action? If not, is it unneeded or unnecessary (trash), or is it something that might need to be referenced at some point or triggered for some later reminder? If it is actionable, what's the next action? And if a single next action won't finish whatever commitment you have made about it, what's the longer-term desired outcome? If the next action can be done in less than two minutes, it should be done immediately; if not, whether it could be done by someone else needs to be clarified.

These are dirty dishes. These are spices. This is bad food. This is still good food. OK, let's deal with each of these as needed.

Organizing

What's clarified but can't be completed at the moment needs to be parked in its appropriate place. Trash goes where trash goes; reference goes where it can be retrieved as needed; reminders of actions to take and projects to finish need to be put in their appropriate categories in some external system.

OK, dirty dishes in the dishwasher, spices back on the spice rack, bad food in the garbage, good food back in the refrigerator.

Reflecting

To determine where to put your attention and what action to take, you do a review of the inventory of options that you have organized and any other relevant content.

What's the time? Where's the recipe for the main course? Are my tools in order and ingredients at hand?

Engaging

Finally, you put your attention and activity in motion, appropriate to the context in which you find yourself.

Get butter out of the refrigerator and start to melt it.

This is how you get your kitchen under control. It's also how you get a team or project under control. And though in the kitchen situation you would run through these five stages naturally and probably quickly, the steps are no different. Most teams and the individuals involved can significantly improve how they capture, clarify, organize, reflect, and engage.

When situations get more complex than cleaning a messy kitchen, more rigor and externalization of this procedure is required. Most people, personally, as well as team leaders and participants, tend to keep much of their self- and team-management in their heads. But the head is a lousy office. Cognitive science research has confirmed that the maximum number of things the mind can remember, remind itself of, prioritize, and manage relevant relationships between, is four. Any more than that produces suboptimal results in everything from not doing as well on tests through to being driven by the latest and loudest inputs instead of intuitive strategic thinking.

We have spent literally thousands of hours implementing this five-stage model with individuals at their desks where they work and at times where they live, and with teams in their office environments. The following is what that typically has involved.

Capturing—The first and essential step

For individuals, we first gather any materials physically in their environment that have their attention—things that ultimately are not where they should permanently reside or about which some decision might need to be made. We have them put those into their in-basket if they fit there or write a note to represent the item and store the note in "in." This is usually stuff on the desk, in the desk, around the desk, and around their office—sometimes producing quite a large stack.

Then we do what we call a "mind sweep" and have the client literally empty their head by writing down on paper anything and everything that has their attention—little, big, personal, and professional.

Everything from "I need a new extension cord at home" to "I've got to decide what to do about a corporate merger opportunity."

This capture process can take on average from one to six hours, and the results of just this first part of our engagement often produce remarkable results for the individual. It can certainly be a daunting exercise, becoming aware of the often hundred-plus things that had their attention. But the relief usually generated by having all their "stuff" in one place is extraordinary.

As we began to apply this model for getting control in team situations, it merely translated to a focus on capturing what has the team's attention, as a team.

What's been produced at this stage is not a to-do list, though it might look like one. And for the process to be most effective, trying to make prioritizing or organizing decisions at this point would filter and limit the freedom for getting a clear look at everything. Optimal capturing should gather it all.

Then what naturally shows up is a question: "What do we do about all this?" This leads into the next step in the process.

Clarifying—Getting clear on what things mean

Once everything that requires some thinking has been captured, decisions need to be made.

Ideally, each item on the gathered list(s) is examined, one at a time, top to bottom. (No skipping around!) The thought process to apply is relatively simple:

What is this thing?

Does it need any action?

If not, is it trash, reference material, or something for later assessment/review?

If it is actionable, then what's the next action?

If there is a next action, can it be completed now in less than two minutes?

If not, can it be delegated?

If neither of those, then it is a pending action to be done when appropriate.

If one action won't complete the commitment, what's the project it will involve?

As straightforward and productive as this thinking formula seems to be, one of the more surprising things we've experienced over the years is how little it is applied for most of what has people's attention. And we're talking about some of the best, brightest, and busiest people on the planet. After most executives we have coached with this method have spent time capturing, they require at least two focused days to be walked through these clarifying steps and make the appropriate decisions about the meaning of all the contents.

A team may need a good bit more time to think about what they have identified than it took to identify what had their attention in the first place. The team should ask themselves the same questions, but with the addition of "Who's got this?" for actions and projects identified, and "Where does this go?" if it's reference information or something the team needs to review with some frequency.

What then follows naturally is the need to organize the contents that have resulted from the clarifying.

Organizing—Putting things where they belong

Once the items that have been captured have been clarified, they need to be organized to keep the situation under control. Much like spices in the kitchen have to be returned to where spices belong, projects that have been identified need reminders in a list of projects, action items need parking where they will be seen in the appropriate contexts, reference materials and information need to go where they can be easily retrieved as needed, etc.

This is where the plethora of organizing options and tools comes into play. For individuals this usually means lists. And those lists can be kept wherever it is most convenient to see the contents when necessary. Sticky notes on the refrigerator for food shopping might be sufficient. As might a loose-leaf notebook, or any one of several hundred personal organizing apps.

For some teams a powerful project management software app might be best. For others a simple Kanban bulletin board of sticky notes might suffice.

The point is, where do you need to park this reminder/content so that there is no concern about the right person or people referencing it at the right time? Frankly, very few individuals or teams have this as optimally implemented as it could be.

Optimal team performance will be the result of both the team and the individuals involved managing this organizing phase appropriately.

Of course, the next logical step in staying in control is assuring that relevant content is reviewed and reflected upon, in a trusted system, by the right people at the right times, and updated as needed.

Reflecting—Maintaining an overview of your commitments

This part of the getting-control process can and often does happen anywhere, at any time, by anyone. We often must step back from hanging out in the weeds and lift our perspective to locate ourselves and orient our focus and activities optimally in space and time. Simply reviewing your calendar for a few days ahead to notice where and when you need to be or do something is a version of this necessary reflection.

If you or your team has captured, clarified, and organized relevant information regarding commitments, some version of reviewing those contents will be important to stay clear and focused. This could range from noticing the sticky notes on your refrigerator before you go to the market to reviewing your annual goals before your quarterly management meeting.

How frequently you do such reviews is dependent on the situation. There are times when a daily standup meeting for the team is required to stay on point. An individual should review the next day's scheduled meetings to ensure there are no missing pieces in what they need to handle before that morning. And some things only need to be reflected on more rarely—weekly, monthly, quarterly, yearly—to feel comfortable that things are on track. But regular reflection is a necessary step to maintain a sense of control.

As we touched on in chapter 4, creating and using reflection time is one of the most important, and most lacking, practices for teams as well as individuals.

Engaging—Making trusted choices about what to do next

The most obvious result of implementing the previous four pieces of the getting-control puzzle is to make trusted choices about where a person or a team puts their attention and activity. When is taking a nap the best thing to do for myself? When is having a team after-hours libation get-together what's needed? When should we have a concentrated sit-down to work on this project plan together? Etc., ad infinitum.

It's much easier to enjoy having guests for dinner if you have captured, clarified, organized, and reflected on the current reality. The point of all that work is to be able to make intuitive choices about what to do next. It's much easier to have difficult and complex situations under control if the same process has been applied in a team environment.

And then, naturally, the question, latent or otherwise, emerges: So how do we get comfortable about the prioritization of our choices about what we're doing?

THE SIX HORIZONS OF FOCUS

As mentioned we need both control and focus to be on course. In addition to the five steps we use to take control, we also need reference points to ensure we're controlling the "right things."

[DAVID] When I began my exploration of personal productivity practices in the 1980s, an inevitable and obvious question was tied to it. With all the stuff to do, how should I determine priorities? I grappled with the best way to answer that question. The rather simplistic labeling of things "A, B, C," though somewhat useful, didn't fully match any reality I was aware of. Watching TV to relax wasn't any one of those letters. Nor did the Eisenhower Matrix of important/urgent—though also useful in certain circumstances—relate to someone taking time to research whether their daughter should take karate lessons. And neither could keep up with the pace of change in most people's lives, as each new message they received in a day could entail a fundamental re-sort of lists based on those models. I did boil the issue down as simply as I could get it. It required the awareness and integration of multiple levels of our agreements with ourselves.

We have a lot more about which we need to "get things done" than a simple to-do list represents. The inventory of commitments we have, personally and organizationally, can be identified on multiple levels—five different altitudes and one on the ground floor. We may or may not be consciously aware of any one of these, but they are there, and they will ultimately determine our priorities and most appropriate focus, seen through their respective lenses.

To be most comfortable about ensuring we're moving on our priorities, as an individual or as a team, we need to make sure our actions are aligned with one or more of these levels of our agreements with ourselves.

These commitment examples can be grouped, from the top down:

Horizon 5—Purpose and Principles

Horizon 4—Vision

Horizon 3—Goals

Horizon 2—Areas of Focus and Responsibility

Horizon 1—Projects

Ground—Actions

Horizon 5—Purpose and Principles

The prime driver for any activity, conscious or not, is the big "Why?" and "What really matters about this?" We need to fix a flat tire because we want to continue driving to our destination safely. We want to test and potentially launch this new product because it could solve a major problem for consumers and create market success. This is obvious stuff, usually, for obvious situations. It's not so obvious, though, in more subtle situations, where a bigger "why" that is lurking should be accessed for optimal creative thinking and prioritizing. For more on this see chapter 5.

Horizon 4—Vision

If I/we were wildly successful in fulfilling our purpose, what would be true? Personally, what would be our ideal career and lifestyle? Organizationally, how do we want to be, and be perceived, in (say) five years? What would wild success look, sound, and feel like, if this project/team won its game?

This is the next, more operational level of thinking and content that gives direction and focus. A purpose could be broad and general, e.g., "do good in the world." The vision of doing that could be anything from "teaching underprivileged kids" to "curing a major disease."

Horizon 3—Goals

This brings the focus to an even more specific and operational level. What are the key things that need to be accomplished within the next year or two to create the vision? This is typically the horizon of annual planning, budgeting, and strategy sessions in an organization.

Horizon 2—Areas of Focus

What are the things that need to be maintained at sufficient levels or standards so we can go forward most effectively? For example: our own education, our technology capabilities, our sales and profitability, our work processes. These are not things that we complete or finish—they are simply the arenas that need to be kept in useful conditions.

Clarified job descriptions and accountabilities also lie here. On a team, this translates to: Who's responsible for which key team activities.

Horizon 1—Projects

As we move even further down to Earth about our commitments, the question becomes: What do we need to complete within the next few weeks or months, to engage appropriately with all of the above horizons? What needs to be handled, completed, researched, implemented?

Most individuals have from thirty to a hundred of these, including both personal and professional areas. Teams have as many as they must to fulfill their role as a team.

Ground—Actions

This is the most operationally granular level of commitment. It's where "the rubber meets the road." What physically and visibly needs to be done—now—about any of the above? And who's responsible for doing it? Such questions are often avoided and unanswered in meetings and planning sessions.

To apply these to a real situation, let's return to the "guests for dinner" scenario we used previously, working up from the bottom to the horizons:

Actions—You're having them for dinner for the simple reason your partner put it on your calendar.

Projects—You want to complete a nice dinner for the guests.

Areas of Focus—Your guests include a new staff person with whom you want to create a more informal and positive relationship.

Goals—You want to ensure that in the coming year you've created a great working team.

Vision—You'd like to be considered for a very senior position in your career because of your track record with superior team building.

Purpose and Principles—You care about being of great service in your work in the world, and to your family and yourself with an abundant and healthy lifestyle.

Now, seeking clarity about any one of those points might be sufficient for you to be optimally present and productive with what you're doing. At the same time, any one of the higher-horizon perspectives might add significant creativity and value to your focus and priorities in what you're doing, even at the action level. The same is true for teams.

Frankly, very few individuals or teams have the inventory of all these horizons complete and current, and even if they did, the inventory will likely change—especially at the lower and more operational levels. When the question of priorities emerges, one or more of these horizons should be revisited—perhaps updated—and integrated in the decision-making process.

SITUATIONAL FOCUS—THE NATURAL PLANNING MODEL

A third key model of GTD is a practice for getting any situation or project under control and appropriately focused. Whereas the Horizons of Focus described above are primarily a current but static descriptor of the realities of the different altitude perspectives, and useful for ensuring an overall context for prioritizing, the Natural Planning Model is more intentionally focused on creating content for optimal productivity in the realities of the moment. It is like the horizons model but is more centered on intentional activity.

[DAVID] Another common question that emerged in my early consulting days was: What's the best way to plan something? I searched high and low for some sort of model or training that answered that question but found nothing that was universal enough for my purpose and interest. I even checked with some corporate training and development people whether they had found any good project management training they trusted. Nothing. Some companies have created their own project management training courses in-house, focused on the specific projects related to that company's business. But there was nothing that could be applied universally.

So, one day (or week—I can't remember) I was thinking about planning, and I realized that we are all planning, all the time. We plan how to dress, how to make lunch, how to talk to a friend or neighbor, and even how to get out of a room, before we do. We have a purpose for doing it, we have an image of having it done, we consider all the things we need to consider, then organize ourselves, and we get moving. We do that naturally. It's a Natural Planning Model.

Could that model be objectified and used universally? You bet. Identify purpose, principles, and outcome (vision); brainstorm potentially relevant information and perspectives; organize the thoughts and focus; and decide (and take) next actions.

We have both spent countless hours using this simple model as a guide for individual and team discussions and decision-making, with surprisingly successful results in every case. What's great about it is how simple and flexible it is—it is equally good for huge initiatives and seemingly simple projects, both personally and professionally.

We unpacked the usage of this model in chapter 10.

A Timeless Approach to Using Collaborative Software

Collaborative software (also known as groupware) for teams has been one of the major IT trends of recent years, as companies strive to facilitate greater teamwork, better knowledge management, and higher productivity than was possible with the previous set of more individually focused tools.

In this appendix we want to offer a way to navigate the incredible number of features and functions that come with the various team software offerings on the market, and show how teams can use them in a way that supports both individual and team productivity. We've included this material as an appendix instead of in the main body of the book because not all readers will have access to, or even need to use, collaborative software, and others already have streamlined, smooth, functional, and easy setups. For both of these groups, the details that follow here would be optional. And, as the digital frontier on this type of software keeps expanding, newer applications could show up any time that might make a rewrite useful.

We also wanted to separate these ideas from the main body of the book because we have leaned heavily on the expertise and thinking of both Robert Peake and Monika Danner, and it felt right to highlight their contributions separately.

Collaborative software can have a significant impact on teams, and on the individuals working on those teams. Whether that impact is highly positive, negative, or mixed usually comes down to how the tool is used rather than the nature of the tool itself.

> If our work environment is easily understood even by strangers, it also makes it easier to collect the wisdom of everyone.
>
> —KIYOSHI SUZAKI

Many applications have emerged with the objective of providing a digitally coordinated focus for a team or group. Initially, many only aspired to provide a shared reference system, but many of those tools now also provide a means to manage the team's projects and assigned actions, and multiple means of communicating as well. We are aware of teams—mostly in tech companies with well-defined workflows—that have made parts of those tools work for them, but by and large the success rate is very low even in optimal conditions. In the more ambiguous world of knowledge work, where projects and processes are less well defined—things like organizing the annual office party, finding the best social media consultant, optimizing governance on the supervisory board, etc.—the outcomes and activities fit even less easily in the available boxes of any given piece of group software.

Despite the major investment in them, these tools have not landed well with most to whom they've been offered. At least partly because of a lack of clear guidance on how to use them, many feel that they end up working for the groupware rather than the groupware working for them. Because these tools have added to an explosion of communication channels, many individuals and organizations are simply shifting their problem with managing email to these new and shiny platforms. The overall impact can seriously undermine the clarity we must establish to effectively manage our individual and team commitments.

Simply creating more places to store information, for example, does not necessarily make it easier to find what you need. And even better storage of information in relation to key projects does not in itself create clear objectives and accountability for those projects. In addition to the supporting material required to collaborate on a project, clear outcomes and an up-to-date "state of play" are necessary to optimally manage it to completion. Three distinct elements—where we are now, where we are headed, and what information we need along the way—must be disentangled from threaded discussions and digital pinboards if we are to do anything besides search endlessly for the things we need.

So it is not any particular feature that is missing. It is the team decision about what its workflow is, and how the tool can support that. What's missing are well-defined protocols about levels of detail that should go into such groupware as well as policies regarding delegation, frequency of updating, etc. The tools can also engender duplication of effort: team projects and assigned activities must be owned by someone, and if they need a reminder in their own system as well as in the team application, they won't be happy about it. It can be highly demotivating to have to input into—and review—dual systems. Part of the challenge of using groupware effectively is getting the information needed for a team overview without impairing individual effectiveness.

There are many pitfalls to these products, but for some it may be worth the effort of at least experimenting with them to see what might work and might stick. But from our experience and observation, we suggest not seeing a new tool as a silver bullet, but rather as a minor piece of a larger solution. With all the hype surrounding game-changing technologies, teams and organizations regularly fall into the trap of thinking that they will solve problems rooted in human dynamics. To paraphrase Bruce Schneier, if you think technology can solve your productivity problems, you don't understand the problems, and you don't understand the technology.

Having a greater understanding of how the pieces fit together between a trusted GTD system and a company groupware solution can help your team make sense of how these two can interact optimally, and more important, how they can use groupware in a productive way.

At a high level most groupware solutions are designed to improve team effectiveness. One way to measure this effectiveness is to see how quickly and easily a team using one of these applications can answer the following four questions:

- What is our goal and who owns it?

- Who will do what by when?

- What is the status of . . . ?

- Where can I find information on . . . ?

Quick and clear responses to these questions support the following:

- Visibility of objectives

- Accountability for those objectives

- Tracking progress

- Effective management of shared reference information

In the modern office we are all fighter pilots.

—PAUL TOUGH

The answers to those four key questions will help you understand how the different elements of your groupware solution can support the work of your team. The questions below will help you understand how the pieces fit together, and how you might best employ your groupware— or only parts of it—to improve clarity in an individual or team system.

DOES THE SOFTWARE OFFER A FAST WAY OF CREATING AND MAINTAINING LISTS AND/OR CALENDAR ENTRIES?

If this is true, the groupware solution could constitute part or all of a personal GTD system. If it can't accommodate all of what is needed for that, team members will have to decide to allocate tasks and meetings between their individual system (for tracking their own outcomes and actions) and the groupware system (which tracks team outcomes and activities). For example, for a salesperson, sales opportunities in the team sales software might represent some or all of their own list of projects they are tracking to completion.

DO PEOPLE POST THINGS IN YOUR GROUPWARE THAT ARE POTENTIALLY ACTIONABLE, AND THAT DO NOT EXIST ELSEWHERE?

If so, in GTD terms, this is an inbox. Team members will need to check this regularly to capture inputs that may become outcomes or next actions in their own system. As a team, you want to agree to minimize the number of places to look in order to spend less time hunting around. One way to minimize inboxes is to transfer the information from a groupware stream intended for many people into one of a select few places where individuals can subsequently clarify and organize the information into their own trusted GTD system. If the software links between the groupware and individual systems allow it, this can be transferred directly. If not, they may need to adopt a workaround (such as emailing screenshots to themselves, or jotting a note for their physical inbox). Worst practice would be to simply leave it where it is as the only trigger for future action. That simply multiplies the places to check before acting and makes prioritization much more difficult.

Filters, rules, and even email notifications can be used to aid the discovery process but can sometimes cut both ways. It is often better to manually scan an important data stream than to rely on imperfect filters to bring you what you need (and hide what it thinks you don't need). This is particularly true if missed information can have critical consequences.

DOES YOUR TEAM ENGAGE IN MEETINGS OR CONVERSATIONS ON GROUPWARE THAT CAN RESULT IN NEXT ACTIONS OR PROJECTS?

Once again, this is an inbox. The key question is this: Are there any commitments as a result of this communication that we need to capture? Just as email has a spam filter, your team needs an "action filter" switched on whenever you communicate. Often in groupware channels you are just socializing or swapping updates—like you would at an in-person meeting or when chatting in the hall. But keep a watchful eye out for what you (or anyone else on the team) have requested, or agreed to do. Someone on the team needs to take notes or otherwise "extract" the actionable commitments from a recording or transcript of each meeting, so everyone can later clarify the relevant outcomes and next actions for themselves.

DO ONE OR MORE TEAMS TO WHICH YOU BELONG GENERATE SHARED INFORMATION RELATED TO SPECIFIC PROJECTS?

If so, wherever it lives, this contains project support information. Team members need to connect this information to the outcome they have defined on their project lists. If the system permits it, this could be through an integration, but, if not, it can be handled by simply pasting in a link or making a note to "See such-and-such folder in shared files."

DOES THE SYSTEM CONTAIN INFORMATION USEFUL FOR COMPLETING NEXT ACTIONS BY THE TEAM?

This contains action support information for the team. They'll want to reference this information in the next action they've defined in their own lists, in a similar manner to project support as above.

You'll want to create links from the "master" lists (in an individual's trusted GTD system) to the team's action support, project support, and waiting-for support information wherever possible. If no built-in technology solution exists for integration, permalink URLs can sometimes be used in a text field. Worst case, duplicate the relevant portion of content using copy-and-paste or screenshots. The key goal is to be able to make choices based on an overview of your own trusted system first, and from there be led into other relevant sources of information, rather than use disparate information in the team system as triggers for personal prioritization.

DOES THE TEAM MAKE STRUCTURED REQUESTS TO OTHERS THROUGH THIS SYSTEM (E.G., LIKE A TICKET TRACKER)?

If it does, this represents waiting for support information. Some prefer to reference this information in their own "waiting for" list, but many simply treat the system as an extension of their own lists. This works fine as long as they are prepared to review it regularly, along with their other lists.

DOES THE SYSTEM CONTAIN INFORMATION RELEVANT TO TIME-SPECIFIC ACTIVITIES FOR THE TEAM OR TEAM MEMBERS?

If yes, this is a calendar. If it's technically possible, it is useful to consolidate or integrate it with any other calendars that team members are running. If not, they'll want to review it regularly as an extension of their main calendar.

DOES YOUR TEAM HOLD REGULAR MEETINGS FOR WHICH YOU WOULD LIKE TO KEEP AN AD-HOC AGENDA OF TOPICS TO RAISE?

If you do hold meetings in groupware, they can be aided by keeping a running Agendas list somewhere accessible to all. This allows for capturing topics members want to raise as they occur to them, rather than trying to brainstorm—or remember—them just before the meeting begins. Any simple shared and easily accessible list system will do.

DOES YOUR GROUPWARE ALLOW FOR STORAGE OF GENERAL INFORMATION THAT IS USEFUL FOR THE ENTIRE TEAM TO HAVE ACCESS TO?

In GTD terms this is general reference. It represents general information not tied to a specific project or action, but should be easily retrievable, as it may be useful—critical even—when needed. As we mentioned in chapter 4, on the five steps of GTD for a team, agreeing upon some minimal standards about where team reference information is located, and how it is labeled and stored, can help minimize time spent searching for it.

Man has an irrepressible tendency to read meaning into the buzzing confusion of sights and sounds impinging on his senses; and where no agreed meaning can be found, he will provide it out of his own imagination.

—ARTHUR KOESTLER

SAMPLE PROTOCOLS FOR THE USE OF COLLABORATIVE SOFTWARE

We hope the above principles and questions will help clarify the kinds of factors you'll want to take into account as you begin using—or become intentional about how you are using—a piece of collaborative software. To give you some sense of how one organization has found a way through, the following is an example of the kinds of documented

To find a form that accommodates the mess, that is the task of the artist now.

—SAMUEL BECKETT

standards concerning team use of groupware that has worked for the culture team at Leroy, which we mentioned in the chapter on working standards:

Principles for the use of our collaborative software at Leroy Way Office (LWO)

Here are some principles for how we use the collaborative software at LWO. The purpose of this tool is to ensure that we have a good flow of information internally in the department. Everyone must be up to date at all times.

Only alert those you wish to reach with your message

It's easy to message everyone using our collaborative software, but in the same way you only send an email to those it applies to, please only message those who really need to know. In contrast to email, all threads will be available to everyone, which means that everyone can find things later if they want to.

Before setting up a discussion thread, think about whether the topic is something suitable for a written discussion

Sometimes a call or a meeting is a more effective solution than trying to resolve a complex issue in writing.

If you are in doubt about where to post something, create a thread!

Our collaborative software gives you two ways to communicate: threads and messages.

When you first start, it can be difficult to know whether to start a thread or send a message. If you are in doubt, the default is to start a thread. The more discussion that happens in public threads, the more public information your team will have access to, and the easier it will be for everyone to do their job.

WHEN DO WE USE THREADS?	WHEN DO WE USE NOTIFICATIONS?
• When we post unpublished status updates • When we propose something new • When you need feedback on, for example, a document you have created • When you need to advertise something	• Quick questions that concern a few people • Quick feedback • Private conversations

Choose the right channel

In our collaborative software we have many different channels. When posting, choose the channel you think is best. Even if you start a thread in the wrong channel, it is not a problem. You can easily move a thread to another channel.

Give the threads clear and descriptive names

As an example, use prefixes like [?] or [FYI] to easily let people in on what you want with the thread you have posted. The prefix [?] means you have a question you want answered, and [FYI] means what you write is for information only, and no response is required.

When necessary, summarize context and content for others in the department if they are asked into the middle of a discussion

While the person can go back and read through the entire thread for context, it can often be confusing for someone to figure out exactly what is needed from them, especially if it is a longer thread. If you take the time to briefly and clearly articulate what is needed from that person, it will be much easier for them to respond quickly.

LIKE THIS	NOT LIKE THAT
@Jonas: We have now assessed the two proposals against each other. Attached is a summary of the advantages and disadvantages of the two proposals. Can you list the days and times that suit you with a meeting to discuss this on video next week?	@Jonas: Please have a look and get back to me on dates.

Close threads and document outages

When the conversations end, you can spend a few minutes closing the thread and adding a detailed conclusion so that others looking for information can quickly understand what the outcome was and why.

Closing threads is also useful for duplicated conversations. When you notice a duplication, do not delete the duplicate thread. Instead, close it and add a link to the original thread in the conclusion. That way, if someone searches for and finds the duplicate thread in the future, they will be able to quickly follow the link to the original.

Manage expectations

When you know you can't respond to a request within the next working day, at least respond to explain why, to manage expectations.

Have fun!

Team communication should not only be about doing things. Getting to know one another via common interests is productive, too! If you've seen or experienced something others might enjoy, share it!

As authors we include the above not as suggestions, but as an example of something that has worked. Their approach might work for your team, and it might not. Whether they are "right" or not is not the point. The point is that this team took the time to discuss and elaborate protocols so current team members have a reference for how to use their collaborative software, and so new members don't have to spend months to understand how to use it.

HANDLING GROUP INBOXES

Finally, we move on to a specific case: the group email inbox. Those familiar with previous GTD books will know what we suggest for individuals: that any inbox is only a temporary collection point that gets emptied regularly. Effective individuals don't try to *work* out of their inbox; every twenty-four to forty-eight hours they *clarify* everything that comes in, take care of two-minute actions, archive references, put good ideas on a Someday/Maybe list for later, then identify clear next steps and desired outcomes from what's left and put them on appropriate lists. Then they can prioritize with confidence and go to work with a clear head.

Unfortunately, more and more people now have a second mailbox. Not a personal one, but one they share with colleagues. Typical addresses for these inboxes start with info@, office@, recruitment@, or sales@. The inbox of a ticket system serves the same function. The names vary, but the principle is the same: If you send something to such an address, you don't know who will answer; it can be one person, or it can be fifteen different people. You don't need to know. As a "customer" all you care about is that you get a prompt response that resolves your query.

For teams with a lot of interdepartmental and customer contact, the advantages are clear:

- Continuous coverage—there is never an "out of office" message like you'd get from an individual

- Consistency of address—even if over time there are many changes in the team responding

- More evenly spread workload—for when there are high volumes of general inquiries for the team

It only becomes problematic when there is no clear accountability for who is doing what (and by when) behind the anonymous address. In the best-case scenario, this "only" leads to multiple readings of messages, occasional redundant replies, and some light frustration among those who process the inbox. In the worst case, the additional inbox becomes a message "cemetery" from which no response is forthcoming because no one feels responsible for answering. Instead of more customer satisfaction it can end up causing more frustration.

To avoid this, if a team is planning to open—or already operating—

a shared inbox, we recommend they ask themselves a few simple questions:

- What should the address be used for?

- Where do we store information and reference material?

- What is the principle for emptying the inbox?

QUESTION: WHAT SHOULD THE ADDRESS BE USED FOR? (SUBTEXT: DO WE REALLY NEED IT?)

Here you want to think hard about what kind of things—requests/mails/information—the team wants to handle in the inbox. In light of that, who should know the address? This will also determine where—or whether—it gets published. Here the possibilities range from "Actually, the address is secret, we only use it to document mails via bcc" to "We no longer have personal mail addresses in the team. Everything now runs via this one address." In general, the broader the filter used, the higher the expected mail volume will be—and the more team resources required to process it.

QUESTION: WHERE DO WE STORE INFORMATION AND REFERENCE MATERIAL?

This question becomes more relevant when the email box must be able to do more than handle just short-term inquiries and is deliberately used as an entry point for information and reference material. For example, the team may need to at least document the status of completed cases. In some situations, a legally prescribed data-protection-compliant filing system might also be necessary.

General rules about the best folder structure are therefore difficult to make, beyond the principle that there should be nothing in the reference material that still requires action, that it should be quick and easy to file and find things, and that any archive should also be tidied up every now and then. As we said with regard to team reference in chapter 4, the best solution we've found is to appoint someone who has responsibility for the system and who occasionally does brief "tours" for the team to provide clarity on what goes where.

QUESTION: WHAT IS THE PRINCIPLE FOR EMPTYING THE INBOX?

Emptying the inbox regularly has many advantages. Everyone wastes less energy because they no longer inadvertently read things twice. The stress of having too many open loops is reduced because unfinished to-dos have clear actions identified. And the inbox is used in the way it was intended, as a place to find new things, and not as a reference system or an extremely ineffective to-do list.

To achieve this in the team, we see three possible ways to empty the inbox. The optimal choice that best suits the team has to do with the expected volume of messages as well as the size of the team—and the response to the first question, "What should the address be used for?"

VARIANT 1: THE ROTATION PRINCIPLE

In this case one person or a couple working in tandem is completely responsible for the mail account for a specified period (a shift, a day, a week, etc.) and processes *everything* that arrives there. This variant corresponds most closely to a ticket system, e.g., in IT support.

One advantage is the maximum customer benefit with the greatest possible anonymity of the processor. This system is successful when requests are very comparable, require uniform handling, and additional expert knowledge is rarely necessary. It is suitable for larger units and the processing of large quantities of incoming mails. To reduce the number of things that fall through cracks, it will make sense to have a handover of cases that are still "open" at the time of rotation.

VARIANT 2: THE "GRAB IT" PRINCIPLE

In this case, all relevant team members check the inbox regularly and independently pick out what they think they can best process (because of time resources, professional responsibility, skills, etc.) Technically, the identified mails can be marked with a personal category or moved to a folder with the name of the person who's taken charge of something on it. Emptying the inbox then works almost automatically.

This requires a lot of consultation within the team to function well. It can work if the overall volume remains manageable and the experts are equally responsible in picking out "their" emails and marking them in the same way. Rules of the game and expectations of email communication should be discussed in the team. For example, what performance promise do we make to the customer in terms of response times? And what is the process—or who is responsible—for handling whatever is left once everyone thinks they've handled their bits?

VARIANT 3: THE DISPATCHER PRINCIPLE

One or more persons (also possible in rotation) are responsible for emptying the inbox and distributing mails to the team. The criteria for distribution can vary according to time availability, equity, regionality, expert knowledge, or some other useful way of sorting the incoming messages.

Technically, this can be done (as an example) in Outlook via folders for each team member: @Tim_action, @Jenny_action . . . When checking the team mail address, the respective agents only look at "their" mails and answer them independently. As soon as they are completed, they are moved (@Tim_done, @Jenny_done), or tasks are marked as completed so the dispatcher sees the released capacity again.

The advantage here is clearly assigned responsibility for incoming mail and the clear allocation of responsibility—without duplicate orders or vague handovers between several people. In addition, in the case of unusual requests, it can be more efficient to assign them to an expert right away, or to enable faster processing through an equal distribution of labor across the team. The critical success factor is the responsiveness of those to whom the dispatcher assigns the work.

With these basic questions discussed in the team, we believe that many of the misunderstandings and frustrations can be minimized for both the team and its clients, whether anyone in the team is a GTDer or not.

Appendix 3

Working Well in a Virtual World

WHAT'S ALL THE FUSS?

For years after the pandemic the world of work was in flux. Finding an optimal mix of remote and home—hybrid working—was the topic du jour in newspapers and professional journals. Employers were casting about, looking for the best formula to get people back to the office part-time, while continuing to offer them the flexibility they'd come to expect after a couple years of mostly working from home.

But this style of working was never anything actually new in substance. Since at least the middle of the twentieth century, consultants and sales reps had worked in the way most people were now only beginning to explore. For those professions, working in the office was neither expected nor appreciated. Both moved to where there was work to do, or where their clients needed them to be. Sometimes that was in the office, but being there too often could be perceived as not selling enough, or skimping on client care. If things were going well, a big chunk of their work was done at client sites. Some work got done at home (because it made no sense to go to the office in the morning if a client lunch was in the opposite direction), and some got done in hotels, trains, and planes. For people who had these kinds of jobs, hybrid working wasn't much of a change; for them, the "new normal" was simply normal.

What was different was the number of people who were being moved to this way of working and the speed at which the change was taking place. Suddenly, knowledge workers everywhere were grappling with where and when to get their work done.

The concept isn't complicated. Hybrid working, and its close cousin, virtual working, are simply working from wherever best suits the individuals concerned, using all available tools to optimize time and effort on a team that doesn't need to consistently intersect in either time or space.

We already know that this way of working is a great fit for certain types of professional activity and for certain kinds of personalities. What is not yet clear is whether it will work for everyone who wants it or is being pushed toward it. Hybrid working has always suited those who are highly motivated, disciplined, and able to structure their work in a way that works for them. But many people have preferred to "go to work" because the structure and hierarchy they found there saved them from having to organize and motivate themselves. We are in the middle of an exceptionally large, long-term experiment to find out whether working from home will be appropriate for them, too, and whether they will understand and accept that this is how work now gets done, and they can no longer count on the structures of an office life to help them focus.

This way of working is not going away, though the name is likely to change. In a few years we believe that "hybrid working" will be simply known as "working." There are those who'd like things to flip back to how they were before, but the flexible-working genie is well and truly out of the bottle. Having shown they can do their jobs reliably—and under significant pressure—from home, most people expect a new deal from their employers. They are willing to come to the office when necessary, but any employer who wants to force them back to their desks will need a very compelling argument, or an armada of recruiters to fill a sea of empty desks.

Barring another global epidemic, a purely virtual setup will remain a rarity. It might be that you only see your colleagues once per week, or per quarter, but for most people some version of hybrid working will be their new normal. The technology is simply too useful, when used wisely. It's not that face-to-face meetings are good, while virtual ones are not so good. For activities requiring human connection or joint focus, face-to-face is probably better, but if you are trying to pull together a geographically disparate group for a critical meeting on short notice, even a "not-so-good" option is preferable to "not at all." Rather than see virtual as a poor cousin to authentic face-to-face working, it will be more useful to see the opportunities provided by virtual and hybrid working as an extension of your options.

One of our clients prefers face-to-face meetings with her team whenever possible but loves the advantages offered by being able to call a quick video meeting for her wider team of a thousand people, spread across the country. Something that would have taken weeks or months and a huge budget to organize—if it was doable at all from a financial perspective—can be pulled together in a matter of days with almost no costs.

[DAVID] In the 2010s we were able to shrink our company to a very small, close-knit group of people—close friends and colleagues over decades, becoming primarily an IP-licensing enterprise. During the pandemic of the 2020s we functioned effectively virtually, located in Colombia, California, Colorado, and the Netherlands. But we were all hungry for the look, touch, and feel of face-to-face with one another. It was worth a serious cash investment for us to create a retreat, in a real destination place, with a tiny bit of time for business and a lot of time for fun and hanging out. It made "virtual" much easier for fun and hanging out, when called for.

CONS

In the initial stages of the mass experiment with working virtually, most organizations just packed up and shipped the existing way of working in the office to each employee's home. If they were in meetings all day at the office, they spent all day in meetings on Zoom. Millions of innocents ended each day completely exhausted without really understanding why. Since then we have come to learn more. We know that it simply isn't productive to use existing technologies to replicate at home what we were doing in the office. If you're doing eight or ten meetings back to back, simply because you can with a click of a button, then you're doing it wrong. Back-to-back meetings weren't a good idea in the office and are an even worse one from home.

We believe that the medium—and the infrastructure it runs on— are amazing. To have enabled hundreds of thousands of people to see one another, communicate, and collaborate from anywhere with a decent connection to the internet is nothing short of a technological miracle. And yet...

We've learned that the medium works well for certain types of communication but not so well for things that have a substantial nonverbal component. The technology will certainly improve, but for now it struggles with some simple elements that are essential in human connection and communication. For starters you can't look at someone and be seen to be looking at them at the same time. When looking at them on your screen, they see you—best case—looking down or slightly to the left or right on your screen to be able to observe their reactions. It is a toss-up whether that is better or worse than the alternative, which is to appear to be looking at them, but be looking meaningfully into your own camera. Your soulful gaze at the lens above your screen may be convincing, but it cuts you off from the feedback on their reactions to what you are saying. Switching between the two through the conversation partly solves the problem but adds a subtle dynamic of your eyes darting around on their screen, leaving you looking like an addict between scores.

That is in a one-to-one. With a screen full of faces, no one has any idea who or what anyone is looking at. These may seem like insignificant issues, but eye contact and reading body language have been the 0s and 1s of human trust for hundreds of thousands of years. Video conferencing offers only a simulacrum. It provides a good enough copy that we have the sense that we are getting most of what we need. But a bit like how watching news about a war zone on a screen gives you the sense that you know what is going on there because you've "seen" it, video calls give a sense that you've met someone, when you really have met them in a very information-poor way.

Information poor, but subtly energy intensive. Part of the challenge is that the medium not only requires extra-focused attention to get anything like the same amount of information from a given conversation or a meeting, but it also leaks focus like a sieve. Distractions come from other programs on the device you're using, of course, but also from notifications coming through on other devices. Oh, and there is an entire world of nondigital reality that each participant is dealing with in their own environment, of which your meeting is—best case—happening on a twenty-seven-inch screen in 180 degrees of their field of vision.

That reality includes their entire domestic life, unless they have the means to have a separate, soundproofed, home office down at the end of a garden. Which raises the privacy and identity implications of having people in your home, seeing your place, and experiencing your domestic life. Some participants will be naturally proud of their homes, and some would prefer that their professional network neither see nor hear anything about their home situation. Conversely, the eyes and ears of their domestic situation are acting as a subconscious brake on what they can or want to say and do in their professional sphere.

All this before we factor in the physical challenges of looking in the same direction, at the same focal point, for hours at a time: back pain, neck muscles taut as piano strings, headaches. And a lack of movement that impairs cognition. It doesn't take much exploration to work out why the medium can leave people feeling hollowed out by the end of a few hours using what is—again—a miraculous feat of human engineering.

All of it adds up to something quite different from what we believe it should be, and this has profound implications for what we should be asking it to do.

OTHER CHALLENGES

Our very human proximity bias means that those who are more in contact with their team and their leadership are likely to receive better treatment than those who are remote. We're all for the egalitarian ideal, but if I were looking to get promoted, I'd be spending as much time as possible in the office, meeting people, building trust and relationships in the way our DNA was built for. You can be terrific at your job, but if you never come to the office because you've decided to reduce costs by moving out of the city, or to a different country, then you run the risk of being replaced by a nice, competent worker in an even lower-cost location.

And that means we run the risk of a two-tier workforce, with the bottom tier made up of those at home more often, disadvantaged when it comes to the inevitable organizational politics, and newer people less able to navigate than those with more time and better existing relationships.

That makes it sound like the more experienced folks are better off, and to a certain extent they are. But another thing that became clear during our global experiment in remote working was that virtual workers connect and work well with those they already know but are less likely to connect with new people. The cost of this is impossible to gauge because you can't know what possibilities won't develop with people you don't meet.

Then there are the structural and discipline challenges that come with working from home. It seems that people use at least some of the time they get back from not commuting to do more work. That's good, perhaps, if you are a business owner, but not so good if you are the one putting in that extra time. In the initial months of the pandemic, there seemed to be a bump in productivity when people began working from home, but more recent studies show that productivity eventually suffers when people have no boundaries around their work life, and the extra work time just ends up producing more sick time.

We are still in the early days of the next phase of this work experiment. Over the course of the next few years there will be a shake-up in the market. Both companies and workers will decide how they want to conduct hybrid working. Certain companies will decide that they want people back in the office full-time, and people who don't want that arrangement will go elsewhere. Other organizations will introduce no-office, super-flexible approaches, and find that those who live alone actually quite like a bit of company in the office. This experiment will continue for many years, and there is much to be decided. Now we have a hot labor market, and talent has the whip hand, so companies are unwilling to say what they really want for fear of losing talent. As a stopgap until they can arrive at a sensible solution, some have gone as far as offering free food on Mondays and Fridays to induce people to show up and amortize the rent.

One can only hope that the eventual decisions for the future of work will not be by fiat but instead based on actual necessity. Ideally, individual teams and departments will make that call for themselves, based on what best supports the achievement of their purpose and vision in a sustainable way.

One of the biggest questions we see is how the virtual/hybrid model will affect the maintenance of company culture and employee loyalty. Will (much) more virtual work fail to foster relationships and company/team loyalty? If you don't really know your colleagues or your boss, and you are mostly working on your own, what is to stop you wandering out the virtual door to work with a new bunch of strangers for 15 percent more per annum? Same desk, same tasks, same pajamas, with a different logo and more money. These impacts will only slowly be seen over the coming years, if they are measurable at all. If the trend to subcontracting and shrinking management layers continues, then it will be even more important that the top team live the behaviors and have the means to communicate culture and values quickly to those who are new to—and may not remain long on—the team.

PROS

So much for the challenges. As we said earlier, we both marvel at the possibilities on offer here. Virtual/hybrid working presents incredible opportunities to both managers and those they manage if everyone accepts a change from managing by observation of work to leading by objectives. By removing the ability to observe work being done, leaders must find a different way to lead their people. There are effectively two options: install spyware on your team's computers to see what they are doing all day, or set clear goals for them and coach them on outcomes rather than inputs. The choice is between control on the one hand and trust and empowerment on the other.

The former might be summarized by the implicit message in making people show up unnecessarily: "Just get in here and sit somewhere that I can keep an eye on you during the time we're paying you." No one will ever speak those words, of course, but they don't have to. Contrast that with the message offered by letting people work wherever and whenever they want, if they deliver the outcomes delegated to them on time: "We trust you to do what we pay you for. Here's what I want when you are finished. When can you get that to me by?"

Such flexibility is highly valued by the workforce. Depending on which study you consult, the flex is worth something like 5 to 8 percent of current salary. That is, people would take a pay cut of that order of magnitude to keep the flexibility they now have. Or—more likely—leave for somewhere else that pays as much but offers more freedom.

Leading virtually is an opportunity for a fundamental shift in the leadership model, from observing and managing how workers use their time, to delegating clear but challenging outcomes. Those familiar with the GTD definition of a project will have a head start in working this way, but any leader can benefit from the approach.

There is an opportunity to move to a more frequent and broader—if shallower—mode of communicating with your team, via weekly broadcast/podcast updates, and with stakeholders via social media. The team gets the ability to work from anywhere, though not everyone can take advantage of it (having children in school tends to cramp digital wanderlust something fierce). Finally, everyone should experience dramatically reduced travel time and cost, with attendant reductions in emissions.

WHAT IT TAKES TO MAKE IT WORK—WAYS TO WORK IN THE NEW WORLD TO MAXIMIZE THE TOOLS AT YOUR DISPOSAL

The most obvious way that GTD supports virtual and hybrid working is in the definition of the work to be done. Rather than delegating tasks, if the team leader—and team itself—take time on the front end to clearly define the expected outcome, and resources available for delivering it, then people can get on with the work that needs to be finished, regardless of where that happens.

Virtual teams need far more clarity on everything from the definition of work, through who's doing what, to when and how they'll meet. A more subtle but important aspect of the GTD model for this new world is in the invitation to define the desired end state of navigating it optimally. What would be true if this new reality was met equally with a new reality of the work culture at hand? The answer to that will undoubtedly be unique to the enterprise and the key people driving it. "How would we be, and how would we be doing it, if this change were no problem, and we were appropriately engaged with it?" This would relate with the vision level of focus, discussed in chapter 7. A few suggestions:

Mix up communication channels to avoid teams being hollowed out by too much time on video calls. Like tech bros who go back to doing things on paper because they prefer the "feel" of it, many have started requesting old-school phone calls instead of video conferences or agreeing to run the video call with cameras off.

Be clear on when people are expected to be in the office, if that is necessary. Telling the staff that they can come in for three days a week, whenever they like, can make scheduling important meetings on a team nearly impossible. Mandating two to three office days and allowing flex on the others seems to be the way that many are finding works well.

Invest in the best possible lighting and sound quality you can afford. Virtual/hybrid working isn't going away anytime soon, so people will be looking at you in your home for a very long time. Three years on from the first lockdown, none of us has any excuses for not having the right tools for our jobs. You'll want a professionally appropriate background, and—if the stakes are high in your work—connective redundancy so that if one path to your meeting is blocked you have at least one other option for getting there on time. You need a contingency plan for when things go wrong. Running on a shared home broadband will look a lot like negligence if your call gets dropped in the middle of a client meeting because your teenage son is stealing virtual cars in the bedroom down the hall.

Level the playing field. Hybrid also applies to most meetings these days. Some people are in the same room, and some are remote. Rather than putting all the people in the same room on one camera, you'll want to have everyone in the room log on so everyone is visible to everyone else. Although this might seem like you are downgrading the entire group to the lowest communications denominator, this approach makes sense if you want better participation from those not in the room.

We see that even mostly virtual companies are finding they need to find ways to build relationships face-to-face for their primarily virtual model to function optimally. Those who choose this model need to be conscious of its strengths and weaknesses. That often means becoming more intentional about nourishing culture and relationships in a virtual environment and keeping a much closer eye on people's mental health in the new ecosystems.

Index

Italicized page numbers indicate material in tables or illustrations.

hybrid working (*cont.*)
 other challenges, 306–8
 pros of, 308–9

ideas, generating. *See* capture
Impact vs. Effort Model, *241*, 241–42
"improvement opportunities," 97
in-baskets, 253, 271
inboxes, 5–6, 27, 295–300
 collaborative software for, 287–88
 emptying, principles of, 298–300
 response times, 129–30, 131, 141–44,
  143, 222, 296
independent contracting, 40, 308
individual skills and team tactics,
  8–11
Industrial Revolution, 39
infectious working standards, 131–35
Institute for East-West Securities
  Studies, 113–14
integrity, 22, 162
interruptions (interrupt-itis),
  27–28, 54
introverts, 59–60
intuition, role in GTD, 102

job descriptions, 75–76, 278. *See also*
  role clarity
job interviews, 76
Jobs, Steve, 155
job titles, in Holacracy, 46–48
Jones, Daniel, 44–45

Kanban, 40, 238, 274
Kaufman, Margo, 40
Kennedy, John, 212
Kettering, Charles, 68
"keystone habits," 132
King, Martin Luther, 110
knowledge and learning, 262–63

knowledge work, 12, 284, 302. *See also*
  New Work; virtual work
 New Work and, 53–55
 purpose and, 194
 "queuing theory," 230–32
 workflow methods, 40, 67, 230–31
"knowledge work athletics," 91
Koestler, Arthur, 291
Korean War, 108
Kouzes, James, 70

Latham, Gary, 166, 168
laziness, 247, 250
leaders (leadership), 211–25
 changing nature of teams and,
  28–29
 critical responsibilities of, 252
 definitions of, 214–15
 delegation, 216–17, 223, 309
 encouraging accountability and
  responsiveness, 219–20
 fluid, 74
 as gardeners, 215–17, 219–20,
  222–23
 getting overwhelmed, 247–48
 Getting Things Done model and,
  221–25
 great vs. effective, 213–14
 managing the team. *See* team
  management
 nuts and bolts of, 212–13
 prioritization, 242–44, 245
 Projects lists, 102
 role-modeling, 217–19
 "softer" aspects of, 212–13
 standard view of, 213–14, 215
 virtual work and, 309
 vision, 154, 212, 215
 working standards and, 133, 134,
  217–19, 224–25